THE IMMIGRATION TIME BOMB

Gov. Richard D. Lamm
and Gary Imhoff

THE IMMIGRATION TIME BOMB

The Fragmenting of America

 TRUMAN TALLEY BOOKS / E. P. DUTTON / NEW YORK

Published in the United States by
Truman Talley Books • E. P. Dutton,
a division of New American Library,
2 Park Avenue, New York, N.Y. 10016

Library of Congress Cataloging in Publication Data

Lamm, Richard D.
The immigration time bomb.
"A Truman Talley Book."
Bibliography: p.
1. United States—Emigration and immigration.
2. United States—Emigration and immigration—Government
policy. I. Imhoff, Gary. II. Title.
JV6455.L35 1985   325.73   85-12886

ISBN 0-525-24337-2

Published simultaneously in Canada by
Fitzhenry & Whiteside Limited, Toronto

DESIGNED BY MARK O'CONNOR

10 9 8 7 6 5 4 3 2 1

COBE

First Edition

This book is dedicated to our late agent, John Cushman, who treated publishing as a gentleman's profession.

Contents

Preface and Authors' Note

Arnold Toynbee, after a lifetime of studying history, observed that "the same elements that build up an institution eventually lead to its downfall." This clearly applies to the wrenching subject of immigration. Immigration policy was once an asset to this country, helping to make us strong. But its current uncontrolled state will seriously harm this country and its institutions.

This is not easy for Americans to accept. The Statue of Liberty is deeply embedded in the American psyche and American institutions. But public policy must ceaselessly change, evolve, and transform. Abraham Lincoln once observed, "As our case is new, so must we think and act anew. We must disenthrall ourselves." America has to "disenthrall" itself from the idea that immigration is an unqualifiedly positive force in our national policy.

I put forth the following heresies:

1. The United States clearly cannot continue to accept twice as many immigrants and refugees as all other nations combined.
2. A basic definition of *sovereignty* is control over a nation's own borders, and we are not now controlling ours.
3. A country cannot have a "no border" policy any more than a house can have a "no door" policy.
4. The problem of finding jobs for our own citizens will be staggering in the near future. Today, 30 percent of black teenaged youth are unemployed, 30 percent of Hispanic teenaged youth are unemployed, and massive immigration will exacerbate this problem.
5. The individual miracle of birth is becoming a collective tragedy. We will add one billion people to the world's population in the next eleven years. The pressure to emigrate to the United States will increase geometrically. The United States clearly cannot take all of the world's surplus population, and it would be insane for us to try.
6. The United States is no longer an empty continent that can absorb endless streams of population.
7. The melting pot, like any pot, is finite.

If I could carve a motto over the state capitol of Denver, it would be, "Beware of solutions appropriate to the past but disastrous to the future." Public policy changes and, as today is different from yesterday, so today's policies must be different from yesterday's. We cannot always fight the last war, as von Clausewitz warned the generals.

All public policy is very heavily influenced, if not controlled, by the assumptions that are brought to it. Our solutions are dictated by the underlying assumptions that we bring to the problem. If the earth is flat, it does not make sense to build ships to explore for new worlds. If the sky is a big cosmic tent with the stars hung in it like lights in a ceiling, we should not build rockets to explore the universe. Much of today's confusion and inability to solve political problems arises from the painful fact that many of the controlling assumptions of our society should be dramatically different from when this country was founded. Europeans found in America a continent with vast resources, a seemingly endless supply of land, and raw materials free for the asking, where population growth and hence immigration were clearly positive public factors. We made the assumptions of the infinite—that there would be infinite room, infinite resources, and the ability to absorb infinite numbers of people.

The glory of America meant there would always be a frontier, there would always be an endless supply of land and water and resources for the asking. One traveler on the Oregon Trail in 1849 symbolized this optimism:

> Buffalo everywhere, as far as the eye can see. The herds number in the tens of thousands. These shaggy creatures, so awkward and lumbering, will provision and clothe America in perpetuity; there is no doubt of it. The most confirmed pessimist could not envisage a lessening of these endless black smears from horizon to horizon. The buffalo will be part of our West till the end of its destiny.

America has changed dramatically since the Statue of Liberty was created. In 1890, the United States had a population of a little over 60 million. Today it is over 236 million. The density of population in the year that the Statue of Liberty was dedicated was 17.8 per acre. It is now over 64. The total budget of the federal government was $318 million, which today is approximately how much it spends on pencils and paper clips. The 1985 federal budget was over $900 billion. We have gone from an agricultural society in which land was free to an industrial society in which massive amounts of capital are needed to create jobs.

We must be very realistic about our ability to absorb the world's homeless. Africa, hard pressed to feed 513 million persons today, must somehow find the means to feed a population of 1.39 billion by the year 2020. Latin America, with a gross national product one-fifth that of the United States, must create twice as many jobs as the United States *averaged* throughout the 1970s, and do so year after year for at least forty years just to maintain its current high rates of unemployment. Already two illegal aliens are apprehended at our border every minute. The economy within our borders can never keep up with the demands or the misery outside our borders. Hard choices are going to have to be made.

Given those realities, we must ask ourselves many difficult questions:

1. How many of the world's dispossessed can we effectively help?
2. How many additional people can we absorb into our economy and assimilate into our society?
3. With high unemployment in the United States and with severe energy, water, and farmland problems of our own, can we continue to be the "home of last resort" to the world's homeless?
4. And, not least, how much more uncontrolled immigration can the American people tolerate?

John Locke said, "Hell is truth seen too late." America has to explore and debate very carefully its immigration policies and decide as a matter of high public policy how many additional people we can and should absorb. The purpose of this book is to explore in some detail the myriad public policy considerations about this problem, one of the most difficult and painful public policy issues facing America.

AUTHORS' NOTE: This book is a collaborative effort; therefore, we have used the pronoun *I* to refer to both of us, as the authors. We have reserved *we* to refer to all Americans.

THE IMMIGRATION TIME BOMB

1

How Many Can America Absorb?

The immigration crisis has grown steadily and slowly, and therefore taken us by surprise. Today, immigration to the United States is massive, and it is out of control. The United States accepts for permanent resettlement twice as many immigrants as do all the other countries of the world combined. Legal immigration is three times as high as it was in the early 1960s; there are now well over 600,000 legal immigrants in an average year. Illegal immigration is estimated to be ten times greater; there are now well over a million apprehensions a year—without any corresponding increase in enforcement activities. Illegal aliens pour into the United States through Swiss-cheese borders. Legal and illegal immigration combined contribute nearly half of the population growth of the United States. And efforts to cope with the breakdown of immigration law or to moderate the high levels of legal immigration are stymied in Congress by an unlikely coalition of the far right and the far left, fueled by a coalition of big business and Hispanic pressure groups.

In the past, moderate levels of immigration have been good for this country and they will continue to be good for it in the future. The leavening effect of immigrants' energy, enthusiasm, effort, and different cultures have improved all of our lives. Few Americans quarrel with the value of immigration. But, at today's massive levels, immigration has major negative consequences—economic, social, and demographic—that overwhelm its advantages.

To solve the immigration crisis, we Americans have to face our limitations. We have to face the necessity of passing laws to restrict immigration and the necessity of enforcing those laws. If we fail to do so, we shall leave a legacy of strife, violence, and joblessness to our children.

Unrestricted immigration to America has been a fine dream, and dreams die hard. In one of his best-known poems, Langston Hughes asked, "What happens to a dream deferred?" He ends with the disturbing question, *"Or does it explode?"* [1] What happens when a dream is lost can be even more disturbing.

Today, we Americans must lose the dream of unrestricted immigration and must face the reality behind the dream. We dreamed of America as a country of immigration, and we identified open immigration with freedom. We believed that someone poor, someone downtrodden, someone persecuted—from any other country in the world—could pull up stakes, come to America, and have another chance. We thought that we were the land of opportunity, not just for our own citizens but also for all the people of the world who wished to come here.

It is a beautiful dream, but it is only a dream. It is possible to dream it only when immigration to the United States is limited, controlled, and kept to moderate levels. It is not a dream we can keep today.

We were taught that the special destiny of America was

to be a country of immigrants. The history we learned was that our country was built by immigration and by immigrants. In fact, this was never strictly true. The white population of the United States, as counted in our national censuses, grew from a little over three million to nearly eight million between 1790 and 1820, in the earliest decades of the Republic. This is a high rate of population growth, but it does not reflect a high rate of immigration. Immigration to the United States during this time was certainly under ten thousand people a year, and the best contemporary estimates place it at between six and seven thousand a year. For most of our history, the extraordinary population growth of the United States has actually been from natural increases—from the high rate of fertility of relatively small numbers of immigrants.

We dreamed of America as a land where immigrants could become successful by an almost magical process. In fact, immigration has always been a bittersweet transition. It has exacted a high price from immigrants, and our current recognition of the pain of immigration signals our awakening from the haze of sentimentality with which we have surrounded and obscured the family stories of the first American generation.

We dreamed of a melting pot where, without effort and without anguish, immigrants would acquire the language and culture of the United States, where they would learn the technical and social skills they would need to survive and succeed here without paying the cost of relinquishing the language and culture and mores of their native countries. In fact, assimilation has always been difficult.

We dreamed, perhaps most of all, of a land of plenty, a New Eden that would be inexhaustible, that would accept all who came here and provide them with a wilderness to conquer and the land and water and all the other resources they would need to make their lives plentiful—with just a little effort and gumption. We dreamed of a country where competition would be with nature, and not with each other; where giving to one would not mean taking from another; where materials and jobs could be made without limit and where there would be room for all. We dreamed of a country where generosity would be easy because there would be so much with which to be generous. The dream seemed to come true, for a time, but that era is over.

We dreamed that the Statue of Liberty would be a beacon to the world—not just the example of liberty, lighting the way for other nations to follow us, but the harbor light which guided immigrants to the liberty that was available on our shores. Emma Lazarus's poem was added to the statue seventeen years after it was dedicated and changed its meaning forever. It is still cited in every debate over immigration. It is the best short statement of the dream.

THE NEW COLOSSUS:
INSCRIPTION FOR THE STATUE OF LIBERTY

Not like the brazen giant of Greek fame,
With conquering limbs astride from land to land
Here at our sea-washed sunset gates shall stand
A mighty woman with a torch, whose fame
Is the imprisoned lightning, and her name
Mother of Exiles. From her beaconhand
Glows world-wide welcome; her mild eyes command
The air-bridged harbour that twin cities frame.
"Keep, ancient lands, your storied pomp," cries she
With silent lips. "Give me your tired, your poor,
Your huddled masses yearning to breathe free.
The wretched refuse of your teeming shore,
Send these, the homeless, the tempest-tosst to me,
I lift my lamp beside the golden door!"

The reality is something else again. Crime rates among immigrants soar in Miami, Los Angeles, and elsewhere;

signs of backlash abound as America tries to absorb these unprecedented numbers and cultures. Ninety-one percent of Americans want to stop illegal immigration completely. America has what Senator Alan Simpson has called "compassion fatigue." Yet the Population Reference Bureau ominously reminds us that immigration will add more than fifty million people to the population of the United States by the year 2025, if today's levels continue without increasing. Clearly, this will further strain and perhaps break America's capacity for compassion.

Some people deny that immigration can ever be a problem. They refuse to let go of the dream. They argue that treating immigration as a problem treats people, human beings, as a problem. In that, they are right: people, large numbers of people pressing against the resources of the earth, are a problem. Especially in the United States, where each individual uses a disproportionately large share of the world's resources, increased population is a lasting problem for this and future generations. To show why this is true, I have to discuss the importance of two curves.

The first curve shows the growth of the population of the world. It is startling. The best estimates we have are that the human population of the world rose at a very slow, almost imperceptible, pace for the first few million years of human history. That is, human population grew to only about half a billion people worldwide from the first time that we would identify a creature as human to about the year 1630. It took another two hundred years and more, to about 1850, before human population doubled to one billion. In that two hundred years, the slow, steady, almost imperceptible rise in population began to curve upward. In the eighty years between 1850 and 1930, the population of the world doubled again to about two billion people, and the curve became visibly sharper. In the forty-five years between 1930 and 1975, the population of the world doubled again to four billion.

CHART 1
THE HUMAN POPULATION OF THE WORLD

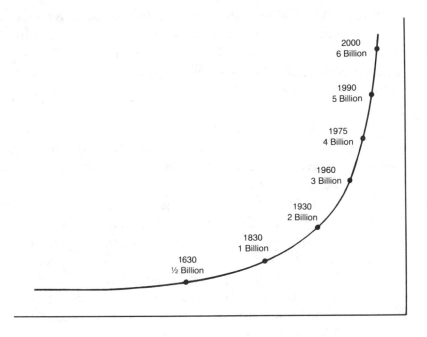

By the year 2000, world population will be over six billion people, and may be six and a half billion. The curve is almost a straight line pointing straight up, almost at a right angle to the line that plots the first few million years of human history.

This startling rise in population is unprecedented in human history. There are no lessons that can be learned from the past about how to cope with this kind of growth, or indeed about whether or not we can cope with it. A shortsighted view of history might tempt us to believe that mankind has always discovered new resources or invented new ways to exploit resources in time to provide for population growth. But this has been true only of a very short period of history—the brief century and a third since 1850—and during that period we experienced both the Industrial Revolution and the Green Revolution in agriculture. What has been true for most of human history, save for that brief period, is that human populations have been limited by the resources available to them. And, except for faith in continued human inventiveness—and not just inventiveness, but quantum leaps in inventiveness—there is every reason to believe that human population in the future will continue to be limited by the resources available to us.

The shape of this human population curve must change. It has to level out. In many parts of the world, birthrates are falling today. But the change will be very gradual, and there is much more population growth ahead of us before the curve turns downward. We are faced with *demographic inertia*. Because so many people are alive, and so many are of fertile age, more children are being born every year than in the year before. And that is true regardless of the fall of birthrates in many parts of the world. At this moment, 200,000 people are being added to the population of the earth *every week*.

The shape of the population curve will not change unless strenuous efforts are made to change it. Birthrates do not fall automatically. Where they do fall, it is because many individuals, organizations, and governments are working hard to ensure that they do.

Closer to home, in North, South, and Central America, especially in Mexico, the population pressure builds up, compounds, and threatens to explode. In the eighty years between 1920 and 2000, the population of Central America alone is projected to increase eightfold, from 4.89 million to 39 million. Though population growth is already straining the social, economic, and political order of the Americas, the brunt of Central America's population growth in this century is still to be faced. Population growth in developing countries is like a rock rolling downhill, gathering speed. Consequently, two-thirds of that eightfold increase between 1920 and 2000 will be added between 1975 and the year 2000. Mexico, with 70 million people, has

300,000 more babies born every year than does the United States, with 230 million people. There is a flood of people rising right outside our door.

The second curve I need to discuss is the resource curve. The availability of most nonrenewable resources can be graphed quite neatly as a bell-shaped curve. At the beginning, when deposits of the resource are just being discovered and methods of exploiting it are primitive, we are at the small end of the curve at the left side of the graph. As more and more deposits of the resource are discovered and as methods of exploiting it are improved, we grow to the top of the bell, the time of widest availability. As the best deposits are exhausted and we move to lower-quality deposits, we move toward the right, the narrower end of the bell.

This curve is true for mineral deposits, ores, soils, and fuels (except solar fuels). Geologist M. King Hubbert was the first to predict that oil and gas supplies would follow a bell-shaped curve. He was derided in the 1950s, when he first drew his curve and when production of oil and gas was growing rapidly, but in fact his predictions have been remarkably accurate for both worldwide and domestic oil production; today it is generally accepted that we are well into the declining end of the curve for domestic oil and gas production. In the United States, further exploration for oil and gas, at least for fuel purposes, will be unprofitable soon after the turn of the century. It will not pay to explore further, both in terms of dollars and especially in terms of any energy profit. We would put more energy into exploration for and exploitation of oil and gas than we would recover from the new oil and gas we would discover. We'd lose energy.

This is the true meaning of running out of oil. There will still be plenty of oil and gas in the ground, and they will be useful as chemical feedstocks to make plastics and other materials. But they will be useless as fuels. And any

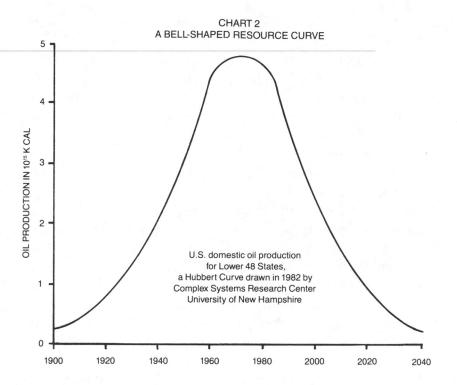

CHART 2
A BELL-SHAPED RESOURCE CURVE

OIL PRODUCTION IN 10¹⁵ K CAL

U.S. domestic oil production
for Lower 48 States,
a Hubbert Curve drawn in 1982 by
Complex Systems Research Center
University of New Hampshire

other fuel that is practical today, which is envisioned to be available by the early years of the next century, has a much lower energy profit ratio than present-day oil and gas. Today, with present stocks of domestic oil, we get twenty times more energy out of the oil we pump from the ground and refine than we put into making it available. The ratio for nuclear energy is at best five to one. Photovoltaics—solar cells—deliver only seven or nine times more energy than is put into producing them. Coal gives better energy profit figures but is a very environmentally damaging fuel. The best deposits of clean-burning coal are nearly exhausted; and synfuels made from coal—as well as from agricultural crops—consume more energy than they produce. They are made at an energy loss.

This decline in fuel quality is important, because it is occurring at the same time that the qualities of other resources are declining. We have to dig deeper and refine lower concentrations of every mineral resource. Agriculture demands ever-increasing supplies of energy merely to feed the increasing number of human beings on the earth. The Green Revolution, that startling spurt of agricultural productiveness in the 1950s and 1960s, did little other than provide new strains of crops that utilized more energy faster—new crops that could use more fertilizer more efficiently to produce more edible grain. If, in the future, we have to put an ever-larger portion of our energy simply into producing energy, then less energy will be available to do all the other things we need it to do. If, because of larger populations, we have to put ever-increasing percentages of our energy into producing food, then we shall have less energy available to produce anything else in our society.

It is not antihuman or antisocial to say that too many people can be a problem. It is simply realistic to acknowledge the fact. Human activity changes the world in many ways in addition to resource exhaustion, and not all of these ways are good even for human beings. People pollute, and too many people living in an area can degrade that area irrevocably. Immigration at high levels exacerbates our resource and environmental problems. It will leave a poorer, more crowded, more divided country for our children.

Immigration at massive levels also creates societal problems. Because the assimilation of new immigrants is difficult, for them and for the host society, too rapid a rate of immigration into an area can strain social relationships and political systems to the breaking point. In many societies less tolerant and less hospitable than our own, rapid large-scale immigration has even led to massive slaughter. Since 1951 over four million Bengalis have migrated illegally to the Indian state of Assam, and since 1979 the Assamese have been protesting the central government's inaction against this migration. Assam is now virtually under military rule; at least 5,000 people, most of them Bengalis, have been killed, and perhaps 300,000 Bengalis have been displaced by mob protests and violence.

In the United States, there has been gang warfare between Vietnamese and Hispanics in Denver; Texas shrimpers have fought immigrant Vietnamese boatmen; black neighborhoods in many cities have seen Korean and other Asian shopkeepers killed in robberies that smacked of cultural resentment; Miami has had a mayoral campaign fought primarily over whether a Hispanic mayor of Puerto Rican descent might be too close to black concerns and a rival Hispanic candidate of Cuban descent more oriented toward the Cuban community. All these rivalries, all these frictions, are primarily over the rate of change caused by massive immigration.

On a less intense level, bilingual education has caused a national debate. The question is whether non–English-speaking students should be taught in English or in their native languages and whether these bilingual programs should be aimed primarily at giving students mastery over English or at maintaining their native languages and cultures. Questions of this sort would simply never be allowed to rise in societies less open than America's—and they would never arise here if immigration were at moderate levels, if there were not concentrations of migrants large enough to sustain their native languages.

At high enough levels, immigration also creates economic problems. In many areas of the world, migrants are moving from less developed to more developed countries. They generally have fewer skills than workers in their host countries, and in those cases migrants move into unskilled jobs at the bottom of the job ladders of those countries. If their numbers are large enough, they displace native workers and—when economies are not vibrant and growing at fast enough rates—they contribute to the unemployment of natives and depress the salary levels for the jobs in which they specialize. In West Germany, for example, certain jobs became stigmatized in the late 1960s and 1970s as "Turkish jobs," performed by temporary migrant guestworkers from Turkey. When certain jobs become stigmatized in such a way, a society loses some of its cohesiveness, a large part of its social mobility, and a degree of respect for manual labor. In the United States, our own garment industry has now been stigmatized as a sector in which illegal immigrants work. Wages have fallen, sweatshops have been revived, a noble union has been corrupted by accepting the existence of "shadow locals" and tolerating the exploitation of illegal workers, and—in a self-fulfilling prophecy—employers have created a class of work that "Americans won't do."

These three problem areas—population and resources, social, and economic—will be covered in these pages. But it should be stressed again that this book is not intended to be a brief against moderate levels of legal immigration, which unquestionably benefit this country. I am, instead, talking about the negative consequences of large-scale legal and illegal immigration and what can be done to bring them under control.

Here are some of the basic facts that have killed the dream of unlimited immigration. The categories of legal immigration which are limited by law admit 270,000 legal immigrants every year. Many more people than that come in categories with no set limits: close relatives (spouses and minor children of American citizens) and refugees. Legal immigration now averages more than 600,000 people a year and has risen to over 800,000 in some years.

Nobody knows exactly how many illegal immigrants come to the United States every year, settle, and live here permanently. But, as economist Vernon Briggs has said, this is true of every serious social problem. If the numbers are all unquestionably clear, we probably know enough about the problem to be well on our way to solving it. Illegal immigration is a crime; those who come here illegally are criminals, and they live clandestinely in America. They are, therefore, not easy to count.

I am going to avoid the dismal swamp, the irrelevant debate over the exact number of illegal immigrants in this country. If one person says there are ten million illegal immigrants in the United States and therefore the problem is serious, another may counter that there are "only" six million and that therefore the problem isn't nearly so serious as the first person thought. Such debates take place every day in other areas of social concern, and they are nearly always distracting. How many people are below the poverty line, exactly? How many people are addicted to cocaine use? How many alcoholics are there? How many people need food stamps? How many burglars are there? In each of these cases, focusing on the rather academic issue of arriving at an accurate, defensible number will deflect us from the serious issue of solving the problem behind the numbers. All we need, in each of these cases, is a rough idea of the magnitude of the problem. With illegal immigration, we do have that idea.

The one hard figure we have for illegal immigration is the number of apprehensions made by the Border Patrol and the investigators of the Immigration and Naturalization Service. In the late 1950s and early 1960s, apprehensions of illegal immigrants were under 100,000 a year. They are now ten times that, well over a million a year, without any significant increase in the number of Border Patrol officers or INS investigators. In 1983, the Border Patrol alone made more than a million apprehensions. If it were adequately staffed and funded—and it is far from being either— it could double or triple that number for a few years, until illegal immigrants became resigned to the increased difficulty of entering the United States and were deterred from trying.

Border Patrol supervisors estimate that for every apprehension they make there are two to three successful illegal entries into the United States. This means that somewhere between two and three million illegal entries are made each year. Since some people enter numerous times, sometimes reentering the country within days of their apprehension and release, that figure should be cut to estimate the number of immigrants who enter the United States illegally—perhaps one and a half million.

In addition, a large number of people enter the United States legally, with passports and visas, and then overstay the terms of their visas. They were legal entrants but they become illegal immigrants. The technical term for them is *visa abusers*. The number of visa abusers is even more difficult to estimate than the number of illegal entrants. Daniel Vining of the University of Pennsylvania has made the best attempt to date to arrive at a reasonable number. Vining took three different sets of records that count the number of people who fly in and from the United States each year. He took the remainder, those who remained within the country, and subtracted legal immigrants from them, and found a yearly deficit of a few hundred thousand people who flew into the United States, entered legally, and didn't fly out.[2] We have no idea who these people are or where they are. We don't know if they are skilled workers or students or potential welfare cases or criminals. They disappear into America.

Of course, some illegal entrants and visa abusers do leave the United States after short stays here. They probably shouldn't be counted as permanent immigrants, though when their stays reach several years the difference between temporary and permanent immigrants begins to blur. A conservative estimate of the number of illegal immigrants who do become permanent residents in the United States is half a million people per year. There is no proof of this number; there is no census (including official U.S. counts by the Bureau of the Census) that locates and counts illegal immigrants accurately. But it is a reasonable and useful approximation of the number of illegals who are added to the permanent population.

Nobody knows, either, how many illegal immigrants compose the "stock" of illegals in the United States today. There is no good way to count them. Estimates have ranged from two million to twelve million, but they are all unverifiable. The Census Bureau, which made a determined effort to find illegals and persuade them to register in 1980, estimated about two million illegals of all nationalities. This number is not useful, since Los Angeles County officials and INS officials in Los Angeles believe that there are as many as two million illegals in that city alone. Relatively sophisticated surveys in Texas have located three-quarters of a million illegals in that state; Mayor Edward Koch of New York estimates that there are at least one million in New York City; advocates of El Salvadorans have estimated as many as four hundred thousand Salvadorans in the United States; and representatives of Hispanic groups, when they estimate their future voting strength, say that there are at least ten million illegal Mexicans in the United States.

Averaging all of the indirect methods of estimating, the knowledgeable guesses, and the attempts at actual counts gives a figure of between three-and-a-half and six million illegals in this country in the mid-1970s. Census Bureau statisticians arrived at that range when they attempted such an average a few years ago. Adding a half-million additional settlers a year to that number increases it by about five million more, giving a working range of eight-and-a-half to eleven million.

Again, the actual number of illegals is not important. What is important is that they are arriving and settling in the United States in large enough numbers and at a fast enough rate to cause real demographic, social, and economic problems. If apprehensions of illegal immigrants were still at the levels of the early 1960s, illegal immigration would not be a serious social problem, the United States would not have to be concerned with it, and we could simply set more moderate, controlled ceilings on legal immigration. But illegal immigration has exploded.

When legal and illegal immigration are combined, over a million people are added to the population of the United States every year. That is equal to the highest level of immigration in our history, which lasted for only a few years in the early decades of this century. It is a level twice that of immigration to all other countries in the world combined.

It is very significant that each of these million-plus people intends to be a permanent resident, a permanent addition to our population. When Pakistan accepts more than a million Afghan refugees it does so once and on a temporary basis, with financial support from the rest of the world, and under the assumption that most of these refugees will be repatriated as soon as possible. The same is true of Ethiopians in Somalia and of any number of other temporary movements in Africa and Asia and Latin America. It is only the United States that attempts to resettle movements of this magnitude permanently and is foolish enough to try to do it continually, yearly, year after year.

At current levels of legal and illegal immigration, we will be doomed to expand our population continuously. Today we add nearly as many people to our population through immigration as we do through natural increase, from births. In the past fifteen years, we Americans have moderated our own fertility rates and brought the number of births down to a level that would allow us eventually to achieve a stable population, zero population growth—were it not for immigration. But with current levels of immigration, we will always be forced to use our resources at a faster and faster rate, to try to expand our economy to make room for more and more workers, to try to spread our suburbs, cutting down the forests and clearing out the farms that used to surround our cities. We shall leave a vastly different America to our children and our grandchildren if we allow this to continue.

The American people recognize these problems. We understand the need for reformulating our policy toward legal immigration and the need for controlling illegal immigration. It is a simple matter of common sense. Advocates of large-scale immigration may argue that immigrants will somehow create more resources by coming here, that they will for some reason not compete with American workers even when unemployment is over 10 percent, that for some reason the descendants of immigrants won't consume as much as the descendants of current citizens. But these arguments do not stand up to examination.

Poll after poll has shown that Americans want illegal immigration brought under control—in fact, polls have consistently shown agreement on this issue by over 90 percent of Americans, an almost unheard-of percentage of agreement on any social issue. Americans have consistently supported lowering the level of legal immigration. Generally, pollsters find that about two-thirds of those they ask think that current levels of legal immigration are too high. And polls have generally used a figure of four hundred thousand a year, not the more accurate six hundred thousand, as the level of legal immigration.

Hispanic Americans—who have been misrepresented by national groups claiming to speak for them—also show overwhelming support in polls both for increased border control against illegal immigration and for lower levels of legal immigration. This should not be surprising, though it is to many people. In many areas, Hispanic Americans are exactly those who are most hurt by massive immigration, whose neighborhoods suffer the greatest impact, and whose jobs are most affected by competition. The most comprehensive poll of Hispanic and black American opinions on immigration was conducted early in 1983 by Democratic pollster Peter D. Hart and Republican pollster V. Lance Tarrance. Hart and Tarrance found that 69 percent of black and 63 percent of Hispanic citizens wanted major increases in spending to enable the Border Patrol to stop illegal aliens from entering the United States; 66 percent of blacks and 66 percent of Hispanic citizens favored penalties and fines for employers who hired illegal aliens; and only 12 percent of Hispanic and 5 percent of black citizens felt that we should admit higher levels of legal immigrants from Mexico. I'll discuss these polls more fully in Chapter 8.

Why has immigration reform been so difficult to achieve, if it is true that large majorities of Americans support the measures that are necessary to achieve immigration control and reform immigration policy? The answer lies partially in the crude economic self-interest of those who profit by employing illegal aliens. Certainly, in agricultural areas of Texas and California, politicians are affected by the pleas of powerful growers who employ illegal migrants at wages much lower than they could pay Americans. And restaurants, taxi fleets, and ununionized "home improvement" firms that employ illegals in our cities certainly profit. The employers' argument is ugly and full of self-interest: they want to be able to hire illegal immigrants in preference to Americans so that they don't have to raise wages or improve working conditions. Surely the employers' argument cannot be powerful. It isn't. Its power comes from the fact that it is allied both to the immigration dream and to the politically powerful and seemingly disinterested forces of internationalism, humanitarianism, and opposition to racism.

Many people oppose immigration reform and argue against controlling immigration because they believe in a new world order, in the rise of internationalism, and in the demise of nation-states. While their vision may be commendable and their ideals unquestionable, their sense of reality is limited. The world is divided into nations. It will be divided into nations for as long as we can see into the future. And the United States, one of the last few nations to accept any appreciable number of migrants, is one of the most desirable nations in the world in which to live. It will continue to attract as many legal immigrants as we allow to come here, and as many illegal immigrants as we refuse to deter.

Another group, the humanitarian idealists, argues that the United States can help deal with world poverty through high levels of immigration. They, too, are probably sincere but unrealistic. The United States is a small part of the world—only 5 percent of the population of the earth. We can voluntarily share the world's poverty; we cannot make the world rich by sharing our wealth.

The immigration laws of the United States should be written and enforced in order to protect and preserve the interests of Americans and of this country. The test of immigration policy must be the interests of Americans. It cannot be whether it hastens the demise of nations, or whether it makes the worldwide distribution of wealth more equitable by lowering the wealth of Americans while imperceptibly raising the wealth of a small proportion of others.

The first priority of any country, the first test for a nation, is to have defined, agreed-upon borders over which the movements of citizens and noncitizens alike are controlled. By that test, the United States today would hardly qualify as a nation. We have not clearly and distinctly set and enforced the conditions under which individuals are entitled to enter this country and become participants in our polity. By failing to do so, we have failed to pay attention to the needs, the desires, and the interests of our own citizens.

The most powerful argument against immigration reform is the fear of acting out of racism. Is immigration reform discriminatory? Is it racist to control illegal immigration or to set ceilings on legal immigration? One fact would tend to support the contention of racism. Twenty years ago, about 80 percent of legal immigrants came from western Europe. Today 80 percent of legal immigrants come from Asia and Latin America, and over half of all immigrants speak Spanish as a native tongue. Opponents of immigration control have contended that this shift in the composition of the immigrant stream, this difference in race, culture, language, and religion, is the real cause of concern over immigration.

But the people who are leading the fight for immigration reform—both within and outside of government—show no signs of racism. In fact they are quite sensitive to racism and work actively to combat any tinge of it in the arguments they make for immigration reform and in the laws and regulations they propose to control and limit immigration. The only mention of racism—aside from a few fringe pronouncements from the Ku Klux Klan that are taken seriously by few Americans and by no one with any involvement in the immigration issue—has come from the opponents of immigration reform.

Charges of racism, being impossible to refute, have sometimes been used to cut off political debate on important issues. When Daniel Patrick Moynihan issued his famous report on the black family twenty years ago, any discussion of social problems caused by the breakup of black families was stifled by charges of racism. Today the problem is of such a magnitude that it cannot be ignored, and all national black organizations are themselves organizing programs to strengthen black family ties.

Irresponsible charges of racism, unsubstantiated by any evidence, cannot be allowed to stall immigration reform. For the past four years, an important start at controlling illegal immigration has been working its way through Congress. It is called the Simpson-Mazzoli bill after its sponsors, Senator Alan K. Simpson (Republican-Wyoming) and Congressman Romano Mazzoli (Democrat-Kentucky). The Senate has passed the bill twice by margins of over four to one—and the House of Representatives has stalled it twice.

The Simpson-Mazzoli bill, simply put, would make it illegal for employers in America knowingly to hire illegal immigrants. This law, called "employer sanctions," was patterned after the recommendations of the Select Commission on Immigration, chaired by a person of proven compassion and concern, Father Theodore Hesburgh of Notre Dame University. It is a simple first step, which must be taken to discourage illegals from coming to the United States. But the first time it came up before the House of Representatives, members of the Hispanic Caucus proposed over two hundred amendments (mostly repetitive and petty) in order to kill it and argued that the law would be a direct affront to Hispanic Americans and would encourage discrimination against them. The second time it came to the House, the Speaker of the House, Thomas P. ("Tip") O'Neill (Democrat-Massachusetts), unilaterally stalled it from coming to the floor for months and made the ridiculous assertion that it would do to Hispanics in America what had been done to Jews in Germany—make them tattoo numbers on their wrists. Chapters 9 and 10 discuss what followed.

Immigration law in this country was once racist; that cannot be denied. It openly and deliberately favored migrants from western European countries, discriminated against migrants from southern Europe and Africa, and excluded all migrants from the Asian Triangle. But that racism has been—belatedly, to be sure—ended. Immigration law is now blind to race, creed, color, and nation of origin. Country ceilings on legal immigration exist only to ensure that there is a mixture in our migrant stream, that no one country or group of countries will again dominate the stream to the exclusion of others. No one is favored and no one is excluded because of country of origin or race. And no one proposing any reforms in immigration law wants to change that policy or has supported any change that would, even inadvertently, affect it.

Senator Simpson and Congressman Mazzoli have worked hard to ensure that their bill would not discriminate against Hispanics or any other group, that its effects would apply evenly to all, and that no employer who was forbidden to hire illegal immigrants would be able to use the law as a pretext not to hire Hispanics. They have succeeded. In fact, their law would offer no support for any discrimination and would ensure that all prospective employees would be treated in exactly the same way regardless of their ethnicity. But false charges of racism have stalled the bill—and will be used against any other measures that are taken to crack down on illegal immigration. I know that, because of my support for immigration reform, I will be attacked in this way. I already have been. But it is necessary to persevere regardless of the unfairness of the attack. The opponents of immigration reform can't win on the facts because they're wrong on the facts. Charges of racism are a desperate, last-ditch attempt to dissuade Americans from joining the movement for immigration reform, to dissuade politicians from voting for laws that would control immigration, to prevent immigration reform from taking place.

I, for one, am not happy about the necessity to limit immigration. Americans cannot, given our history and our humanitarianism, be happy about the need to patrol our borders better, to locate visa abusers within our borders better, to control legal entry into this country more carefully. But it is our duty to ourselves and our children to protect this land, to preserve our inheritance for the coming generations.

It would be wonderful, indeed, if we could control immigration without law enforcement, if international aid and development made other countries of the world so desirable that their people would not want to come here. We are working to accomplish that goal; but it is, at best, a very long term goal. Mexico, to take only one example, is a pretty rich nation by Third World standards. But how long will it take economic development and international aid to make Mexico so attractive a country that its poor people will not want to come to the United States? Will fifty years be enough, or seventy-five? What are we to do in the meantime? And will it ever happen? International development, sharing the wealth, is a visionary solution to our present-day migration problems. Until that millennium comes, immigration to the United States will continue to be controlled by enforcement measures about which we shall all feel some measure of ambivalence.

I propose that we take the following simple enforcement measures immediately:

1. Increase the Border Patrol. In 1984, only about three hundred Border Patrol officers were on duty at any time along the two-thousand-mile border between the United States and Mexico. Some modest increases are now taking place, but doubling or tripling that number and stationing the officers along the most traveled crossing points between the two countries would go a long way toward showing illegal immigrants that we are serious about enforcing our laws—and it would be a long way from "militarizing" the border, using undue force, or altering our friendly relationship with Mexico.

2. Computerize the Immigration and Naturalization Service. Chronically short of funds and workers, the INS still conducts most of its business and keeps most of its records on paper. Computerizing records would not only increase the efficiency of INS employees and enable them to track visa abusers

more easily, it would also enable them to serve the public better.

3. Make it against the law to hire illegal aliens. It is against the law for illegal immigrants to enter the United States and stay here, and it is against the law for them to work here. It is against the law to harbor illegal immigrants or knowingly to give them shelter, food, or aid. But, through a loophole in the law, it is legal for employers to hire illegal immigrants in preference to American workers. Closing this loophole with the Simpson-Mazzoli bill or a similar bill would let the INS concentrate its enforcement efforts on the few large-scale employers of illegals who openly flout immigration laws. By making the employers responsible, the INS could use its resources more effectively. Today, the INS is trying to locate illegals within the United States one by one, and it is unable to move against employers who openly hire them. This situation is analogous to trying to stop gambling by allowing bookies to operate openly and legally while attempting to locate individual bettors. It makes no sense, and it is unfair.

4. Limit family preferences in legal immigration to immediate relatives: spouses and children of permanent resident aliens and U.S. citizens. Our system of extended family preferences in today's immigration law ensures that fewer than 5 percent of legal immigrants are admitted because they have some special skill, talent, or education that is needed in the American work force. If labor skills are one of our major criteria for choosing among applicants for immigration, then we should limit other categories in order to expand this one. Or we should admit that legal immigration is open only to relatives of

people already here and to refugees—that others need not apply.

5. Set a ceiling on legal immigration—including relatives, workers, and refugees—of about 400,000 a year. This is a generous number, equal to immigration to all other countries in the world put together, but it signals that we are determined to get legal immigration back under control. For the fifty years from 1930 to 1980, legal immigration averaged under 275,000 a year, and that includes the very high decade of the 1970s. Four hundred thousand is not a magic number. It is supported by no scientific study that has determined it is best in any way. It can be compromised up or down. The important thing is to put all categories of immigrants, including refugees and close relatives of permanent resident aliens and citizens, under a comprehensive ceiling that gives us back control over the number of legal immigrants who come to this country each year.

These simple steps are all aimed at regaining control over immigration. They are not designed to "seal the border," "stop illegal immigration," or "end immigration altogether." As I have already said, moderate levels of legal immigration have real benefits. And the measures designed to control illegal immigration are like all other laws—they are not expected to stop crime but to bring it under control. Those who oppose tighter border controls and employer sanctions often argue that the magnitude of the problem is so great that no laws can stop illegal immigration. That's true. It's also true that no law can stop burglary and no police force can prevent murders. But reasonable laws and adequate police protection can reduce burglaries and murders to bring them under control, and reasonable laws and adequate immigration law enforcement can reduce illegal immigration to levels with which we can live.

Attorney General William French Smith, speaking in 1982 in San Antonio, exhorted his listeners to understand the importance of immigration law enforcement, something that Texans need little exhortation to understand. In his speech, he told a story that could stand as the sum total of this book: "Some years ago an Indian delegation visited Washington, D.C. Their leader, Chief Ben American Horse of the Sioux Indians, stopped at the Capitol to visit Alben Barkley, who was then vice-president of the United States. After a long discussion, the chief rose to leave. He looked the vice-president in the eye and said: 'Young fellow, let me give you a little advice. Be careful of your immigration laws. We were careless with ours.' "[3]

2

The Dispossessed

In May 1984 three women in Laredo, Texas, pleaded guilty to charges of smuggling babies into the United States. They had purchased the babies from impoverished Mexican mothers, smuggled them into this country, and sold them to American couples.[1] They promised to testify against Nelda Colwell, a Lawton, Utah, woman who procured the babies for sale.

Certainly someone with a defective sense of morality could construct excuses for what the Laredo women did. Such a person could argue that the babies would have a richer and possibly a better life in the United States than in Mexico, that the babies' mothers would be better off (wealthier) because of the payment they would receive, and that the American couples who received the children would be happier.

But this is just rationalizing an obvious evil, something most of us would find odious. It is irrelevant that the mothers would freely choose to sell their children for money or that the children would be richer in the United States. Selling and smuggling babies is simply wrong. It is degrading and immoral.

Baby smuggling and selling is a fitting symbol for all of illegal immigration. It is a small part of the trade in human flesh, but its morality stands for the whole. Exactly the same kind of exploitation that goes on in this case of baby selling occurs throughout the whole system of illegal immigration. What is astounding is that exactly the same lame rationalizations, the same transparent justifications of exploitation that I suggested above as possible apologies for baby smuggling are actually made by the apologists for illegal immigration.

The people of the United States have higher standards than that. The exploitation that is an integral part of illegal immigration offends and outrages us. This is not to say that all illegal immigrants are exploited in the United States— certainly some, and perhaps most, are not. Some illegal immigrants arrive here without adverse incident, obtain decent housing at a fair price, receive honest wages for an honest day's work, and are subjected to no discrimination. As I shall point out in a later chapter on job competition, some illegal immigrants can make out very well. But many illegal immigrants from Mexico are forced to run a gauntlet of bandits, double-crossing smugglers, sadists, and rapists on both sides of the border. Many illegal immigrants from all countries find that they are expected to pay exorbitant rents for unsanitary, overcrowded, perhaps condemned city apartments, or in rural areas are forced to live in shacks or even to camp in the open fields that they are to harvest. And many illegal immigrants are forced by the threats of unscrupulous employers to work in unsafe workplaces at wages well below the minimum.

It angers me that some people try to excuse this exploitation, to deflect our righteous outrage about these actions in our own country by arguing that illegal immigrants would earn even less money in their home countries, or that they would be no better housed, or that their governments would not offer them any more protection against abuse. The people of the United States are not responsible for how other governments treat their citizens or for the living standards of other countries. (That doesn't mean the United States shouldn't assist with development programs in the Third World or shouldn't care if other governments ignore the basic human freedoms of their citizens—it means exactly what it says: that we in the United States are not *responsible* for the existence of those conditions in other countries.) But we are responsible if we let Americans exploit any people in this country. We are responsible for the standards we set ourselves for the treatment of workers, for the housing of tenants, and for the protection of lives and liberties in our own homeland. If other countries fail to treat people well by our standards, that is not a reason for us to lower our standards.

The problems faced by illegals are seemingly endless. For illegal immigrants from Mexico the problems start at the border, when they attempt to sneak into the United States. For them, the biggest border danger isn't the U.S. Border Patrol—far from it. The Border Patrol now makes over a million apprehensions a year, but it probably catches only a third or a quarter of those who attempt to cross. And if the Border Patrol catches an illegal immigrant, he or she will be held in custody for a few hours or a few days at most, charged with no crime, given no punishment, and released back into Mexico. After some inconvenience and a little delay, the illegal will then be free to attempt to cross the border again.

Certainly illegals don't want to be caught by the Border Patrol, just as no one wants to be given a speeding ticket, but being caught isn't necessarily a terribly serious matter. The Border Patrol doesn't steal from illegals. It doesn't rape, beat up, cripple, or kill them. The Border Patrol, in sum, is the least of the worries of those Mexicans who attempt to cross the border.

The greatest of their worries is, or should be, the border bandits who prey upon them. The bandits are predominantly Mexicans; they are occasionally Mexican Americans. Sometimes they wear the uniforms of the Mexican municipal police, or they pretend to be (or are) the *judiciales*, the Mexican state police, or they are the Mexican immigration police—for all of whom robbing illegals is just another form of the *mordida*, the bribes that the Mexican police traditionally take as their right.

The border bandits who are not members of the police forces of Mexico commit crimes on the Mexican side of the border if they must, but they prefer to operate on the American side, in the no-man's-land that the United States has ceded to illegals, their smugglers, and their parasites. American law is so much more lenient, criminals are so much less likely to get beaten up when they are in the custody of the American police.

Lines and Shadows is Joseph Wambaugh's picturesque and compulsively readable account of one American attempt to deal with the crimes committed against illegal aliens coming into the United States. For a brief period between 1976 and 1978, the city of San Diego tried to patrol the no-man's-land in the United States between it and Tijuana. The experiment began because the number of maimed illegals and unidentified murdered bodies being brought into the city from the no-man's-land had gotten too great. The San Diego Police Department's daily occurrence sheets quoted by Wambaugh tell it all:

Saturday, 2300 hours. Spring Canyon, alien robbery. Two males armed with a gun. Three victims.

Saturday, 2100 hours. Deadman's Canyon, three suspects, two victims. Knives and machetes used.

Wednesday, 2000 hours. Alien robber, E-2 Canyon. Clubs and rocks used. Ten victims. Five suspects.

Wednesday, 1930 hours, alien robber, Monument Road. Three victims. Armed Tijuana police officer ambushed them.

Wednesday, 2245 hours, alien robbery. Three victims. Monument Road. Border Patrol interrupted robbery. Tijuana auxiliary policeman (unarmed) in custody. Other uniformed officer (armed) escaped into Mexico.

Friday, 0700 hours. Alien robbery. Three victims robbed in gully by two male suspects dressed in Tijuana police uniforms.

Wednesday, 0950 hours. Body found ⅓ mile east of Hollister, 200 feet north of border fence. Male, Mexican, 30's, throat cut.

Friday, 1430 hours. Border Patrol found body on mesa near mouth of Spring Canyon. Badly decomposed male.

Tuesday, second watch. Border Patrol says Tijuana Police Department notified them of murder by soccer field in Spring Canyon, 0100 hours.

Wednesday, 2300 hours, alien robbery, San Ysidro View Park. Victim struck from behind. Face beaten in. Hospitalized.

Friday, alien robbery, 0100 hours, 8 male susps, 17–20 years. Armed with knives and clubs. Two victims and their children robbed.

Saturday, 2300 hours, Border Patrol chopper interrupted gang rape. Five suspects. Spring Canyon.[2]

The San Diego Police Department created the Border Crime Task Force—better known as the Border Alien Robbery Force (BARF)—to go into the desert canyons as decoys, as make-believe illegals, to flush out and arrest the Mexican bandits.

Most Americans are not privy to official internal police or Border Patrol listings of crimes. But Wambaugh's recountings of the crimes committed against illegals convince me that something had to be done to combat them. There were endless robberies, rapes, beatings, and murders seemingly at the whim of the bandits. But his account of the two-year crusade of the Task Force (BARF) also convinces me that their job was impossible. The illegals hid from the Mexican police. They hid from the American police. They hid from both countries' immigration police. They deliberately chose to cross the roughest, least defensible terrain—because they were members of the underground. And in that indefensible terrain they met much rougher, more brutal members of the underground who chose them as victims because of their lack of protection.

After two years, San Diego did what the late Senator George Aiken said the United States should have done in the Vietnam War—it declared victory and withdrew. But the San Diego police didn't withdraw from a foreign country. They withdrew from territory of the United States— territory that has been conquered not by force of arms but by the massive lawlessness of illegal immigration. And that lawlessness has spawned, has created, the Mexican bandit gangs that now truly own Deadman's Canyon and the rest of the wasteland south of San Diego.

If the illegals are able to evade the bandits, they still have to make it past their own smugglers. Many Mexican illegals do not use professional smugglers; many of them have been to the United States before, or have friends who have told them how to come, and they do not need the services of someone who would act as a guide. But many Mexicans and most of those of other nationalities who choose to enter the United States illegally do use smugglers, and smugglers do not generally possess high moral character. Outside the American Southwest, newspapers rarely carry articles about the illegals who are robbed, beaten, or abandoned by their own smugglers, or about the illegals who die from being trapped in overcrowded, unventilated trucks or from inhaling gasoline fumes as they were locked in car trunks. Outside Florida, it is rarely news that the body of another Haitian thrown out of the boat by a smuggler has washed onto the shore. Such events are commonplace to the members of the Border Patrol, who regularly rescue illegals from their unscrupulous smugglers, and to the members of the Coast Guard, who patrol the sea between Florida and Haiti, but they are largely unfamiliar to most Americans.

Occasionally, however, such events are so horrendous that they make national news. In 1980, over the Fourth of July weekend, fourteen Salvadoran illegal aliens died after they were abandoned in the desert by their smugglers. That made news. In April 1984, it made news when at least four Salvadoran and Mexican aliens were killed and seven were injured when they were trapped on a long, narrow train trestle in Texas and hit by a train. (I say "at least" because it is not at all sure that the Border Patrol was able to find all the bodies or all the injured.) Those aliens, also, had been led by smugglers who had taken them on a forced march for eighteen to twenty hours without food or water.[3] And it occasionally makes news when another boatload of Haitians attempting to reach the Florida shore is killed by their smugglers for the few dollars they may be carrying.

The problems of illegal aliens do not end after they have evaded the bandits and their own smugglers and entered the United States. After they have arrived, aliens have to contend with the unscrupulous American employers who would hire them in preference to American workers. The old stereotype of illegal immigrants was that they were predominantly migrant workers in the fields of large agricultural plantations. We are familiar with the exploitation of migrant workers, but we may think of it as being something from the past, something this country has outgrown. But exploitation in any job category will never end as long as there are people who are forced to do the work because of desperation or fear.

Among migrant workers the stories of Guillermo Valdivia and Jesus Alvarez Hernandez are common enough to be typical. As John Kendall reported in the *Los Angeles Times*, these two seventeen-year-olds from Atotonilco, Mexico, believed the promises of a labor recruiter/smuggler who brought them to Riverside, California, to pick citrus fruits. They were told they would be paid six dollars an hour, less twenty-five dollars a week to their smugglers, and that their food, shelter, water, work clothing, and picking equipment would be provided free.

In fact, they and the other illegal immigrants on their work crew were given plastic sheets in a field as their homes. They were told to cook over open fires and to try to keep warm (in January, with temperatures below freezing at night) with the single blankets that were sold to each of them. They worked from 7:00 A.M. to 4:30 P.M.—dawn to dusk in the California winter—with a half-hour lunch break, and they were charged exorbitantly for the eggs, beans, and tortillas that were their only provisions. In fact, they were never paid for their labor because the Blue Banner Co, Inc., their employer, deducted inflated and fictional charges from their promised pay for their food, shelter, tools, and smuggling fees. And, reported Kendall, "when Valdivia, Alvarez, and the others refused to work unless conditions were improved, their blankets and picking equipment were taken away."

The only thing that makes the Blue Banner story different from many others like it is that it became public knowledge that Inland Counties Legal Services coaxed the workers out of hiding and persuaded some of them to file suit against their employers, charging that they had been held as "virtual slaves through economic bondage, physical threats, and fear of discovery, jail, and deportation."[4]

At the end of a very similar incident, on February 6, 1984, Federal District Judge William M. Steger of Tyler, Texas, pronounced sentence on three defendants who admitted they practiced slavery. These are the facts in the case: Steven Crawford and Randall Craig Waggnor, two Texans who had a contract with the Texas State Department of Forestry to plant pine trees in Center, Texas, arranged with Joe Gonzales, a professional broker in human beings, to deliver nineteen Mexican illegal aliens to them as a work crew. They bought the men from Gonzales for fifty dollars each and then held them captive at riflepoint. They forced the nineteen aliens to live in a single, tiny, fourteen-by-twenty-foot unheated shack that had no windows, insufficient beds and blankets, and no bathroom or toilet facilities. They made them work from morning to night for no pay, and they gave them almost no food. When some of the Mexicans attempted to escape, Crawford and Waggnor recaptured them at gunpoint.

Crawford and Waggnor were arrested after the aliens finally escaped and were able to call the police, and they were convicted on more than a dozen counts including conspiracy, transportation of illegal aliens, and involuntary servitude—slavery. Then Judge William Steger pronounced upon Steven Crawford, Randall Craig Waggnor, and Joe Gonzales what he believed was the proper sentence for holding human beings in slavery in America in the year 1984: each one got five years' probation and a thousand-dollar fine. Steven Crawford's lawyer, Weldon Holcomb, approved of the sentence: "I believe," he said, "this was the proper sentence, based on all the facts and circumstances surrounding the case." Mr. Crawford, after all, he said, had his reasons: "He was trying to get ahead.

The young men just used bad judgment." And who could blame Americans, after all, reasoned Holcomb: "The Mexicans on the border just sell these people like cattle."[5]

In another incident, on January 24, 1982, the Immigration and Naturalization Service and the Federal Bureau of Investigation apprehended twenty-six Indonesian illegal immigrants in Beverly Hills. But they did not stop there in this case: they also indicted their various employers. The employers were charged with paying the workers minimal, or no, wages and with keeping them in their homes and businesses against their will through intimidation and through confiscation of their passports and visas. The employers were accused of having contracted with smugglers to supply them with workers. The workers were brought into this country, predominantly as legal visitors, sent to their prospective employers, and then held in subjugation. It was, simply, a case of twentieth-century slavery in Beverly Hills.

It was slavery that was made possible by the system of illegal immigration. If the illegal aliens protested, if they tried to escape, they were subject to deportation because they were here illegally. They felt, therefore, that they had to accept their fate—they had to accept the conditions their employers forced on them. Alvin Michaelson, a lawyer for twelve of the eighty homeowners and business "employers" who were subpoenaed to testify in the case, took an attitude that foreshadowed what Weldon Holcomb would say two years later in Texas. Michaelson was quoted as saying that his clients had "simply wanted good help." And he defended his clients' actions by saying that they had done nothing "more serious than what happens every day in L.A. with the hiring of Salvadorans, Guatemalans, everybody."[6]

The terrible truth is that Michaelson's defense of his clients is a correct one. This kind of intimidation is widespread wherever illegal immigration is widespread. The employers, the exploiters of the Indonesians, were not doing anything unusual. Instead, they were doing something that their lawyer could accurately characterize as an everyday occurrence, something everybody does.

Sasha G. Lewis has written a useful book on the bondage of illegal aliens in this country's workplaces.[7] Lewis's view of slavery is not mere imagery, nor is it exaggeration. She documents case after case of illegals who were brought to the United States by unscrupulous employers and their employment agents, who were promised good jobs at what seemed to them to be generous wages, and who were cheated out of their pay and held in bondage.

This slavery is not confined to migrant labor fields or to Beverly Hills. The increasing dependence of Sunbelt industries on illegal aliens is reminiscent of the dependence of the Old South on slavery. The urban work force is also experiencing an influx of illegals and, therefore, an increase in exploitation. One of the most distressing cases of worker exploitation reported in recent years was in Elk Grove Village, a suburb of Chicago, where the Film Recovery Systems Corporation operated what Cook County State's Attorney Richard Daley described as "a huge gas chamber" for its illegal alien workers. In February 1983, Stefan Golab died from breathing cyanide fumes. His death led to an investigation of the company. For over two years prior to his death, the company had made a practice of hiring illegal aliens. The work they engaged in was inherently dangerous: they recovered silver from used X-ray film by pouring sodium cyanide solution over chips of the film. The solution would act on the film to create silver cyanide, which was then pumped into electroplating tanks to separate the silver. Two by-products of the separation process are cyanide gas, which is used in some states for executions, and cyanide sludge, which is poisonous if absorbed through the skin.

The Film Recovery Systems Corporation plant had no

windows or fans in the vat room, where seventy large, open vats sat with cyanide fumes billowing from them and cyanide sludge sloshing over their rims. The workers were not provided with gloves or face masks or required to wear them. The workers could not read English, so they could not understand the warning labels printed on the barrels of sodium cyanide they used. And the skulls and crossbones printed on the labels were painted over or scraped off. The plant's managers, for obvious reasons, worked in another building. Its operators had never applied for the permit that Cook County requires to run such an operation, and had misrepresented its business to the county, so it had never been inspected by the Cook County Environmental Control Department before Stefan Golab died. And the workers, of course, had never heard of the U.S. Occupational Safety and Health Administration.

The firm, Richard Daley said, preferred to hire illegal aliens because "they could not understand English and were afraid that their illegal status would be exposed." Over the years, nearly ninety Polish and Mexican illegal aliens worked at the Film Recovery Systems Corporation; around twenty to thirty worked there at any one time. As in the fields of Texas and in the mansions of Beverly Hills, it was the illegal status of the workers that made their exploitation possible. Even after Stefan Golab's death, when the head of the Cook County Environmental Control Department arrived at the plant to ask the plant officials to allow their employees to submit to blood tests, the employees fled from the plant and hid. Another time, when the police arrived at the plant to help medical personnel, the managers gathered the Hispanic employees and locked them in a hall.

This much can be said in favor of the company's owners and managers; they did provide Alka-Seltzer for employees who complained of stomachaches and headaches.[8]

I would think that this kind of blatant, murderous exploitation would surely be sufficient to discredit any employer in this country—but apparently it is not. Cook County indicted five officials of the firm on murder charges as a result of Stefan Golab's death. One of these officials, Michael MacKay, was vice-president of Film Recovery and president of B. R. MacKay and Sons, Inc., which owned Film Recovery. Michael MacKay lives in Utah. And Utah's Governor Scott Matheson has refused to extradite MacKay to Illinois for trial in the case, calling him "a responsible and respected businessman." Obviously, making illegal aliens work in a gas chamber isn't enough to destroy a businessman's respectability or to cause him to be thought of as irresponsible.[9]

After having been nearly wiped out by decades of hard work and organizing against them, garment manufacturing sweatshops have returned in the United States. Both in the New York–New Jersey area and in southern California, where illegal aliens are readily available for sewing jobs in sweatshops, wage exploitation and substandard working conditions have returned. Veteran journalist Rinker Buck covered the sweatshops for *New York* magazine in 1979. He found evidence of women working in New York City who earned two dollars a day making shirt collars; he interviewed women who made a maximum of ten dollars a day and who were happy to get that much out of their employers. Buck estimated that in 1979 there were as many as 4,500 garment manufacturing sweatshops nationwide, and that anywhere from 50,000 to 70,000 illegal aliens were employed as garment workers in sweatshops in New York City alone. "Minimum-wage and overtime violations . . . ," wrote Buck, "unlawful piecework taken home, and child labor are the norm, not the exception. There are even documented cases of sweatshop managers' refusing to pay a worker's wages simply because they know that their predominantly alien work force has no way of seeking redress for their grievances."[10]

In Los Angeles in 1979, City Attorney Burt Pines

brought suit against twenty manufacturers and landlords in the garment district. Pines reported that his investigation had disclosed that a majority of the 110,000 workers in the apparel industry were illegal aliens who worked under unsafe conditions and received substandard pay, and that their co-workers who were new immigrants with legal status were largely unfamiliar with their rights under the law and were therefore easy to exploit. He reported the following specifics of exploitation: 83 percent of the 1,674 firms inspected did not pay the minimum wage or overtime; 96 percent did not keep adequate work records; and violations of health and safety laws included such things as rodent feces in workplaces, toilet stoppages, leakage from a sewage pipe, and frayed wiring on pressing irons.[11]

Buck explains why these conditions are allowed to continue:

> The sweatshop system relies on the grudging complicity of a whole population of both workers and managers, united by strong ties of family, friendship, and national origin. They see the paternalistic system under which they work as the only way to begin the climb up the economic ladder. True, they are victims, and the wages they earn here are a pittance by American standards, but for the most part it's a fortune compared to what they once earned in Hong Kong or Panama City. So more often than not, the last thing they want is for "Justice" to barge through the sweatshop doors in the form of an immigration agent, a Labor Department investigator, or a union organizer.[12]

In other words, the very presence of illegal aliens who are disposed to accept these conditions and who are prevented by their illegal status from protesting them makes ending the conditions impossible. If we want to end the sweatshops, we have to remove illegal aliens from the work force. The International Ladies' Garment Workers' Union (ILGWU) has attempted to fight abuses by organizing illegals and attempting to bring them into the union and to represent them. But all they have achieved by this tactic, aside from isolated temporary successes in some few subcontracting shops, is to increase the institutionalization of illegal aliens in the industry and to speed the lowering of work standards and wages. They have promoted the replacement of American workers by illegals.

The garment manufacturing industry could have modernized; it could have improved its practices and workplaces had the union chosen instead to defend its American workers. After a difficult adjustment, American clothes manufacturing could have competed again in an international market against the cheap labor of Asia and South America. Today, however, after the union and exploitative subcontractors have cooperated for more than a decade to cede it to illegal aliens, it is doubtful that American garment manufacturing can ever again become an industry in which American workers can receive respectable work and honest pay.

As the volume of illegal immigration has grown over the past two decades, the number and types of abuses of illegal immigrants have grown. We have tried, futilely, to attack these abuses without attacking the basic system of illegal immigration. As crime at the border has mushroomed, we have attempted to counter it by putting more American police at the border—police who had to fight the border bandits and ignore the illegal immigrants on whom the bandits prey. We have tried to counter the bad housing in which illegal immigrants are concentrated by increasing the power and numbers of city housing inspectors and by passing new laws to improve living conditions for migrant workers. We have tried to protect illegals and the Americans next to whom they work against poor working conditions and substandard wages by sending

Occupational Safety and Health Administration (OSHA) inspectors to patrol workplaces and Department of Labor enforcers to police wage and hour standards.

But the evils inherent in the system of illegal immigration cannot be ameliorated. I am convinced that we cannot correct the multitude of evils created by this system unless we smash the source of the evils. We cannot eliminate the seeds of the weed unless we uproot the weed itself.

Illegal immigration introduces people into this country under conditions that exclude them from our society. It creates a subclass of people who are here, but forbidden to be here: second-class noncitizens. Illegal aliens are outside the law; therefore they are also outside the protection of the law. By tolerating the system of illegal immigration for so long, we have allowed millions of people to enter the United States and to live here outside the protection of our laws. We cannot ignore, we cannot tolerate the system of illegal immigration and at the same time find ways to ease its inherent abuses.

We only waste our energies and resources when we devote them to attempting to protect people who are outside the law, people whose very presence in this country is illegal. They cannot be adequately protected by our laws. Their destiny is to be abused, to be mistreated, to be exploited; and it is worse than naïve for the apologists for illegal immigration to pretend to be shocked by the exploitation inherent in the system they defend. Because we are a decent country, because we want all people in this country to be protected by our standards and our laws, we shall continue to try to protect illegals against exploitation; but all our labors will be Sisyphean, endless and ultimately unavailing.

Illegal immigration makes modern-day slavery possible, and slavery as practiced in the United States in the seventeenth through the nineteenth centuries does in fact present a very close parallel to the contemporary system of illegal immigration. Slavery was also a system of exploitation, of abuse. The apologists for slavery also believed that its evils could be ameliorated without affecting the system itself. It could well be true that most slave families were not forcibly separated by slave auctions, that most slaves were not beaten, or even that most slaves were allowed adequate diets. But these issues would be irrelevant to any attempted justification of the system of slavery. Had most slave owners treated their slaves humanely and exerted societal pressure on their peers to ensure humane treatment of slaves, that also would have been irrelevant. Had there been a "Slavery OSHA" inspecting plantations for good working conditions and humane treatment, that would have been irrelevant as well as ineffective—because slaves were outside the legal system. They were a subclass who were, by their inherent status as noncitizens in a slave-owning society, subject to exploitation and abuse. They were largely unprotected, and it was not possible to protect them against overwork, underpay, beatings, robbery, rape, or abuse.

Because no system of laws or social prohibitions could be adequate to protect slaves, there was no "moderate" cure for the evils inherent in slavery. There was only a radical cure: abolition. If Americans were truly offended by the exploitation of slaves, there was only one course for us: slavery had to be abolished.

The same is true of illegal immigration. There is no moderate cure for the abuse of illegal immigrants. There is only a radical cure: the abolition of the system of illegal immigration. There are, however, two ways to abolish the system of illegal immigration. The first way would be to open the borders of the United States to all comers, to declare that there will be no restriction on immigration to this country and that anyone who wishes to come here and to work here will be welcome. The second would be to enforce existing laws against illegal immigration vigorously and thoroughly, and to pass new laws which would make the campaign against illegal immigration easier to pursue.

The first way does have the virtue of simplicity, and it wouldn't require us to increase the protection we give to our borders. Sasha Lewis, the author who identified so many abuses of illegal immigrants, would recommend it. She believes that we can solve the problem of illegal immigration by simply abandoning all limits on legal immigration. But this solution has one flaw: in the real world, it is impossible to open the United States to all comers. We would be overwhelmed by the hundreds of thousands, the millions of people who would take advantage of our foolish invitation, and we would quickly be deluged by the masses of its grateful accepters. Within a very few years, we would either withdraw the invitation or find ourselves reduced to the standard of living of Pakistan or Bangladesh—at which time massive migration to this country would cease to be a serious problem (though emigration from it would no doubt set record levels).

Those who want us to give illegal aliens free entry into our country imply that they have a monopoly on sympathy for the plight of illegals. But they don't. I also sympathize with exploited illegal aliens. But I believe that those who truly want to abolish this exploitation must strongly support enforcement of the laws against illegal immigration. The difference between the advocates of illegal immigration and its opponents is not that its advocates are more revolted by unfairness and exploitation, but that they also advocate an unrealistic and unworkable solution (and therefore no solution at all) to the problems of unfairness and exploitation.

U.S. growers contend they can't operate without illegal aliens. "No one will do stoop labor!" they cry. But this argument ignores the fact that America was built on American stoop labor—hard field labor. Even today most stoop laborers in this country are U.S. citizens, and U.S. growers can hire American workers if they provide them with decent housing and working conditions. The current system produces a harvest of misery as well as of crops—and we do not have to exploit misery to pick our crops.

The only possible way to abolish the abusive, exploitative system of illegal immigration is to enforce the laws against it. The only practical way to reduce the crimes committed against illegals—because of illegals' status outside our system of laws—is to reduce the number of illegals within our society and to reduce the entry of illegals into this country.

What will the future hold if we allow this exploitation to continue? One thing is certain: by tolerating large-scale illegal immigration and the inevitable accompanying abuse of illegal immigrants we are creating a massive problem for our children and grandchildren, who will have to deal with the children and grandchildren of illegal immigrants.

I relied on Vernon Briggs, the distinguished economist of immigration, for much of the information in Chapter 7 of this book. He said to me,

Aside from the economic effects of illegal immigration, even if there were no displacement of American workers, the main reason to be concerned about illegal aliens is the creation of a subclass of rightless persons in our society. That's a time bomb. There are people within this country who cannot vote, who cannot hold political office, who are constantly in fear of a knock on the door, even though that knock may never come, who are in fear of being stopped on the street, who are in fear of any contact with government officers, who are abused, taken advantage of, whose rights can be violated on the job, who can be discriminated against in one way or another. It's just not a healthy thing to have a subclass of that kind in this country. And their children, who may or may not have been born here, are going to grow up and resent the society, the circumstances, under which their parents had to live. The parents may be grateful to be here, even with all these problems. but their children won't be. That's the lesson of the civil rights movement of the 1960s.

The U.S. House Select Committee on Population said in 1978 that illegal aliens may

become wedged into an inferior status, part of a substratum in American society that is outside the education and social service systems. Although illegal aliens—because of their self-perception as natives of another country who expect to earn money here and return to their country of origin—may be willing to accept these circumstances, comparing them favorably to the far worse conditions from which they came, their children are unlikely to accept the same exploitative conditions and low-paying, "dead-end" jobs.

The children that illegal aliens bring to the United States, although lacking U.S. citizenship, will think of themselves as Americans with rising expectations and dreams of upward mobility. . . . Continued illegal immigration under such conditions may in time produce a second generation of alienated, frustrated young people in our society, capable of producing hostilities, disturbances, and protests like those of the 1960's.[13]

And in 1979 Secretary of Labor Ray Marshall said,

We have come too far in this century to turn back the clock. Long ago, we decided to improve the working conditions and pay for all workers. We enacted standards for employers, and we must enforce them. It is repugnant that millions of workers in America are in a lifelong second-class status, without legal protections or civil liberties. It is not only repugnant: it is dangerous to our society and a problem which can come back to haunt us with a vengeance. . . . Undocumented workers may be desperate and fearful enough to endure this today. But what about ten years from now? And what will their children be willing to endure? Is there any doubt that their children will be disadvantaged because of the extralegal status of their parents? I am convinced we are sowing the seeds of a serious future civil rights struggle, and we would be better off if we were to confront it now.[14]

Slavery's aftermath was a century of discrimination and of protest against that discrimination. It was a century of wasting the contributions that black Americans could have made to this country; it was a century of twisting the souls of white Americans by imbuing them with prejudice against their black compatriots. But we have that lesson, now, behind us. We can learn from that history. We can profit from that bad example, and we can prevent there ever again being an organized system of abuse of our fellow human beings in the United States. Because illegal immigration has until the past two decades been both localized and under moderately good control, the abuses that are inherent in it have not previously shocked the national conscience. Now, however, illegal immigration has grown beyond those bounds. It has become national in both its scope and its extent, and it has become large in both its numbers and its effects on us. We must face these abuses now and eliminate them.

We do not fight discrimination and exploitation simply out of goodwill and morality. We also fight them in our own interests, and in the interests of our children and grandchildren. We fight them because a society that would tolerate this exploitation and the conditions that created it is not a good society for us, either.

On August 24, 1984, the leader of the women who smuggled the Mexican babies into the United States was sentenced in Laredo, Texas. Federal District Court Judge George P. Kazan sentenced Nelda Karen Colwell to three years' probation and a one-thousand-dollar fine, for which community service could be substituted.[15]

3

Lawlessness

As far as we are from solving our own crime problem, we cannot afford to ignore the lawlessness that comes with the breakdown of our borders. Our immigration policies are exacerbating our national epidemic of crime. The most striking recent example of that lawlessness was the 1980 Mariel boatlift. Almost all of the 127,000 Cuban illegal immigrants in the Mariel boatlift will be given special treatment and consideration for permanent resident alien status, yet there is good evidence that 40 percent of them were criminals or had histories of criminal behavior or of mental illness.

I want to admit that the subject of crime and immigration makes me uneasy. No aspect of immigration is more sensitive, more liable to misinterpretation, and more problematic than the issue of immigration and crime. In the past, many Americans argued against allowing the immigration of certain groups or nationalities by associating them with crime. The Know-Nothing Party fought in this way against southern and eastern Europeans in the 1850s, as did the Dillingham Commission against these groups and Asians in 1921. Throughout our history, some people have held that the criminal classes were disproportionately migrating to the United States, or that certain races or nationalities were constitutionally inclined toward crime, that they were naturally criminals.

Arguments of this sort have clouded any contemporary discussion of crime and immigration. Not many respectable criminologists or immigration researchers would have the temerity to undertake a study of this interrelationship or would enter into a discussion of how many members of any particular immigrant group were criminals. The relationship of immigration and crime is by general, unspoken agreement a taboo subject for researchers and for the popular press. There are many examples of how it is generally avoided. Here are a few:

- A hotel in upstate New York burns down, and many people die. A bellboy is accused of arson. It is alleged that he feared losing his job and wanted to act like a hero by rescuing fleeing guests. Only the most careful reader of the last few paragraphs of the longest follow-up newspaper stories will discover that the bellboy is an illegal immigrant from Central America, and the television coverage of the disaster never mentions it.
- A child in Florida is brutally murdered by a madman who had just been released from an institution in Massachusetts. The mental institution is widely accused of unforgivable carelessness for releasing a man who falls into uncontrollable rages and hears the voice of God telling him to kill. But there is no public outcry against the institution for not reporting the man, an illegal immigrant from the Caribbean, to the Im-

migration and Naturalization Service for deportation.

- Gangs of young Chinese immigrants terrorize Chinese
shopkeepers and restaurant owners in the Maryland
suburbs of Washington, D.C., and gangs of young
Vietnamese immigrants ply the same protection racket
against Vietnamese store owners in the Virginia suburbs. But the long chains of bullying and threatening incidents are mentioned for only a day or two on
Washington television and radio stations, and the
Washington Post dismisses them with only the most
perfunctory coverage.

- When *The New York Times* reports in 1984 that the
Customs Service arrested five people for conspiring
to smuggle more than one billion dollars of classified
high-technology military equipment to China, it is not
until the eighth paragraph that the reader learns that
three of the five were naturalized American citizens
from China and that the other two were citizens of
the People's Republic.

- A nationwide ring of Nigerian nationals is engaged
in credit-card fraud, bank fraud, life insurance fraud,
student loan fraud, counterfeiting of documents, and
smuggling and drug trafficking. But when the Atlanta police hold a seminar for law-enforcement officials to alert them to this organized criminal activity, the Nigerian Consul General sends protest letters
to the mayor of Atlanta and the governor of Geor-
gia, calling the seminar "dangerous, racist, unlawful, and blatantly prejudicial to the rights of Nigerian citizens in this country."

- It takes more than a month for it to be revealed that
the worst mass murderer in Dallas's history, a Mo-
roccan national, was able to enter the United States
with a criminal record that included convictions in
thirteen assaults and one child beating, two invol-

untary hospitalizations for mental health disorders and alcoholism, two jail terms, and a probated sentence of five years.

- And, in the most widely publicized rape trial in a decade, six men in New Bedford, Massachusetts, are accused of raping a woman in a barroom. Wide publicity is given to the false accusation, the mistaken belief, that patrons in the bar looked on and cheered. But no publicity at all is given to the fact that the accused men are Portuguese immigrants. That is, no publicity is given until Portuguese residents of New Bedford and Fall River form the Portuguese American Defense League to support the accused rapists. Sixty percent of the population of New Bedford and Fall River are of Portuguese descent. Thousands of them ignore the fact that the raped woman is of Portuguese ancestry and that the prosecutor is the son of Portuguese immigrants, and join the committee in demonstrations to support the defendants and castigate the press for reporting the rape. They contend that the men are on trial only because of prejudice.

These reactions partially explain why the press shies away from identifying criminals by their immigration status or national heritage. But an additional reason is that the conscience of the American press on the matter of race is uneasy. It was not many decades ago that few newspapers in either the South or the North took any note of the weddings, births, or deaths of Negroes. But almost all papers prominently identified the race of any Negro involved in a crime. And any standard history of immigration to the United States is replete with examples of the press associating migrants with criminality. For example, the Dillingham Commission, which performed much of the background research for the passage of the 1921 Immigration Act, did much admirable, straightforward, and scientific research on the economic and sociological effects of migration to the United States. But the public impact, the popular press's coverage of the Dillingham Commission was much more concerned with the pseudoscientific theories it propounded about the inherent criminality of southern European "races."

After all of this is said, however, it must be added that the reaction against this prejudice has been, in many cases, rather extreme. In 1961, the Federation of the Italian-American Democratic Organizations of the State of New York attacked the television series "The Untouchables." The program had been committing an unpardonable slur (in the eyes of the Federation) by portraying many members of the Mafia in the 1930s as having been of Italian heritage. Since the success of the Federation's campaign to force the series to portray Mafiosi as though they were primarily White Anglo-Saxon Protestants, it has been unusual for any television or film drama to portray villains who are not WASPs.

And yet I am convinced, even though I know my concern with the issue will be widely misunderstood, that it is important to discuss the relationship between immigrants and crime. We make a terrible mistake if we sweep the subject under a metaphorical rug. A "gentleman's agreement" not to discuss a subject because it is difficult or disturbing is a prelude to disaster; it is exactly the subjects that are most sensitive which are the most likely to cause social problems.

It is probably true throughout the world that most immigrant groups commit crimes at a higher rate than the general population. And there are many reasons for this. Immigrants, after all, are displaced persons; many avenues of success in their new societies will be closed to them. They will have difficulties adjusting to their new countries and learning the language and the mores of their new societies, and they will encounter discrimination which could engender resentment and ill will toward their new country. Most immigrants will also be poor, and in all societies there is a higher incidence of crime among the poor.

In Colorado, the percentage of all arrests of the foreign born grew by almost a third in the five years between August 1978 and August 1983. And the Colorado Bureau of Investigation found that it accumulated new files for more than 8,500 foreign-born criminals in those five years. In June 1983, three of the ten most-wanted criminals in Denver were illegal aliens.

In the United States, immigration is associated with crime in at least four ways. First, illegal immigration is itself a crime, which millions of people commit yearly. For an illegal immigrant to work in the United States is another crime, which millions of people commit continuously. Some people do not take illegal immigration seriously because they consider it to be a "victimless" crime. No individual is hurt by the act of another individual's crossing the border, they say, and it is difficult to become very disturbed by any one person's overstaying a visitor's visa or walking across the border. As long as individual acts of illegal immigration are considered in isolation, illegal immigration itself may be thought of as a relatively harmless form of lawbreaking. Only in the mass, only when hundreds of thousands of individuals commit the crime, does its seriousness become evident. In this respect, illegal immigration is much like prostitution. Many take a rather relaxed attitude toward the enforcement of laws against prostitution because, if we set aside the important issue of whether many prostitutes are initially coerced into their profession, it is a relatively "victimless" crime. But a growth in prostitution which makes it highly visible—such as the opening of massage parlors or outcall services that advertise openly, or obvious solicitation by streetwalkers—will create public concern and calls for the enforcement of the law.

Second, as I showed in Chapter 2, illegal immigration

is surrounded by many other crimes, which it encourages by the very nature of its secretiveness. The border gangs that prey upon illegal border crossers, that rob, rape, terrorize, beat, and even kill them, are paralleled by the pimps and thieves who prey upon prostitutes. In both cases, the reluctance of those who are outside the law to call upon law enforcement agencies makes them easy game for more vicious criminals.

Third, illegal immigrants are frequently assisted and preyed upon by one unique class of criminals, the smugglers who arrange for their passage into the United States. While there are folk tales of "honest smugglers" who deal with their clients fairly—who break the law while operating under a criminal code of honor, as it were—these tales should be classed with stories about "gentlemen thieves" like Raffles. There aren't many gentlemanly bandits and honest smugglers in real life. The real people who smuggle illegal aliens into the United States are the same kind of people who smuggle drugs and other contraband. They are smuggling people because it is easier and less dangerous, because the United States is lax about enforcing its immigration laws, because they are less likely to get caught, and because their punishment will be light if they are caught. (In fact, the increasing integration of drug smuggling and alien smuggling is creating the growing practice among illegal alien smugglers of using the aliens as "mules" for carrying drugs.)

And fourth, as I mentioned at the beginning of this chapter, crime and immigration are associated in one way that stands out strikingly in American history in the case of the criminals who entered the United States in the Mariel boatlift. It may be useful to give a short history of the boatlift. In April 1980, a small group of Cuban political dissidents claimed asylum in the Peruvian embassy in Havana. The group began to grow, and when Fidel Castro agreed to let them leave the country it mushroomed to over ten thousand. The United States agreed to accept a portion of the group if they would first be screened in Costa Rica, in Central America. But Castro outmaneuvered the Carter administration by announcing that Cubans would be free to leave the country only if they were to go directly to America by boat from Mariel Harbor. By the end of April, the boatlift had begun. Private individuals and ad hoc groups in the Cuban community in Dade County, Florida, and Jersey City, New Jersey, became active in financing boats that traveled from Miami and Key West to Mariel. Some wished to pick up friends and relatives, while others had a generalized desire to help any of those who wanted to leave Cuba.

The initial reaction in the United States was that the communist government of Cuba was terribly embarrassed by the exodus, and there was an initial public wave of support for the "Freedom Flotilla." But even before the end of the first month it was obvious that Castro was using the exodus to get rid of Cuba's criminals, and stories began circulating that some people were being expelled and that boat owners and captains were being forced to take criminals, mental patients, and other undesirables.

While initial public support for the "Freedom Flotilla" waned and turned to distrust rather quickly, the Cuban community in Florida continued sending boats and financing the boatlift for months. The Carter administration was unwilling to take strong measures to prevent them from supporting the boatlift for several reasons: President Carter did not want to appear to be preventing the escape of political protesters from a communist regime; he did not want to oppose the strong Cuban constituency in a state that might be vital to the Democrats in the 1980 election; the Republican candidate, Ronald Reagan, was vocal in his support of the Mariel boatlift and would have excoriated Carter had he moved to close it down; President Carter's primary opponent in the Democratic party, Senator Edward Kennedy, was even more enthusiastic about the boatlift (and he remains the strongest congressional supporter of granting all the Marielitos permanent resident status); and the traditional American myth of free and open immigration paralyzed liberals in the Carter adminstration and prevented them from taking strong moves against an obvious, massive, public flouting of immigration laws.

The boatlift lasted through September, until Castro himself closed Mariel Harbor. About 125,000 Cubans entered the United States during the five months that it lasted.

Even today, it is unclear how many of those in the Mariel boatlift were professional criminals. It is also unclear how many were expelled from Cuba for being prostitutes or homosexuals or how many had communicable diseases. But the problem of importing criminals is the most troubling of all. One of the foremost experts on Mariel criminals is Detective Richard Alvarez of the Harrisburg, Pennsylvania, Police Bureau. Detective Alvarez himself, however, told me that he doesn't claim to be an expert. "Nobody knows much about them," he said; "nobody knows enough." But Alvarez is the co-founder and organizer of METS, the Mariel Entrant Tracking System, that aids police forces nationwide to identify the Mariel criminals whom they have apprehended. Through METS, Alvarez also consults with police forces in many cities to help them understand the problems they are encountering with the Marielitos. He calls himself "a cop of Cuban heritage": his father was born in Cuba and his mother was raised there.

When the Mariel boatlift started, Detective Alvarez said,

I was enthusiastic just like Jimmy Carter; I thought it was the greatest thing to come down the pike. I remembered the difficulties my parents had had trying to get some of my family out of Cuba in the 1960s, and I envisioned being able to travel there and having more trade there, and maybe the possibility of my being able to go back there. I haven't been back since the 1960s, and I have a lot of relatives there, half of whom I've never known.

But Fort Indiantown Gap, one of the internment reception centers that housed the Mariel refugees, was within twenty minutes of Harrisburg. One of the higher echelon coordinators there happened to be O. Frank DeGarcia. DeGarcia was born in Cuba. He came to the United States as a refugee at the age of fifteen. He had been active in law enforcement as the state director of welfare fraud investigations, and the state loaned him to the State Department to be a work force coordinator at Indiantown Gap. He supervised most of their food, medical, and survival-type services. He saw the Marielitos much earlier than the rest of the country did, therefore, and at his first opportunity he came back to Harrisburg and started briefing the police department.

At first, what he had to say about the people who had arrived wasn't given much credence. But as things progressed, and as the riots started at Fort Indiantown Gap, the chief of detectives, Richard Vajda, who is now the chief of police, started to pay some attention. DeGarcia was able to get a program started in which the Hispanic patrolmen on the Harrisburg police force—there were five of us then—were rotated through the detective bureau. Harrisburg has a fairly large Hispanic community, so that was an additional benefit of the program. When I was brought up to the bureau, I was still pretty much a young guy—I had only been a cop for five years, three years in Harrisburg and two years somewhere else. I was a patrolman then, and I was the second of the Hispanics who began to work in the detective bureau for three months.

One Wednesday, after I had been in the Detective Bureau for only two or three days, I was in early in the morning, just drinking a cup of coffee and clearing out the cobwebs, when we got a call that there was a shooting downtown, in broad daylight, and a fatality as a result of that shooting. I ran down and found the body of a man who had been identified as a black male. Some of the cops even thought he was a fellow they knew who had grown up in Harrisburg. But when I looked at the man, I saw that he had tattoos on his eyelids. The tattoos read *te vi*, which in Spanish means "I saw you," and I realized that he was a Mariel Cuban refugee.

The criminals in Cuba had an elaborate system of tattoos which identified their criminal specialties; this was unique, and no American criminals wore such public badges.

The M.O. behind that robbery was that two Cuban Mariels went into a pawnshop, handcuffed the elderly proprietors, and pistol-whipped them. One man set off a silent alarm, and one of our foot officers responded by walking into the store. In Harrisburg, a robbery in broad daylight on a business day is just highly unlikely; it's very uncommon. So the cop really didn't expect to find anything, and he was met by a hail of gunfire. He wounded one of the robbers and retreated. He was outside, reloading in a safe place, when the second robber came out. The cop challenged him; the man turned with a pistol in each hand and tried to shoot the cop, so the cop dusted him.

That was the start. That investigation revealed that in Harrisburg we had anywhere from twelve to twenty Mariel Cubans who had recently come from the Bronx. They had been involved in one shooting in the Bronx, and one fatal shooting in Newark, and were into drugs at that time. Looking back, we realized what had hap-

59

pened. The shooting in New York, the initial shooting, had occurred in early April. That spilled over into New Jersey, where there was the fatal shooting. By the next day, we had reports of shootings in Harrisburg, but the cops would find nothing when they got to the scene. The following day, we had the robbery, with the other fatal shooting. I got in touch with the detectives in New York, and I went down there with my photo array book, which then had photos of thirty-six Cuban refugees. Out of the thirty-six photos, their informant in the Bronx knew thirty of them by name, nickname, description, and M.O. And we verified it, and I knew he was telling the truth—you can't tell height by a photo. Not all of these thirty were involved in the one gang, but there was mobility back and forth between gangs.

That started the ball rolling. We, DeGarcia and myself, attended a seminar in December 1980 in Manhattan that was held by the New York Police Department, and we realized then that we had a whole lot more information than they did in terms of identifying these characters and of having some background on them, and that we had the data processed. Because of the mobility of these gangs and the manner in which these guys changed names and had no verifiable identification, and because of oversights on the part of the federal government, they were not identifiable to law enforcement. We decided that night on the way back to Harrisburg that it might be appropriate to develop a central repository where we could collect photographs, assist in identification, and assist in locating fugitives for other departments. We gave it the name METS then.

The system, the METS system, started developing as the Mariel crime problem began to manifest itself, and as law-enforcement agencies began to recognize the Mariels. Gradually, we built a list of about 150 contacts throughout the nation in law-enforcement agencies at the local, state, and federal levels, who dealt with Mariels. They sent us photos and descriptions, and we helped them when we could. Mostly, this happened informally, on an individual basis, rather than through the bureaucracies of the various departments.

Within a few months we started conducting seminars. We had a series of six to ten of them which were very well attended and well received. We started distributing literature and any information that we could find. But, after a year or a year and a half, we had to suspend the seminars because we still had to address our local problems. They—the Mariel refugees—were driving us crazy here. I was trying to wear two hats, to be a criminal investigator and to run METS at the same time, and you can only put in so many hours before you start getting ulcers.

More recently, we've begun the seminars again. Our last seminar in Harrisburg had people come from the LAPD, L.A. county sheriff's office, Indianapolis, Atlanta, Rochester—literally from all over the country. We're in contact with many major cities and a lot of smaller cities that would surprise you.

Now we have printouts of all the Mariels who arrived, so when one is in custody, the police department can call us and say, "I have a guy here who claims to be 'Juan Valdez Garcia,' with this date of birth, who entered through Fort Chaffee," and so on. We try to verify that, to see if there is any individual who fits that description, and then we can direct that agency to where the fingerprint cards are for that individual, to see if they have the right man. That's part of it. All of this time, we've been trying to get some funding so that we could buy additional computer hardware, put the data base on it, and employ a clerk to cover the evening shift. We still haven't gotten that.

The public impression of criminals within the Mariel flow was formed within the first few months after Mariel, and it was shaped by federal assurances that there were only 2,000 criminals at most—1.5 percent—within the Mariel group, and that many of those criminals had been in jail in Cuba only for political reasons, only for opposing the government. The ongoing agreement with Cuba to allow repatriation of Mariel criminals, reached in late 1984 and suspended in mid-1985, will eventually apply to fewer than 2,500 criminals who are now in custody.

Detective Alvarez continued: "During the time that METS was in its infancy, that it was being formed, we wanted to educate not just the law-enforcement officials, but also the American public. We wanted them to know two things: these sons-of-bitches aren't Cubans like the old-school Cubans, first; and second, to be careful of them because they are violent and very, very dangerous." But the federal government was claiming that there were at most 2,000 criminals in the Mariel boatlift, that many of them had been "political" criminals, and that there was no public danger.

So we very early on started contesting the government's claims, and saying that, from our information, there were forty thousand people within the Mariel flow who had been prisoners—and not political prisoners. That was a guesstimate, of course, but it was based on good information: on incidence of arrest per population locally and in New York, on our contact with recidivism, on our Mariel informants, on the whole thing. That figure is still our public figure, although I, with all my heart, believe that the real figure is much, much higher. I can think of four Mariel criminals I talked to recently who, when I asked, "Hey, how many of these characters who came along with you were out of Cuban prisons?" admitted that almost everybody was. Recently I was talking with one of the two Mariels whom I've met whom I trust—I have two cousins who came over in Mariel, and my father swears that they're okay, but I haven't met them yet, and I'm from Missouri these days. Anyway, this guy told me that during the time he was in Mariel harbor, for every legitimate refugee placed on a boat twenty-five cons were put on. We've had others tell us a hundred thousand, and others tell us 80 percent, which is all roughly the same. One man was in a prison with eight thousand inmates, and by the time the Mariel boatlift was over there were eight hundred left. I've talked recently with some immigration officials—lower-level officials who can survive without all the bureaucratic whitewash, who are upset with the whitewash—that it looked to them like almost everybody in the Mariel boatlift was a con. We haven't said that publicly because we can't support it yet and because of the reaction we would get. We already get quite a reaction when we say forty thousand.

When the boatlift occurred, there were reports from Cubans who were in jail in Cuba that the jails were being emptied, and there were legitimate refugees among the Mariels who tried to tell the immigration officials, "That guy's a murderer, this guy's an agent." That wasn't isolated. I talked to a guy the other day who was an official at Fort McCoy who said that after most of the Mariels there had been sponsored, and they had about 3,100 left, they interviewed them and found that 3,000 of them had been in prison.

I didn't really want to believe that it was that bad. I still don't want to claim it. And documentation is extremely difficult. When an agency as sophisticated as the Los Angeles Police Department only recognized the Mariels a year and a half ago, when they've been here for four years, how do you compile any statistics? The LAPD is a hell of an outfit; I had a man from them here in December, and the man can run rings around me as far as being a cop—but the LAPD didn't realize that a lot of the crime in the city was Mariel-committed. They thought it was American blacks, or other Hispanics, or even Caucasians. They didn't know what to look for.

Another difficulty as far as statistics, as far as arrests here in the United States, is that they change their names so frequently. About a year ago, the New York Police Department gave me a list of five thousand names of Mariel Cubans—identified as Mariels through tattoos, through their own admissions, through other identifications—and asked me to do a random sampling of them. I picked four hundred names at random, and found that only 20 percent of them gave verifiable identities. The federal government misread my data and claimed that that proved the five thousand weren't Mariels, and that they were other Hispanics. Oh, no. They were Mariels.

The Mariel criminals are used to surviving a very repressive criminal justice system, where because of the revolution there are eyes and ears everywhere that see where you are. They've fine-tuned methods of smuggling, of dealing with contraband, of dealing in the black market, of lying their way out of situations, because there it's literally a matter of life and death. I mean, if you're arrested for a crime there, or suspected of a crime, they'll start thrashing you from the very start. They have no human rights there. Because of the extreme measures taken by the Cuban police, the Cuban criminal is a lot more violent than the

American criminal. I would say just the average Mariel criminal is more hard-core than some of the worst we have in this country.

The first two thousand hard-core Mariel criminals were put in the Atlanta federal penitentiary. Bernadette Hernandez is a detective in Atlanta. She reviewed their psychological profiles, and found that out of the 1,100 who were there when she did her research, only 50 were considered normal, were sane. In New York City, 214 Cubans were arrested in the year prior to the 1980 boatlift. From the time of the boatlift it jumped to something like 2,000 or 3,000. Over 9,000 Cubans have been arrested in New York now and they're averaging 250 arrests of Mariels a month. In Las Vegas, Mariels are something like one-tenth of 1 percent of the population; they're responsible for 11 to 12 percent of the homicides. In Harrisburg, well over half of the Mariels have been involved in some fairly serious criminal activity.

We were very critical of the federal government and of INS at one time, and maybe rightly so. But with time I've tempered my criticism of the government and of INS, because I understand that processing 125,000 people in four or five months was an impossible job for them. But it is only recently that we are getting some cooperation from INS, and we still don't get cooperation from the real high brass; they just want to forget about the whole thing.

When Mariel refugees entered the United States, the Carter administration realized that they did not fit the criteria for refugee status the government had instituted just a few months earlier. They had not been persecuted for their political beliefs or activities; they were not in danger from their government because of opposition to it. The administration, therefore, did not give them a blanket refugee status. Instead, it instituted a new, extralegal status that did not exist in immigration law. It used the attorney general's parole power to admit individuals into the United States and called them Cuban Entrants/Status Pending. (In fact, because the administration believed that Haitians who had entered the United States illegally were in essentially the same position as the Cubans who had entered illegally—neither group was eligible for refugee status, but neither group was likely to be deported wholesale—it paired the Cubans with the Haitians and gave them the same status: Cuban/Haitian Entrants/Status Pending.) This state of limbo was supposed to last for only six months, during which time the Congress could take steps to legalize their position in this country. To date, Congress has not done so, and the Cubans and the Haitians remain in this country without any legal basis whatsoever. The Immigration and Naturalization Service, under pressure to find a way to regularize the Cubans, began in late 1984 to regularize their immigration status by using the long-superseded and outdated procedures set up to handle the Cuban refugees of the 1960s.

One thing Immigration instituted very early on was an avenue to revoke the status of Mariel criminal offenders in the United States. The Cubans are, essentially, federal parolees. There are terms of parole, and if they violate the terms of parole they can have detainers put on them and they can go through exclusionary hearings to be expelled from this country. The INS has a procedure under which, if a man commits a felony and serves his sentence, it will revoke his parole and send him to a federal penitentiary. But INS never told anybody—they never let police departments or prosecutors know about the program. That was part of what we did—we spread the word that revocation of parole was possible. We tried that early on in Harrisburg, and had about a dozen taken out of here, but I got disgusted when I found that a few months later several of them were out of the Atlanta prison and were back here. Federal District Court Judge Marvin Shoob was ordering the release of Mariel prisoners because the federal government couldn't show that they were ever going to release them or get them taken back by Cuba.

In any case, the INS is making progress; it is beginning to help. And there are some avenues available to ID Mariels through the INS that I'm just now becoming aware of. That was part of the problem, of course; the help they had available never filtered down to the local levels. As far as other national departments or systems—nothing. There is no national program or federal help for law-enforcement agencies which have to deal with Mariel criminals.

I'll give you a general typology of Mariel criminals. On the first rung you have a whole large group of very, very violent people, a lot of psychopaths, a lot of people who for a number of reasons don't think twice about taking a human life. When they first hit the streets, they needed more money than welfare gave them, and they needed it quickly. So one of the very first manifestations we started seeing was very violent, very brazen armed robberies. One example close to here was in Reading, Pennsylvania. Three of them walked into a Mom-and-Pop grocery store, shot and killed the owner, and the proceeds of the whole damn robbery was one pack of cupcakes. It was just craziness. Or they'd try something like the stunt I told you about here, and they'd get away with nothing or they'd get away with two or three hundred bucks. They were basically working with prison associates, people with whom they had done time in Cuba or people from the same hometown in Cuba. Because, remember now, if we're emptying out prisons, and we empty one which might have eight thousand prisoners, all of whom are from the same province, and if we empty it out within a matter of days, most of them will end up in the same internment camp in the United States. So all we've done is replace the prison population, relocate it. And when the first one gets out, he turns around and sponsors ten of his buddies in the internment camp, and all at once you have an instant gang.

These are some slick dudes, and the organization then was based, and to a degree still is based, on who was toughest. Your basic thuggery. Whoever was toughest was the head high honcho, and then you had your pecking order, and that was your organization. They'd commit a crime, break up that gang, and then do other crimes with different partners, different participants. Over the years, they've become increasingly organized. Armed robberies were the first manifestation. Second were residential and commercial burglaries, tied in with auto theft rings run by other, more established Hispanics. The random sex crimes—an awful lot of real heavy perverts among these guys, too—rapes and assaults you wouldn't believe. And of course your violent crimes, your aggravated assaults, your crimes of passion, and your homicides.

But every year robbery has dwindled, at least on the East Coast, and in fact everywhere that I know of except Los Angeles. And it has been displaced by the drug traffic. The organization there at times is extremely sophisticated. You have your old-school, right-wing Cuban refugees from the sixties, some of them CIA-trained. Groups who had to seek an alternate financing method for their paramilitary activities when the support from the U.S. government dried up. And that financing method is basically cocaine. So you have established, sophisticated people who now have a complete labor force available to them of some really rough-ass characters. And they fit right in.

Another type of leadership that we have in drug traffic is the Cuban operative. There are about four hundred Cuban operatives who were sent to the United States from Mariel to set up a drug ring. About a year ago, at the invitation of the New York State Select Committee on Crime, DeGarcia and I attended a New York State Senate hearing at One Federal Plaza to give testimony. One of the other witnesses testifying was a Federal Drug Enforcement Administration informant. I don't know what his real name is; they've changed his name a million times, and he's under very tight protection—the security was incredible there. He testified that he was a Cuban operative prior to the boatlift, but that he had been caught smuggling drugs from Cuba. He had offered to give state's evidence, and his testimony and information led to the arrest of a bunch of other people, including the indictment of a vice-admiral in Cuba's navy. During the boatlift he was placed among the refugees with three thousand operatives, of which he was among a smaller figure, four hundred, assigned solely to the importation and smuggling of drugs. In one year's time, either 1981 or 1982, he smuggled in cocaine, quaaludes, and marijuana, and turned over seven million dollars to Fidel Castro's government. One out of four hundred, and he turned over seven million in a year. He also testified at that point that there were fifty thousand hardcore dudes among the boatlift. I really believe now that there were more than that.

But you now have three levels of leadership: one, the established, right-wing Cubans who are renegades; two, the operatives; and three, the guys who for one reason or another are able to make the connection themselves. Their operation might be run by Mariels just for profit's sake alone. One guy we did a little work-up on just recently was tied to a Mafia family in New York—if you remember, under Batista the Mafia was involved deeply in Cuba, so some of those ties go back years and years. Back about two years ago in Miami, they were having Mariels posing as Metro Dade police officers, equipped with radios, uniforms, and cars. They'd run up to a drug dealer's house, flash what looked like a search warrant, announce they were police, rip off the drugs, and then take off. Miami had a 120-man commercial burglary ring—I have the photos here. They're ingenious people. A couple years ago, DeGarcia and I had a difference of opinion. He never could see them really getting organized. He thought they didn't have the family structure that the Mafia did, and so on, and so on. And I said that they would organize. They had the prison associations; they had the clearly defined pecking order; and they had people emerging as kingpins. Finally, the other day, after about two years, DeGarcia told me he had talked to some people, heard some things, and he said to me, "Alvarez, you were right." I compare them to the Mafia during prohibition. I constantly relate them to the TV show, "The Untouchables." The reckless abandon, you know, the gunfire. They don't care who gets involved, who gets hurt.

Alvarez believes that not only was there a deliberate policy of emptying the prisons in Cuba, but that there were other motives for getting the criminals out of Cuba and into the United States.

Of course, Cuba is hard-pressed for hard currency, especially in trying to finance its military ventures throughout the world. The drug smuggling, of course, is a good source of income. You know, I used to be a young liberal in college, and a McCarthyite (Gene McCarthy, not Joe McCarthy), and the whole bit. And it used to drive me crazy that people attributed everything to a communist plot. But the more I look at this, and the more I'm active in law enforcement with the Mariels, the more I really believe in a communist plot. This is not only a drain on our economy because of the drugs; but also the Cuban refugee almost anywhere is an inordinate percent of the prison population; and we've heard talk of people who are here to cause uprisings within the prisons. It taxes the criminal justice system; it taxes all of our systems. We're talking not only about prisons being emptied, but also mental health facilities. And we're talking about the streets being swept to get rid of prostitutes, pimps, and anybody who Castro considered undesirable.

I fully suspect that some other operatives are involved in technology theft, computer theft. When you have a bunch of real hard-core characters like the criminals coming across, and then you have a highly educated former Cuban official come here and begin to work immediately in a sensitive high-tech industry, you really start to wonder. In Cuba, you only get an education and good jobs if you belong to the Party; and Fidel Castro won't invest that kind of money in you and then let you leave the country. There are hundreds of examples of people like that. God only knows what their motives were. But I'll never forget them.

Cuba landed, literally, the equivalent of more than three Marine infantry divisions on our shores with that boatlift. A hundred twenty-five thousand people. The chaos itself was incredible; the personal suffering was incredible; but I think there's more to come. I can't say definitely that I know saboteurs are out there, but I fully suspect it. If I'm right, if there are saboteurs among them, I don't know why they haven't struck yet. When I look back at the invasion of Grenada, I was sitting on pins and needles, because I expected all hell to break loose. I don't know why it didn't; maybe Castro didn't want to provoke us to take more action. I do have information from Dade County that three years ago one group of operatives whose sole mission was civic disruption was amassing a whole lot of weaponry—hand grenades, automatic weapons. I'm not saying the typical Mariel bandito criminal is coming here with a mission. He's not intentionally doing this for Castro. Castro just knew what would happen.

There is a real danger that all Cubans, or even all Hispanics, will be stereotyped, will be tarred, by the actions of the Mariel criminals. And it is inescapable that the reputation of all Marielitos will be damaged by their association, no matter how brief or accidental, with the criminals in the boatlift.

The way I deal with that is that every time I open my mouth to talk about the Mariels I give a disclaimer. We're not talking about all Mariels, we're not talking about all Cubans, we're not talking about all Hispanics. We're talking about a specific group of convicts, of mental cases, and of undesirables that Castro put on our shores. I think the only way to combat the stereotype, to keep it from spreading, is for the Cubans, the Hispanics, to really crack down on the Mariels themselves and to exert a lot of pressure themselves to get this mess cleaned up. The way to take away the stigma is to make the criminals exiles, exiles within this country and within the community.

I get two messages from the Hispanic community, especially from Cubans. You have to understand that when Castro came into power the professionals, the middle class and the upper class, came to the States. I know that in my family we had doctors, attorneys. Ironically, one of my uncles was the mayor of our hometown, and a communist. But when Castro came into power, the hardware store that my uncle owned was confiscated, and he pulled up roots and came to the States. These people who were coming over, professors, high-ranking officials, found themselves pushing brooms, washing dishes, and doing the most menial labor. They busted their humps for years in order to reach the level of living they had been accustomed to, in order to get recertified and reenter their professions. They have worked hard for twenty-five years, and have become a very wealthy, very ambitious group, on the whole. In fact, all my Cuban cousins embarrass the hell out of me, because they're making three times the money I am.

But these Cubans, and myself among them, remember the prejudice. I remember being called "spic" when I was young. I'm not crying on anybody's shoulder, but it wasn't fun. But this group went through that, and is, by necessity, sensitive to any discrimination. And now, to have these guys come in here, and to have them cause this ruckus, and to have the reputation of the group be downtrodden, and to see the old racist innuendos returning, makes Cubans very defensive, very combative. That's why, if anybody who isn't Hispanic talks about it, they—we—get defensive. But by and large the established Cubans know what the Marielito criminals are. The word in Spanish is *escoria*. That's the word Fidel Castro used. It might explain what I'm saying. It means "scum." Again, of course, when I say *Marielitos* here I refer to the criminals, not to the family that came here because somebody bailed them out, because somebody in the family who hadn't seen them in twenty-five years came with a boat from Key West. I'm not talking about the legitimate guys. But the established Cubans have learned.

There's an awful lot that can be done about the Mariels if the government is willing, number one, to admit to its error, and, number two, to spend a whole lot of money. We still have the parole status on these guys. I think the ideal thing would be for the law-enforcement officials in local communities to round up the Mariels who have proven to be disruptive and to put them back into internment camps until they can be forced back down Fidel Castro's throat. I don't know how you do that. People want to send them down to Guantanamo and force them across the line. That sounds unreasonable, and I know it will never happen, but I don't know what else would be a complete solution. I think the federal government recognizes that, and that that's why they've maintained the posture they have, hoping that in a few generations they'll be assimilated. Maybe they will be, in a hundred years, but there'll be a lot of suffering in the meantime. It was a terrible blunder, a terrible blunder.

You know what the bottom line is in all this? And this is my heartfelt conviction. The Mariels are a drop in the bucket right now. Because of our immigration policies, because we can't or won't enforce our laws, we've opened the door to everybody. We're not screening at all. I fully believe that we're headed toward a breakdown.

As Detective Andrew Lugo of the Bronx said, "Letting these guys in was like Custer calling for more Indians."[1] But what is the lesson of the Mariel boatlift? To me, the lesson is simple: immigration laws are meaningful and useful and they protect our society. Mariel was a massive breakdown of our immigration laws. And because of that it was a disaster for our law enforcement agencies and, of course, for the citizens of the United States who will suffer at the hands of the criminals who were admitted.

Mariel demonstrates that immigration laws—with teeth—are vital. It is vital to have not just immigration laws that limit the number of people who will be admitted each year, but also laws that screen those immigrants for their suitability to enter this country. Many of the Marielitos— tens of thousands of them—should never have been let into the United States under any circumstances. But they were admitted because they successfully evaded our immigration laws and the screening procedures that these laws mandate, and once they were here our government felt powerless to expel them.

Mariel was a breakdown of the system, and a dramatic one. Pictures of dozens of men crowded on the deck of a small boat steaming into Miami made for powerful television. But Mariel was minuscule compared with the volume of illegal immigration that occurs every year. Marielitos—all of the entrants who came in the boatlift—were fewer than one-tenth of the illegal immigrants who entered the United States in 1980, and who enter every year. And those illegal immigrants, just like the Marielitos, are unscreened, unseen by any representative of this country. In the volume of illegal immigrants who come to America, Mariel is being repeated every single month of the year. Our government's toleration of that illegal traffic is an open invitation for more of the same.

4

The Splintered Society

I love America, and I want to save and preserve it. To most people, that sentence would seem a bland and noncontroversial bit of flag-waving. But when the subject is immigration, a lot of people would object to it strenuously. When confronted with the social stresses and strains that large-scale immigration place on our country, some people just want to ignore them, want to deny that they exist. Others are less well disposed to the culture and the mores of the United States and don't believe that we should save and preserve them.

Let me say it directly: massive immigration involves serious and profound social and cultural dangers. The United States is not immune to the trends that have affected and altered all other human societies. Civilizations rise and civilizations fall—and there are certain universal pathologies that characterize the fall of history's civilizations. Ethnic, racial, and religious differences can become such a pathology; they can grow, fester, and eventually splinter a society. The "melting pot" society is clearly an exception to history's lesson, and we make a serious mistake if we think that all our differences can and will harmonize (or homogenize) without our work and care.

I believe that America's culture and national identity are threatened by massive levels of legal and illegal immigration. Admittedly, there are good historical reasons that some people remain complacent in the face of massive migration. After all, there were adjustment difficulties in earlier periods of peak migration, but the fears of Americans that migrants would permanently change the basis of American culture were unjustified, as were their fears that migrants and their children would not assimilate. And the yearly inflow of immigrants to the United States composes a lower percentage of our total population today than it did in the 1910s. Therefore, it is easy to assume that we're unjustified if we worry about the social effects of large-scale migration today.

I know that earlier large waves of immigrants didn't "overturn" America, but there are at least five reasons not to be complacent, reasons to believe that today's migration is different from earlier flows. First, the yearly inflow of immigrants is a small portion of our society's total population, but immigrants are not evenly dispersed throughout the country. They settle in a few big cities, and they constitute large proportions of those cities. The culture of Kansas and Nebraska is not much affected by the small influxes of migrants they receive, but the cultures of Miami, Florida; Los Angeles, California; and Washington, D.C., have been and are increasingly affected, visibly and markedly.

Second, the peak migration years of the 1910s were ended in 1921 by a new immigration law that set annual ceilings on migration levels. The peak immigration years of the 1970s and 1980s are continuing—and there is not now any plan that promises to end them. The migration stream of the 1910s would not have been assimilated had it continued unabated, had it been augmented by decades of followers.

Third, earlier flows of immigrants were well mixed by language groups, and no single group predominated. As Michael Teitelbaum pointed out in an influential article: "While there were substantial concentrations of a particular language group in past decades (e.g., 28 percent German-speaking in 1881–90 and 23 percent Italian-speaking in 1901–10), previous immigration flows generally were characterized by a broad diversity of linguistic groups ranging from Chinese to Polish to Spanish to Swedish. Furthermore, those concentrations that did occur proved to be short-lived." But, Teitelbaum points out, today's migration stream is quite different: "The INS reports that, in the period 1968–77, approximately 35 percent of all legal immigrants to the United States were Spanish-speaking. If one adds to this figure plausible estimates of Spanish-speaking illegal immigrants, it becomes clear that over the past decade perhaps 50 percent or more of legal and illegal immigrants to the United States have been from a single foreign-language group."[1] And this concentration shows no sign of changing in and of itself at any time in the near future.

Fourth, today's migrants come after the impact of the ethnic pride movements in America, after the death (or at least during the long critical illness) of the melting pot ideal. During the last peak of immigration to the United States, our society insisted on immigrants' assimilation. If adult migrants who settled with others of their own nationality were not required to learn English by the circumstances of their lives, at least their children who entered public schools were certainly expected—by their parents as well as by society—to make English their primary language. Today, with ever-growing language group subcultures, assimilation is controversial, and pressures within immigrant communities countervail against the attractions of assimilation.

Fifth, the argument that we need not worry about the assimilation of massive migrant groups ignores our actual experiences with immigration over the past decade. In fact, there have been numerous and profound problems in cities where recent large movements have settled. There has been a recent and threatening history of cultural clash and conflict, a record of widening community rifts, a new splintering of our society that results directly from large and continuing immigration—legal and illegal.

I'm not going to dwell on these incidents, but here are just a few examples: Vietnamese shrimpers have fought with Texas fishermen who accused them of overfishing. Vietnamese refugees in San Francisco have trapped squirrels in public parks for food and have encouraged their very young children to work as peddlers on the city's streets. Gangs of blacks and Hispanics have fought one another in Denver. Lawrence, Massachusetts, has been racked by firebombings, looting, and fighting between those of Hispanic and of French-Canadian descent. Many more examples could be cited from every large city and from many small towns.

But so far there have been relatively few incidents in the United States, compared to other countries. "The fact that there are so few incidents speaks well of our tolerance, our ability to relate well to all sorts of people," Gerda Bikales told me. She is the executive director of U.S. English, a Washington-based organization, which was founded on the belief that the English language is the most cohesive force in American life, and which promotes the use of English in the United States. Most of those active in its affairs, from its founder, linguist and former senator Samuel Hayakawa, to Ms. Bikales herself, are themselves immigrants to the United States. U.S. English is especially concerned with promoting immigrants' fluency in English in order to help them achieve assimilation more easily.

"In the earlier years in the United States," she says,

> we reacted much more violently against people who were much closer to us culturally. There were hangings of Italians in New Orleans at the beginning of their immigration there. There were incidents, though very few, against Jews. So the fact that there are not a multitude of such incidents, that there are not more cultural clashes, speaks well for us. But we fear that if we as peoples within the United States become too different, too separated, we lose all possibility of communicating and of identifying with each other as citizens in a polity. Then we may revert to some of these ugly patterns, to some of the xenophobia.

Gerda Bikales sees a sixth reason that today's migrant stream will not assimilate as easily as earlier ones.

> Primarily, I'm inclined to put the blame on very unwise government policies that tend to discourage acculturation and assimilation—specifically, government support for bilingual education and voting. Frankly, I think that assimilation is no longer a goal, if what you mean by that is some sort of total blending in. Until the late fifties and early sixties we did expect assimilation. Now what we expect from migrants is accommodation, acculturation. We still expect, and we should expect, that migrants accommodate themselves to us so that there isn't any obvious clash, so that we can communicate, so that we have some things in common, so that, when push comes to shove, we can relate to each other as citizens with a shared vision of the national interest.

Can a country's national identity really be endangered by immigration? Let me give one example: Barbados. Barbados is an island nation of about 250,000 people. Barbadians are worried about immigration from other Caribbean islands, not only because of economics, demographics, and environmental degradation, but also because the tens of thousands of newcomers are eroding the distinctiveness of Barbadian culture, overwhelming the native culture of their homeland.

Another example is Belize. Leon Bouvier, an eminent demographer with the Population Reference Bureau, has written about this small Central American/Caribbean country. "Tiny Belize, with a population of fewer than 150,000 people and independent of Great Britain only since September 1981, is faced with massive refugee and immigrant movements from El Salvador, Guatemala, and Nicaragua. Predominantly black and English speaking, Belize could easily become Hispanic through immigration."[2]

Barbados and Belize are afraid of becoming another Hawaii. In Hawaii, Filipino, Japanese, Chinese, and American immigrants have made the native Hawaiians a tiny minority and preserved their culture primarily as a tourist curiosity. In an important sense, Hawaii is no longer Hawaiian. It is pan-Asian and it is American, but it is not Hawaiian. Barbadians, with good cause, do not want their country to become pan-Caribbean; the people of Belize do not want to become indistinguishable from Honduras and Guatemala.

Americans can understand and sympathize with Barbadians' desires to preserve their unique and distinctive culture against the changes wrought by immigration. We may even have an amused tolerance for France's efforts to preserve its culture against "contamination" by American food, music, and words. But, curiously, some Americans are embarrassed by American efforts to defend American culture, to defend the melting pot. Ramon Santiago, the director of Georgetown University's Bilingual Service Center, has said that "the melting pot concept has been discovered by many sociologists as not representative of U.S. society. Instead, the salad-bowl or mosaic concept has been preferred."[3] But what Santiago did not say was that this shift of organizing metaphor has been predominantly a political, as opposed to a sociological, change.

"America" and "American culture" are real. They sometimes seem to be amorphous concepts, but there is an America; there is an American culture. And this country and its culture are not—to end the food imagery—composed of undigested chunks in a salad lying side by side, unaffected, unflavored, and unchanged by each other, held together only by a thin dressing. Succeeding waves of migrants to the United States have subtly altered this country, but they have been changed in turn. And that process—until some twenty years ago—has created a common culture and a common political ethos that is generally shared by all but the newest immigrants.

On the other hand, as Nathan Glazer and Daniel Patrick Moynihan asserted in *Beyond the Melting Pot* in 1963, "The point about the melting pot . . . is that it did not happen. . . . On the contrary, the American ethos is nowhere better perceived than in the disinclination of the third and fourth generation of newcomers to blend into a standard, uniform national type."[4]

Glazer and Moynihan were part of the leading edge of a new movement in American thought—a movement that corrected some of our misconceptions about the American immigrant experience. For generations, we had pretended that people moved to the United States, assimilated, and became just like each other—that Italians and Irish, Czechs and Chinese learned English and American history and left their differences behind them. Our national myth had been that of *The Melting-Pot* of Israel Zangwill's 1909 play. The play, which popularized the term *melting pot*, showed ethnic groups that had been enemies in Europe becoming friendly and united in the New World. Glazer and Moynihan reminded us of the remaining differences which that myth ignored.

Soon after the publication of *Beyond the Melting Pot*, parts of the civil rights movement evolved into the black pride movement. Born in reaction to white racism and to the slow pace of progress toward equality in the United States, the black pride movement rejected the ideal of integration into the dominant society and glorified the differences of black from white Americans. And throughout the rest of the 1960s and 1970s the movement grew among different groups until it became the ethnic pride movement, accentuating and celebrating each group's differences from other Americans. At their most extreme, proponents of this theory advocate a kind of genetic determinism of culture, a belief that, simply put, blacks are born with the rhythms of Africa and Italians are born appreciating opera. And its proponents, consciously or unconsciously, denigrate American culture—or deny that America even has a culture—and deplore assimilation. Every step toward assimilation, these ethnic pride advocates claim, is a loss of individuals' heritage, their "natural, inborn culture." They believe that the grandchild of immigrants who cannot speak the language of the old country, who does not appreciate the art or traditional values of the old country, has lost more than he or she ever gained through the process of being Americanized.

The ethnic pride movement was a necessary corrective to our easy belief in the melting pot; certainly it has deepened our understanding of the diversity of Americans, of the strong tugs of our various ethnic traditions. But in its insistence on the "unmeltability" of ethnics, and especially in its self-conscious dismissal of an American culture, the ethnic pride movement has profoundly misjudged the American ethos.

America's culture is deep, rich, valuable, and immensely attractive. We Americans find it difficult to appreciate or even to recognize American culture because we are so immersed in it, but our American culture, our American style, has spread throughout the world. The French Academy fights a rearguard action against the invasion of American-English words into their language, American food into their cuisine, and American music into their teenagers' stereos. The national dress of Mexico is a T-shirt emblazoned with the name of an American football team. International culture is shaped by American films and American television shows, the liveliest, most stylish, most interesting entertainment available in any country.

And yet, some Americans doubt American culture. Some are embarrassed by it. Why would some Americans be reluctant to defend our common culture against the divisiveness of pluralism? First, we Americans are tolerant of the differences among cultures, more open to accept the values of other cultures than any other society on earth, and reluctant to impose our own culture on others. That's laudable—unless it prevents us from preserving our culture for our own descendants.

Second, some Americans are afflicted by a lingering doubt about the worth of American popular culture. While American culture is so vital that it, along with our economic success and freedom, is a major attraction for immigration from all over the world, some Americans are so unsure of its value that we hesitate to "impose" it even on those who migrate here to become permanent residents. We hesitate to assert the primacy of American culture—including the English language—even within parts of the United States.

Third, many Americans are unwilling to believe that

there can be any real danger to American culture and society. Admittedly, this contradicts what I've said in the beginning of the chapter, but both things are true. Walt Whitman, that most American of poets, wrote in "Song of Myself," "Do I contradict myself? Very well then I contradict myself. (I am large, I contain multitudes.)" Very well, then, I'll contradict myself: just as we question the worth of our own culture, so do we believe it to be invulnerable. American culture is strong; it is resilient. It is hard to believe it could ever be undermined. Our history is so rich and our optimism so abundant that we think America has a special destiny. "America is eternal," brags President Reagan, ignoring the historical fact that no country ever was or could be eternal.

Most of us would not want the United States to become unrecognizably different from the way it is today, but neither can we envision that kind of change happening. The United States is not a small, underpopulated, defenseless country like Belize or an island like Barbados, neither is its migration large enough to swamp us natives.

But if you don't believe that unassimilated immigrants have the power to change America, go to Miami, in Dade County, Florida. You could find similar stories in any number of other American cities—New York, Chicago, Los Angeles, Washington—but the example of Miami is particularly dramatic. Before 1960, Miami was best known for being next to Miami Beach. It was a quiet, undistinguished city that was just beginning to grapple with resolving the problems caused by the segregation of black Americans. But in 1965 Cuban prime minister Fidel Castro opened the port of Camarioca to Cubans who were discontented with the revolution. About 5,000 of them left in the month the port opened, and most of them came to Miami, only ninety miles away. On December 1, less than a month after Camarioca was closed to emigrants, the "Freedom Flights" from Havana to Miami began. In the seven and a half years that the Freedom Flights operated, until April 1973, 261,000 emigrants left Cuba, and most of them settled in Dade County. In April 1980, Castro opened the port of Mariel for those who wished to leave Cuba and for those he wished to expel from Cuba, and, in the five months until Mariel was closed in late September 1980, another 125,000 Cubans arrived in south Florida, most of them to remain there. And the State Department is now negotiating an agreement with Cuba that may bring additional hundreds of thousands of Cubans to the United States—undoubtedly mostly to Miami.

These waves of migration have changed Miami. The first cohort of Cuban migrants was professional, upper- and middle-class Cubans who were displaced by Castro's communist reordering of Cuban society. These early Cuban migrants are often credited with having caused a period of economic growth and economic prosperity in Dade County. This is partially true. But it shouldn't be overlooked that the Cubans who came to Miami received massive amounts of federal resettlement aid. Over two billion dollars of federal resettlement money, an amount that dwarfs all combined governmental and private efforts to aid Miami's blacks, were pumped into southern Florida's economy in a few years following the 1965 wave. When Congress investigated the resettlement program in 1979 and 1980, it found that some Cubans were still receiving resettlement aid fifteen years after they had arrived in this country. A separate issue is that an undeterminable part of Miami's economic boom can be credited to the massive profits made in illegal drug traffic from Latin America. Because of the connections of Florida's Latin community—not just Cubans, but also Colombians, Salvadorans, and others—south Florida became the center of American drug activity in the 1970s.

The second wave, the Mariel boatlift entrants of 1980, did not have the educational and financial advantages of the first wave. They were largely lower class and, as I pointed out in Chapter 3, they included a large number of criminals and other undesirables. Many of them have faced real hardships in adjusting to both American society and Cuban-American society, and many Cubans who migrated earlier have had significant problems with the Marielitos.

Cuban migration to Miami has had an economic impact that goes far beyond any growth it may have stimulated. Cuban migrants, arrivng in large numbers, unable to practice many of their professions in the United States and frequently without English-language skills, were forced down the job ladder. They competed for semiskilled and unskilled jobs with black Miamians who, with the lessening of traditional racial prejudice, for the first time had the opportunity to rise in the formerly segregated Southern city. Because of the magnitude of new migration to the city, blacks were simply frozen out. Miami, unlike many other Southern cities, did not develop a black middle class of lawyers, doctors, professors, and business owners.

There are over 500,000 Hispanics in Dade County, and 85 percent of them are Cubans. Of the 800,000 workers in Dade County, about 350,000 are Hispanic and a little less than 200,000 are black. On January 18, 1983, Jan Luytjes of Florida International University, the leading demographic researcher of Dade's Hispanics, was quoted as saying: "There is no doubt that blacks have been and are being displaced from jobs by Cubans and Haitians in large numbers. And, although it is not out in the open, there is racial tension because of it. The internationalization of Miami alienates blacks even more. While Hispanic businesses and neighborhoods have thrived and spread across the city, blacks are still isolated, locked into old neighborhoods."[5]

After the Cuban migration to Miami, black machine operators dropped from over 10 percent of the black working population to just over 2 percent; service workers fell by more than 4 percentage points, and even household workers fell by almost 5 percentage points. Blacks who held jobs as clerical workers dropped from more than 13 percent to a little over 11 percent. At the same time, the number of blacks doing general labor, at the bottom of the economic heap, more than doubled, from 12.4 percent of the black population to 25 percent. Bruce Porter and Marvin Dunn came up with these statistics for their book *The Miami Riot of 1980.*[6]

"Particularly galling to blacks," write Porter and Dunn, "was the fact that much of the capital that Hispanics needed for their business success was provided by the United States Government. Because the Hispanics qualified as a minority group, their businesses got special consideration from contractors who did business with the Federal Government and had to use a certain proportion of minority-supplied goods and services." In fiscal 1978, for example, Hispanic firms got 53 percent of the minority construction contracts in building the METRO rapid-transit system. Firms owned by women got 35 percent of the contracts. And firms owned by blacks got only 12 percent of them.

> An even greater disparity exists in loans granted over the years by the U.S. Small Business Administration. From 1968, when the agency first began keeping racial and ethnic statistics, to 1979, Hispanics received $47.3 million, or 47 percent of the total, over the twelve-year period. Whites got $46.8 million, or 46.5 percent; blacks got $6.5 million, or 6.4 percent. Comparing the money each group received from the SBA with its representation in the general population, one sees that blacks, whose strength in the population is half that of the Hispanics, received only one seventh of what the Hispanics got from the SBA.[7]

T. Willard Fair, the president and chief executive officer of the Urban League of Greater Miami, wrote in *The Miami Herald* that

Black Miamians may be the most disadvantaged blacks in the country today. We have more competition for everything. It started twenty years ago. Hotel managers on the Beach didn't want a brother from Liberty City as a doorman when they could get a former attorney from Havana who spoke Spanish, English, and French. In 1982, we find ourselves competing with a dramatic influx of Haitian and Cuban immigrants for jobs, services, goods, and housing. . . . Blacks really have no role of importance in Dade County. In most communities, blacks, even unskilled laborers, have a role. Here we are simply not needed. While the press, instant black leaders and white community leaders are so concerned about the Haitians at the Krome Avenue camp, cocaine cowboys, and Miami's sagging image, the black community is going backwards. Certainly I am concerned about the deplorable living conditions in Haiti and the horrendous infringements on human rights and freedom in Cuba. My people know and understand poverty and oppression very well. However, Krome is no more inhumane and disgusting than some portions of Liberty Square, where people live in boarded-up, abandoned units and in abandoned cars—people born in Miami. Blacks do not have the right to become preoccupied with other issues at the expense of black Americans.[8]

Miami's assimilation problems were exacerbated by an influx of the Haitians mentioned by Fair. Most of the Haitians in Miami migrated there from the late 1970s to 1982. They came almost entirely illegally, often in small and dangerous boats. And they created enormous economic and assimilation problems. Their children were difficult to educate, since they spoke a creole patois that few Americans knew, and they were, by and large, illiterate in all languages. Their living styles were frequently unsuited to a modern American city. Their customs and even their reli-

gious practices—including ceremonial animal sacrifices—
were often unfamiliar and offensive to their neighbors.

And the Haitians also posed enormous philosophical
and legal problems. Were they political refugees fleeing
oppression, economic refugees fleeing poverty, or environmental refugees fleeing the overpopulation of their
country and the erosion of their agricultural land? Should
they be admitted to the United States when they landed
here illegally? Would the implication of admitting them be
that every poor person who lived under a repressive government—about half the world—would be eligible for refugee status in the United States? But only about 30,000
Haitians in total migrated illegally to the United States, or
at least to Dade County, during this period. And the major
problems, as in all immigration questions, are caused not
by the nationality of the immigrants but by the size of the
migration. Compared with Cubans, Haitians presented only
minor practical difficulties to Miami.

Miami's Cubans retained their emotional ties to their
island, and they organized politically around the issues of
United States–Cuban relationships, communism, and Fidel Castro. The nearness of Cuba and the long-held dreams
of the overthrow of the communist regime and repatriation to Cuba prolonged the isolation and insularity of the
Cuban community. But the primary factor behind this prolonged isolation is the sheer numbers of people involved
in the move and the proportion of the host community that
they constituted.

The Cuban migration to Miami has created within the
United States a major city that many Americans experience
as culturally and socially foreign. Editor Phillip Moffitt
commented on an *Esquire* article on "The Latinization of
America":

The genesis of the article on Hispanic Americans occurred two and a half years ago, when two of our ed-

itors made the following observations. One described walking out on the terrace of his midtown New York apartment one Saturday morning and looking down at the people on the street. Most of them were anything but your sterotypical Americans. "Where am I?" he caught himself thinking. Another editor, while describing his stay at the Omni, one of Miami's best hotels, noted how much easier it was for Spanish-speaking people to get attention and service. He, too, experienced that sensation of being in a foreign country.[9]

Thomas B. Morgan, the author of the original article, interviewed Miami's mayor, Maurice Ferre, whose situation in Miami is an interesting illustration of modern-day ethnic politics. He has been the mayor of Miami since 1973 and has won six elections. He is a national spokesman for the Hispanic community, but his position in Miami is somewhat tenuous; he is not Cuban but Puerto Rican. In 1983, Cuban-American Xavier Suarez was Ferre's most important opponent. Suarez ran a campaign based on Cuban unity. Its underlying themes were simply that Maurice Ferre wasn't Cuban, and Maurice Ferre was too concerned with the black people of Miami. Suarez's charges united black and non-Latin white Miamians behind Ferre, enabling him to win his sixth term in a run-off election, but if Ferre's studied indifference to black economic and political needs— symbolized by his joining the Hispanic majority of the City Council to fire Miami's black city manager in 1984— demonstrates too much concern, there is little hope for blacks' future in southern Florida.

Ferre agreed, in his interview with Morgan, that it was possible to live in Miami without ever speaking English, and his comment seems to betray a certain pride in that fact: "You can be born here in a Cuban hospital, be baptized by a Cuban priest, buy all your food from a Cuban grocer, take your insurance from a Cuban broker, and pay for it all with a check from a Cuban bank. You can get all the news in Spanish—read the Spanish daily paper, watch Spanish TV, listen to Spanish radio. You can go through life without having to speak English at all."[10]

Gerda Bikales views that kind of separatism with alarm rather than pride. She also points to the growth of foreign language electronic media as a central element of the new migration. "In the first decades of this century," she told me, "there was a vital foreign language press, and foreign language newspapers were numerous, lively, and interesting. But the impact of newspapers is small compared with that of the electronic media. Now, in most cities, there are radio stations conducted entirely in Spanish and an expanding national television network in Spanish. . . . So I think you can isolate yourself more comfortably, more completely, now, in a non-English world."

Thomas Morgan came away from his interview with Mayor Ferre with one question: "To hear Ferre tell it, fifty years from now the Cubans will be both integrated and still speaking Spanish. But how could they assimilate without learning English?"[11] It is an unanswered question.

In 1980, by a two-to-one margin, Dade County voters approved a referendum making English the official language of the county. Many Cubans opposed this referendum, and took this to be an insult directed at them. A *Miami Herald* survey in late 1983 found that 80 percent of Cuban Americans wanted Dade County to print official brochures and signs in both Spanish and English, while 75 percent of non-Latin whites opposed it. But there is another trend which is just becoming visible. The survey found that a third of Cuban Americans who were under thirty-five opposed official bilingualism, double the percentage of those over thirty-five who opposed it. And 85 percent of Cuban Americans agreed with the statement, "People who live in the United States should be fluent enough in English to use that language in their public dealings."[12]

I would be more hopeful if I thought that this shift in attitude among younger Miami Cubans presaged a greater willingness to assimilate, to join American society. But I remain skeptical. The great majority of Miami Cubans still want bilingualism. And less than a third of non-Latin whites and blacks interviewed in *The Miami Herald* poll called Dade County a very good place to live—even in the face of its good climate and natural beauty and newfound prosperity. More than 40 percent of non-Latin whites under thirty-five years of age plan to move from Dade County within five years. And the factor that is pushing them out is the cultural clash, the feeling of being a foreigner within one's own country, that Miami gives to non-Hispanic Americans.

Miami, as well as large parts of Los Angeles, New York, Chicago, Washington, and other major American cities, is an example of how unassimilated large-scale migration can alter the face of America. It is fair to ask what kind of assimilation I would propose as its alternative. Assimilation into American society does not mean that all ethnic differences will be erased—far from it. Sociologist Milton Gordon, one of the intellectual forerunners of the ethnicity movement, makes an important distinction among kinds of assimilation. Gordon writes that the choice is not between assimilation and pluralism; it is among assimilation, liberal pluralism, and corporate pluralism. In this typology, *assimilation* is a demand by our society that the cultures of subgroups be abandoned in favor of the culture of the majority. *Liberal pluralism* means that individual differences are tolerated, accepted, and appreciated by the society as a whole, and that among the differences that are respected are those stemming from ethnic heritages. And *corporate pluralism* means that rights and identity within the society as a whole are determined by the subgroup to which one belongs, by the ethnic, racial, religious, or other subcommunity with which one identifies.[13]

When most Americans say *assimilation*, we don't mean the kind of assimilation Gordon describes. We really mean something closer to what he calls *liberal pluralism*. But many people who belong to ethnic groups in the process of assimilation fear that Americans demand of them the kind of total and immediate loss of group identity that Gordon describes.

On the other hand, most members of ethnic groups don't want a corporate pluralism, under which they would derive all their rights and societal identity from their respective ethnic groups. But the general society fears that that is exactly what the representatives of ethnic pride movements advocate. In fact, most of those who have already assimilated into American society as well as most of those who have not could probably agree on what Gordon calls *liberal pluralism:* a state of accommodation that the general society can interpret as a gradual assimilation and that ethnic subgroups can interpret as a long-lasting retention of the traits they hold most dear.

There are groups and ethnic group spokespersons who do advocate corporate pluralism, even separatism, and we are right to treat them with suspicion. For example, the National Council of La Raza operates today as a mainstream political group, but its El Plan Espiritual de Aztlan calls for a revolutionary nationalism for Chicanos and assumes that "social, economic, cultural, and political independence is the only road to total liberation from oppression, exploitation, and racism."[14] Even the best-intentioned calls for affirmative action plans based on ethnic or racial group membership arouse fears of corporate pluralism, of individuals attaining favor or position because they belong to certain subgroups, and these fears account for the deep hostility that affirmative action plans have aroused.

We are right to treat calls for corporate pluralism with suspicion and to shun them. They would make unassimilated cultures the rule, not the exception, and they would create splintered societies. And even in America, growing immigrant ethnic groups have the potential to be ethnic power bases for splinter groups. And thus they are attractive targets for those who, with overdrawn rhetoric and appeals to a separatist pride, would aim for political importance. The world, sadly, is filled with many examples of splintered societies:

- In February 1983, 3,000 people were killed in India's northeastern state of Assam when native Assamese rioted against illegal immigrants from Bangladesh. It took 150,000 Indian troops to keep a tenuous peace in this tension-filled area. And the 1984 assassination of Indian Prime Minister Indira Gandhi resulted from her actions against violent Sikh separatists, and was followed by indiscriminate retributive violence against all Sikhs.
- France, facing an intense anti-immigrant backlash, adopted a program to pay foreign "guestworkers" $4,000 apiece to leave France, and a new proposal includes a "repatriation package" of benefits that totals nearly $16,000 for each worker willing to return home.
- In Belgium, the pressure of 850,000 guestworkers complicates the problems caused by existing tensions between the Flemings and the Walloons.
- The United Kingdom and West Germany, with 2.1 million "commonwealth" immigrants and 4.6 million guestworkers respectively, have experienced severe social strain and tensions.
- Canada, Belgium, Malaysia, Lebanon, and dozens of other countries have faced internal turmoil in recent years. Pakistan and Cyprus have been partitioned. France faces the separatist demands of Basques, Bretons, and Corsicans. Spain faces autonomy movements from the Basques and the Catalans.

One further thought about assimilation: one reason that the splintering of the United States by unassimilated groups is not inevitable is that many ethnic groups in America are not "natural." They are creations. Identity is an idea, and ethnic identity is a rather abstract one. As sociologist Nina Glick Schiller has written, "An ethnic group is an interest group whose members interact in some organized fashion. Members of ethnic groups—as opposed to members of other interest groups in American society—interact around certain common cultural symbols. These may or may not have been part of the original ethnic culture. . . . Once such a group is organized, members of the ethnic category may choose to identify with the group on certain occasions and for certain purposes. This phenomenon can be called ethnic identity." [15]

There are many incidents that demonstrate how American ethnic identities have been invented and how they can center on artificial constructs. For example, Kwanzaa, a "traditional" black festival, was developed in the 1960s by Ron Karenga in California to replace the celebration of Christmas. Most of the costumes worn by celebrants of various ethnic festivals are imaginative creations, not what would authentically be worn by ancestors in "the old country," and most of those who wear the costumes could not tell the difference.

At this historic moment, Hispanic immigrants to America are inventing a "Hispanic" ethnic identity. Hispanic immigrants do not come from a single cultural tradition, as many Americans believe. They come from dozens of distinct cultural traditions, from countries with different histories, which may even have warred among themselves. Puerto Ricans, Cubans, Spaniards, Mexicans, Salvadorans, and Argentinians come to the United States feeling as alien to each others' countries and cultures as to the United States and its culture. It is only after their migration, after their meeting in the United States, that a

"Hispanic" identity that includes them all is created. (Even the use of the word *Hispanic* to designate all Latin Americans is a very recent invention.) This Hispanic identity is created consciously, purposefully, by those who wish to use the tool of ethnic identity to forge a power base. It is as artificial as a "Caribbean" or a "European" identity would be—and it is as natural a reaction to the migration process as any other ethnic group's reaction has been.

It is not useful to praise or condemn ethnic groups or the creation of ethnic identity. What we must do is support the assimilation of ethnic groups—or the liberal pluralism that makes the assimilation process possible and least painful for those individuals undergoing that process—and oppose the pluralism (or corporate pluralism) that militates against assimilation.

Leon Bouvier strikes at the heart of the question when he asks, "Is it proper for a nation to insist that its culture remain as it is? If the answer is yes, is this a subtle new form of racism or is it a laudable expression of cultural identity?"[16] Probably everyone will accept that it is proper for Belize and Barbados to attempt to preserve their cultures, and that their attempts are not racist but are laudable expressions of their cultural identities. And I believe it is just as proper for the United States to emulate Belize and Barbados and France and England and every other country in the world, and for us to preserve our culture.

If we recognize this, and work to ease the assimilation of new immigrants into American culture, the United States need not become a splintered nation divided by separate languages, separate cultures, separate traditions. This will be possible when immigration is brought back under control, and when ethnic groups are allowed to undergo the natural process of assimilation into the United States as earlier groups did. Then the danger of splintering will be averted.

Certainly, the culture of the United States will change

in the future. It has changed in the past. Our culture and social organization have evolved in many ways. Every immigrant group has changed America just as every group has been changed in the process. Current waves of immigrants will change this country. What is important is the pace of change. We in the United States wish to regulate the pace of that change, to ensure that it will be an evolution rather than a revolution based on population changes. We wish to enjoy the healthy invigoration we experience from absorbing new residents from many cultures; we don't want to suffer the radical overturning of our way of life or the clash and conflict of differing cultures within our country. And only a reasonable, moderate pace of immigration into the receiving cities, already saturated themselves with problems and splintered culturally and economically, will ensure that we can meet that ideal.

5

Language:
The Tie That Binds

Official federal government policies that encourage bilingual and bicultural education delay the assimilation of new immigrants. Of course, such was not the intent of the federal educational bureaucrats who designed bilingual programs or of the members of Congress who voted for them, but that is the result.

I believe that it makes no sense for the government to discourage foreign-language speakers from speaking English. I am concerned about the dangers of countries in which two language groups clash. I think about the problems caused by Quebec's separatist movement, founded upon the French language. I think about the tensions even within peaceful multilingual countries: the cantonization of Switzerland and the division of Belgium. Language is clearly the cause of some of the world's most severe tensions and disputes. And I know that the United States makes few demands upon its new citizens, has few common elements shared by all Americans—and the English language is the greatest of these common elements.

Our language embodies everything we believe, every aspect of our concepts and our culture. English is the glue. It holds our people together; it is our shared bond. We cannot communicate with those who do not share our language; we are reduced to signs and charades. Likewise, migrants to the United States who do not know English also have an attachment to their languages that goes beyond mere sentiment. Giving up a language to speak another is not like changing hairstyles or clothes styles in order to fit in with a new society. Giving up a language—even learning a new language just to use in the public sphere, among strangers—is giving up part of oneself. The problem of splintered Miami is that Cuban and other Latin immigrants insist on the right to live their lives in Spanish words and in Spanish concepts, and English-speaking Americans react to the rejection of America and its language by the immigrants who were welcomed here and live here (and who call English-speaking Americans "Anglos" in our own country). In this era of massive immigration, it is everybody's problem.

Consider some actual problems faced in many classrooms throughout this country today: Imagine that you are a migrant child in a classroom. You know little or no English. Your parents know none. Your teacher and most of your classmates, on the other hand, know little or none of your language. It does not matter whether that language is Vietnamese, Portuguese, Tagalog, or Spanish. You will feel isolated, and you are likely to retreat to the safety, the warmth, the acceptance of your fellow immigrants. Only the understanding encouragement of your teachers and parents can make the transition to English easier, less painful. Assimilation, after all, is a bittersweet experience, and something of your parents' past must be given up if your American future is to be won.

Imagine that you are a school administrator who must deal with migrant children. You must provide for the children's learning English, making the linguistic transition, and also cope with the ethnic demands (discussed in the last chapter) that the children's home languages and cultures be respected and—possibly—preserved. You may be in Brownsville, Texas, where 95 percent of the children come from Spanish-speaking homes and where nearly 18 percent of them are immigrants to the United States, many of them illegal immigrants. Or you may be in Alexandria, Virginia, where children from over sixty countries, speaking forty languages, constitute 14 percent of the students in elementary schools. Their assimilation will be a bittersweet process for you, too, and a difficult one.

Mexican migrants have had a particularly difficult time in American schools. A recent study by the Urban Institute comments on Mexican students in southern California schools:

> The generally poor performance of many Mexican students can be attributed at least in part to factors beyond the control of the school system, such as low parental education level, limited parental English competence, and membership in a large family. Because most parents speak little English, they are unable to help their children with homework or to become involved in most school activities. Reading test scores suggest a linkage between neighborhood characteristics and school performance. Holding other factors such as income and parental education constant, children who speak English proficiently do not perform well in neighborhoods where the adult population has a limited command of English. Being in a large family also increases the economic pressure on youngsters to leave school early and begin working. Finally, since most large families live in cramped quarters, fre-

quently with several persons to a room, youngsters have little privacy or space available to read or prepare school assignments.

Conversations with teachers and students at numerous schools, however, suggest that, to these external factors must be added limitations at the schools themselves. Perhaps the most serious problem identified is a shortage of bilingual teachers; as a result teacher aides act as "translators." The use of aides reduces the effectiveness of most teachers and slows the educational process. Language barriers also limit communication between students and teachers outside the classroom. The inability to communicate causes friction between Mexican American and other immigrant children. Both students and teachers cited fear of failure among the factors causing poor performance and high dropout rates.[1]

The institute paints a penetrating and accurate picture of the plight of Mexican children in American schools, but its suggested solution—more bilingual education—would only worsen the problem. The study assumes that, unlike earlier waves of immigrants and unlike Asian and other migrant groups coming to the United States today, Mexican and other Spanish-speaking children will have insurmountable problems if they are taught in English. It assumes that they must be enrolled in bilingual programs and taught by bilingual teachers in order to profit from their education.

The bias toward bilingualism is not confined to this one report; on the contrary, for the past decade many, if not most, Americans have believed that Spanish-speaking migrants should be taught by bilingual methods. But there are at least four different educational methods of teaching English to foreign-language speakers. The first, the traditional method, consists of doing nothing special to aid the foreign-language student. Today, it is derided as the "sink or swim" teaching of English. If the student is bright enough, he will catch on and learn the language. In fact, all of us learn our native languages in this way, and it is generally successful with younger children. But it is emotionally difficult, and there are many casualties, many students who will not learn but who will be frustrated by their inability to learn and drop out of school if they are not given some special assistance.

The immersion method of teaching English is one such type of special assistance. Business executives and State Department officials normally learn foreign languages by the immersion method, and it can be a tremendously effective and rapid way to learn a language. While it may appear similar to sink or swim teaching, and while proponents of bilingual education may denigrate immersion teaching by encouraging confusion between the two methods, they are actually quite different. Immersion language teaching is a method that uses only the language to be taught. It augments conversation in the new language with reading exercises, flash cards, language films, and numerous other tools, but it deliberately shuns the use of the students' native languages, considering it a crutch.

English as a Second Language (ESL) is a pedagogic method that has no special political support or theory behind it. It simply attempts to teach English in an intensive way, using methods developed in both immersion and bilingual language teaching. It uses the students' native languages as one tool among many to teach English, but it aims toward early predominance of English and toward teaching all school subjects in English.

Bilingual education, on the other hand, aims first at teaching the students' native languages. After those languages are mastered, they are the primary means through which the new language is learned. While students are learning the new language, all other school subjects are taught in their native languages, and the process of transition to the new language can be excruciatingly slow. Students now spend an average of about three years in bilingual programs. But advocates of bilingual education generally agree that the programs should last between five and seven years—and some even believe that it would be ideal if students were to spend all twelve years of their elementary and secondary schooling in bilingual education. Miami's schoolchildren can take twelve years of bilingual education without even a pretense of its being transitional to the use of English. Obviously, at its extreme, bilingual education becomes a "maintenance program" aimed at preserving the students' original language, rather than a "transitional program" that has the teaching of English as its primary goal.

The education of children is at the center of all social cohesion. During earlier periods of large-scale migration to America, it was accepted that the older migrants would remain outsiders forever, that, to some extent, they would always be "foreign." But in this country, which has uniquely accepted migrants for permanent settlement, it was always widely believed that the second generation, the children of these first migrants, would become identified with their new home, their new country, their new citizenship. The education of the young migrants, therefore, the schooling of migrant children, was aimed toward enabling them to assimilate as quickly and as painlessly as possible.

Since our colonial days, the United States has been thought of as a country of the young. Colonial historian Bernard Bailyn says that it was the young migrants, the young settlers, who first learned how to deal with the new country. In any migrant flow, it is the young who learn the language and the customs faster, and it is the young who, in a reversal of normal family organization, mediate between their families and the outside world. The young become the guardians of the old; they become the knowledgeable ones. Since the early days of this country, the schools have prepared young migrants for this responsibility.

But today's schools have a much more difficult task than did those at the turn of the century. First, the majority of new immigrants speak just one language, Spanish, and a school in which a large percentage of students speak Spanish presents a far different problem from that of a polyglot school in which English is the only reasonable choice as the language of instruction. Second, a small but very vocal minority of Spanish-speaking migrants resists education that tends to assimilate or "Americanize" their children. And third, present-day standards prevent schools from failing or expelling students who cannot keep up with their classmates. Today we have a commitment to universal education, to giving every child the opportunity to complete high school. In earlier periods, immigrant children dropped out of school in great numbers, as Colin Greer has shown in *The Great School Legend*.[2] The brighter, more diligent, more persistent children stayed in school and succeeded; the rest, less able or less patient, simply left school and went to work. Today all children are expected to stay in school, and a great effort is made to ensure that almost all children graduate from high school. This places a heavy new burden on the American school, and it places great new strains on immigrant children, who are already undergoing the normal strains of adaptation to a new society.

These three pressures shaped the bilingual education movement in the United States. Schools in the grip of bilingual education are expected to preserve and even promote the divergent cultural and language backgrounds of their students in addition to preparing migrant children for life and citizenship in their new country. The Los Angeles Unified School District has 118,000 students of limited English ability. Hispanic students are 49 percent of the school population. Spanish-speaking students in the district are taught English as a foreign language and take their basic subjects in Spanish. In Dade County, Florida, 39 percent of the students are Hispanic, most of them from Cuba, and about 25,000 students take English as a second language while being taught math, science, and social studies in Spanish. In Texas 260,000 students, twice as many as in 1980, are enrolled in bilingual education classes. In New York City 63,000 students—Dominican, Salvadoran, Colombian, Venezuelan, Honduran, and Mexican, as well as Puerto Rican—speak only Spanish and are enrolled in bilingual programs.

Of the 45 million children in school today in the United States, 3.6 million have only limited knowledge of English, and 75 percent of the children in bilingual programs speak Spanish as their native language. But only a fifth of those students who could be enrolled in bilingual education are receiving it. One reason is that we would need 67,500 to 72,500 teachers to provide bilingual education to all students who have limited English-speaking ability, and in the entire country only 2,000 qualified teachers are certified each year. We could not teach Spanish-speaking children solely by bilingual education even if we wanted to, unless we also wanted to condemn even more of them than at present to an inadequate education. Most Hispanic children who do not understand English must be taught by other methods.

So why has bilingual education been supported by the federal government as the preferred—and the only federally funded—method of teaching students with limited English-language ability? The 1974 Supreme Court decision in the case of *Lau* v. *Nichols* is usually cited as support for this policy. The Lau plaintiffs were the parents of Chinese-speaking children in the San Francisco school district. Their children did not receive any special assistance in learning English, and they believed that they therefore

had been shortchanged by the district and had not received an adequate course of instruction. The Supreme
Court agreed and ruled that schools did have to give some
special help to students whose ability to speak English was
limited. But the court ruled that "teaching English to the
students of Chinese ancestry who do not speak the language is one choice. Giving instruction to the group in
Chinese is another. There may be others."[3] It is obvious
that the Lau decision does not mandate bilingual education; in fact, it explicitly makes it only one option among
many.

The 1974 Equal Education Opportunity Act did not
specify bilingual education either when it required educational agencies to take "appropriate actions" to ensure that
language barriers were overcome. The Department of
Health, Education and Welfare, however, followed the Lau
decision with guidelines, issued in 1975, mandating bilingual education to the exclusion of ESL or immersion methods. The Lau guidelines implied that English as a Second
Language and immersion methods were inappropriate and
ineffective ways of teaching students English. And the Bilingual Education Act of 1968, also known as Title VII of
the Elementary and Secondary Education Act, has mandated federal financial assistance for bilingual education
programs. There is no federal program to sponsor other
methods of language teaching, but some members of Congress are currently attempting to amend this act by expanding its coverage to include other methods.

If the federal government supports one method of
teaching English to students who speak a foreign language—bilingual education—and doesn't support, or even
forbids, other methods, it should have a good reason. It
should do so only on the basis of sound educational research. But the evidence on bilingual education does not
support any claim of greater effectiveness. Iris Rotberg of

the National Institute of Education surveyed the research that has been done on bilingual programs. Her conclusions are striking:

> It is not possible to select an optimum educational approach for all situations. . . . The achievement results of Title VII programs which were evaluated in their fourth or fifth year of operation, however, do not show that transitional bilingual education programs—as implemented by school districts—were better or appreciably worse than regular school programs. . . . All of this suggests that there is no educational basis for selecting an optimum instructional model for a country as large and diverse as the United States and that current findings do not indicate that the transitional bilingual-bicultural approach advocated by the Lau Remedies and Title VII is better on the average than other models.[4]

And Rotberg points out that bilingual programs may, in fact, encourage segregation of Spanish-speaking children within schools, though she believes that further research must be done on this effect.

The U.S. Department of Education sponsored another careful survey of the research findings on bilingual education, which was issued in September 1981. The following excerpts indicate their conclusions:

- Schools can improve the achievement level of language-minority children through special programs.
- The case for the effectiveness of transitional bilingual education is so weak that exclusive reliance on this instruction method is clearly not justified. Too little is known about the problems of educating language minorities to prescribe a specific remedy at the

Federal level. Therefore, while meeting civil rights guarantees, each school district should decide what type of special program is most appropriate for its own unique setting.

- There is no justification for assuming that it is necessary to teach nonlanguage subjects in the child's native tongue in order for the language-minority child to make satisfactory progress in school. However, if nonlanguage subjects are to be taught in English, the curriculum must be structured differently from the way the curriculum is structured for monolingual English-speaking students.

- Immersion programs, which involve structured curriculums in English for both language and nonlanguage subject areas, show promising results and should be given more attention in program development.[5]

There is no good educational reason to prefer bilingual education over other teaching methods. That is the message. Bilingual programs have held sway for political, not educational, reasons. Bilingual education gives jobs and local power to members of the non–English-speaking community who work in the schools. It reinforces childrens' identification with members of their own ethnic group. And it preserves the distinguishing characteristics of those ethnic groups, which gives a power base to those who identify themselves as leaders of those splinter groups.

Political lobbying for bilingual education comes almost exclusively from the Hispanic community. Although the bilingual education movement is composed of teachers who work in many languages, bilingual teachers alone would be insufficient political support to prop up an expensive method of education whose success is unproved. Immigrant groups other than Hispanics provide little support for bilingual education. Most immigrants who do not speak

Spanish have no illusions that they will preserve their language in this country. And even among Hispanics, support for bilingual methods is far from unanimous.

Mario Obledo, the president of the League of United Latin American Citizens (LULAC), strongly supports bilingual education and goes even further than most: "I think," he has said, "every American child ought to be taught both English and Spanish."[6] And Ramon Santiago, the director of the Georgetown University Bilingual Service Center, answers critics of bicultural programs by saying, "If they mean that Hispanics as a group have retained more of their language and culture, I would say more power to the Hispanics."[7] But at the community level, Hispanic groups have begun to question the unhesitating support for bilingualism that their national leaders would encourage them to express. *The Wall Street Journal* has noted a "new pragmatism" in concerns about the performance of bilingual programs. *Journal* reporter Burt Schorr covered the Coalition for a Better Education in San Diego, a coalition of Chicano organizations which monitors bilingual programs and which is troubled by the persistence of high dropout and failure rates for Chicano high-school students. Schorr quotes Gus Chavez of the coalition as asking, "If we have all of this great bilingual program in place, why weren't our kids doing better in school?"[8]

Schorr has also covered the pilot project of English immersion teaching that has begun in McAllen, Texas:

> Previously, the school district's transitional bilingual classes were conducted partly in Spanish and partly in English up to the third grade. But the pilot project seems to be showing that youngsters can make a faster transition to speaking, reading, and writing English if they are "immersed" in English almost from the start. . . . The progress is significant because here in the palm-shaded Rio Grande Valley, McAllen's large ma-

jority of Spanish-speaking residents and the closeness of Mexico—as a source of new immigrants and as a place to visit Spanish-speaking relatives—have helped to discourage many youngsters from acquiring full English skills.[9]

Let me concede this important fact: school dropout rates for students with limited English ability are lower when bilingual programs are used. That is the most frequently made argument for bilingual programs and the one with the most validity. La Raza, for example, argues that bilingualism must be used because a technological society cannot afford a high rate of dropouts.

Certainly, we should try to educate as many students as possible as far as they can advance in our school system. But La Raza's argument is self-defeating in the last analysis. The adaptation of new migrants to our society— even if we recommit ourselves to speeding their assimilation—will take one or two generations today, just as it has in the past. That process of gradual adaptation is an integral, inescapable part of migration, and a certain amount of confusion is inevitable. If we can't afford school dropouts, who are a natural by-product of displacement and cultural shock, then we can't afford immigration. Certainly, the ill effects of displacement and cultural shock must be recognized, and students should be helped through them. But the measure of success cannot be that students enrolled in any special program for those with limited English-language ability have the same degree and amount of success as those with no language handicap. That is an unrealistic and unreachable goal.

I would propose an alternate goal: reasserting the primacy of English in American schools. The term *primacy of English* comes from *Making the Grade,* a 1983 report on federal elementary and secondary education policy from the Twentieth Century Fund. The report was written by a prestigious panel of educators, headed by Robert Wood of Wesleyan University, gathered by the fund as a task force. Its section on bilingual education cannot be improved on:

> Our political democracy rests on the conviction that each citizen should have the capacity to participate fully in our political life; to read newspapers, magazines, and books; to bring a critical intelligence to television and radio; to be capable of resisting emotional manipulation and of setting events within their historical perspective; to express ideas and opinions about public affairs; and to vote thoughtfully—all activities that call for literacy in English. Accordingly, the Task Force recommends that the federal government clearly state that the most important objective of elementary and secondary education in the United States is the development of literacy in the English language.
>
> A significant number of young Americans come from homes where English is not the first language, and many now live in neighborhoods in an increasing number of states in which languages other than English are spoken. Although this nation has become more aware of the value of ethnic identities than it was during previous influxes of non–English-speaking immigrants, anyone living in the United States who is unable to speak English cannot fully participate in our society, its culture, its politics. This is not because of prejudice but because most Americans speak, write, and think in English. English is, after all, our national language.
>
> We recommend, then, that students in elementary school learn to read, write, speak, and listen in English. As children advance in grade, these skills should be continually improved. By the time they finish high school, students ought to possess such advanced cognitive skills as reasoning, critical analysis,

the ability to explain and understand complex ideas, and to write clearly and correctly.

Many different methods have been proposed for educating children who are not literate in English. It is not the role of the Task Force nor is it the responsibility of the federal government to instruct our schools and teachers on which pedagogy is most appropriate. The federal role, we believe, is to guarantee that all children have equal educational opportunity. Therefore, the Task Force recommends that federal funds now going to bilingual programs be used to teach non–English-speaking children how to speak, read, and write English. Local school districts may decide to teach children in more than one language or to teach them a language other than English. Although we believe that the failure to recognize the primacy of English is a grave error, that is their prerogative. The distinctive nature of the federal role, we believe, derives from the premise that all of us must be able to communicate with one another as fellow citizens.

Accordingly, the Task Force recommends that the federal government promote and support proficiency in English for all children in the public schools, but especially for those who do not speak English or have only limited command of it.[10]

The English language is a basic element of American citizenship. I don't mean to say that anyone who speaks English with an accent is un-American, or to imply that those who do not speak English are unwelcome here. But I do say, along with S. I. Hayakawa, that "the language we share is at the core of our identity as citizens, and our ticket to full participation in American political life. We can speak any language we want at the dinner table, but English is the language of public discourse, of the marketplace, and of the voting booth."[11]

113

Gerda Bikales, who heads Senator Hayakawa's English advocacy group, U.S. English, emphasized the importance of language to citizenship when she explained to me the major objection she has to lengthy courses of bilingual education:

> I think the second generation will, by and large, learn English. I think that even with bilingual education a child of normal intelligence will learn English. Even if you put obstacles in his path, the child will learn. But I am not sure to what extent, even if they learn English, the second generation will feel comfortable as Americans. After children have been isolated in bilingual education classes for many years, three years, four years, five years—and LULAC [the League of United Latin American Citizens] is advocating six or seven years as the proper time for transition from bilingual to all-English education—after they have been segregated for so many years, isolated within their language group, I really wonder what the quality of assimilation, of Americanization, is. I wonder if they're ever going to feel really at home here, or if they are always going to be strangers in our midst.
>
> English doesn't have to be your primary language for you to be "American." Not at all. However, it cannot be totally strange to you. It cannot be so strange to you that you cannot pull a lever in a polling booth marked "Democrat" or "Republican." If it's that alien to you, then you really are estranged from the American body politic, and it is questionable whether you are really able to cast either an informed vote or, more importantly, an independent vote. It isn't essential that English be your primary language, but English can't be so utterly foreign to you that you can't cope in a voting booth. The English language isn't what makes

us citizens of this country, but it is our greatest commonality. This country has so few commonalities that the few we have must be very dear to us. A rejection of English eliminates you, it seems to me, from the polity.

In 1981, when he was still in the U.S. Senate, Hayakawa introduced in Congress a proposed amendment to the Constitution to make English the official language of the United States. In one sense, this proposed amendment would change nothing: it would not prohibit anyone from using a language other than English in any nongovernmental situation. It would not forbid the showing of foreign-language films, or the printing of foreign-language books; it would not attempt to drive the use of foreign languages underground or to outlaw them. But, in another sense, the bill is important: it reverses the long-standing process of the federal government's promotion of bilingualism. It emphasizes the centrality of the English language to citizenship, to belonging to this polity.

Official bilingualism is most important when it comes to voting, to the decision making in the voting booth to which Bikales refers. Current federal law mandates that areas in which there are significant minorities of foreign-language speakers must provide ballots in their languages. If nothing else, an English-language amendment would certainly mandate that voting be done in English.

Some people think that bilingual voting is a civil rights issue. They believe that people in the United States must be allowed to vote in the language of their choice. But this is a very strained and stretched interpretation of civil rights. To begin with, under our naturalization laws, a permanent resident alien must be literate in English before he is given citizenship. Certainly, this law has not been enforced in recent years, and many immigrants gain citizenship without more than a nodding acquaintance with English. But that is no excuse for further erosion of the standards of English usage.

And an immigrant who is unable to understand the labeling of voting levers as *Democrat* or *Republican* is unlikely to understand many of the issues that separate candidates or underlie referenda, as Gerda Bikales pointed out. Proponents of bilingual voting say that many people who do not speak English can follow issues in their foreign-language press or on foreign-language television stations or through their community leaders. They are able to be informed voters, they claim, without knowing English. But are they able to be independent voters? Gerda Bikales has said that "the ethnic leader fights for his leadership by fighting assimilation." He also preserves his power base by assuring that he is the primary, or even the sole, source of political information.

This is nothing new in American life. Certainly, earlier immigrants to the United States were influenced by their ethnic leaders. The entire histories of some city governments could be written in terms of ethnic groups' vying for power. But if earlier generation of voters were able to vote in English, they were also able to receive political information from a multiplicity of sources; they were not limited to what their foreign-language leaders allowed them to receive through their separate media.

On November 8, 1983, San Francisco voters approved Proposition O, an initiative that opposed multilingual voting. Proposition O read: "The Board of Supervisors shall adopt, and the Mayor shall sign a Resolution urging the Congress and President of the United States to amend Federal law so that the City and County of San Francisco need print ballots, voters' handbooks, and other official voting materials only in English." San Francisco is a city known for its tolerance for diverse life-styles and its welcoming of divergent people, but 63 percent of the voters—

89,740 to 55,924—agreed. A ballot in San Francisco can't change federal law, but it was obvious that San Franciscans were tired of elections held in English, Spanish, and Chinese, with Tagalog to be added soon. And on November 4, 1984, California voters passed a similar statewide initiative by a 72 percent approval margin.

An English-language amendment would do one other important thing. It would support actions such as that taken on June 16, 1983, by Mayor Thomas G. Dunn of Elizabeth, New Jersey. Mayor Dunn had received complaints that some workers in City Hall were speaking in foreign languages, so he added an afterthought to one of his memos: "May I add further that English is the primary language to be spoken in the official conduct of city business. Other languages should be used only when helpful to citizens or visitors who are handicapped because of a language barrier. Furthermore, it is most discourteous for city employees to converse in other than English in front of other city employees."

The reaction to this rather innocuous request was interesting. No city employee or union official had any complaint about it. In fact, the president of the Elizabeth City Hall Employees Association, Peter Tarranova, said, "I agree with the memo. This is the United States of America. Don't we have the right to have our national language spoken in the offices of the government? Is that too much to ask? I don't think so." But the Puerto Rican Legal Defense Fund filed a complaint with the Equal Employment Opportunity Commission; the Hispanic-American Political Association called the order insulting; and the president of the Elizabeth Latin American Chamber of Commerce said that the mayor had "created a tremendous division in the city among Hispanic and Anglo people."[12] Hispanic-American organizations cannot have it both ways. They cannot proclaim that the motive behind their support for bilingual-bicultural education is to assist students in learning English and

117

simultaneously protest against the preference for the use of English in official government business and in government offices. That very protest belies their commitment to English.

The startling fact is that many Hispanics who support bilingualism do not accept the predominance of English in the United States. In California the chief of the state's Department of Education Office of Bilingual-Bicultural Education received a letter in late 1983 from Ms. Mary G. Murphy, an elderly Californian who had written to support the Hayakawa amendment. To illustrate the need for it, she described the difficulty she had at her senior citizens' lunches communicating with immigrants who had learned no English. State Department Chief Guillermo Lopez answered her:

> You are directly experiencing the cultural and linguistic enrichment of the U.S. brought about by the immigration to our shores of people from all over the world. . . . Many schools have been successful in having recent immigrant students share their language with their English-speaking friends. They learn English as they help others acquire Spanish, Korean, Portuguese, Japanese, etc. Such cooperation exemplifies the positive spirit with which we should approach our future in an international economy. Perhaps this kind of language sharing could help you and your non-English-speaking peers at your lunches better understand and help each other.[13]

And when he was California's secretary of Health and Welfare, the president of LULAC, Mario Obledo, advocated not only teaching Spanish to all children in all grades and making Mexican history a mandatory school subject but also reorganizing the "Immigration and Naturalization Service in such a manner as to exclude its law enforcement activities" and converting "the Border Patrol assigned to the Mexican Border into a resettlement agency with information and referral services advising economic refugees on living, educational, and employment opportunities."[14]

The growth of Spanish in the United States, promoted by the federal government, raises fears—legitimate fears—that the country is being rejected, or culturally annexed, by its newest immigrants. Eugene McCarthy, an original and independent liberal thinker, has asked whether America is "the world's colony." "A more subtle manifestation of neo-colonialism is the challenge to the status of the English language in the United States," McCarthy wrote.

> There has been both a practical and legal submission to demands that at least some parts of the country should become bilingual or multilingual.
>
> Imperial nations traditionally impose their languages on subject or colonial people—or try to do so— as did the Portuguese in Brazil, the Spanish in South America, the British and the French in their African possessions, and in less successful efforts, the British with the Boers in South Africa.
>
> The process is more subtle in the United States. It is being done in the name of civil rights, of good citizenship, and of economic and cultural equality. Yet it runs contrary to historical evidence of the dangers of bilingualism in a country.[15]

At the present time there may be little danger that English will be replaced by Spanish in the United States, or even that Spanish will gain much support as an official, or semiofficial, second language. But the danger is not nationwide; it is localized. An amalgam of English and Spanish, generally called *Spanglish,* is already developing as a regional dialect in Miami and California, in parts of New York and New Jersey, and especially along the border with

Mexico. The different reactions of the two countries to this development is instructive. On its side of the border, Mexico is reacting against it by creating a governmental Committee for the Defense of Culture and Language to weed out English words and usage. The United States, on the other side, is doing nothing.

Professor Manuel Carlos of the University of California at Santa Barbara has said that "we are already in the process of developing a third language," and that, though the process could take a hundred years, Spanglish will be accepted as a language "when the border areas become powerful enough that political candidates must use this language to campaign in. This is already happening in Texas, where you see Anglo candidates using 'Spanglish' to campaign in the southern part of the state."[16] Again, it is not necessary for the development of Spanglish, or the growth of the use of Spanish, to be national in order for it to be a national problem. In fact, the truth is probably exactly the opposite. This development would be less troublesome if it were occurring nationwide at the same rate rather than being regionalized. Division occurs when regions are distinctive. Lincoln's belief was that "a house divided against itself cannot stand, nor long endure," and the division of regions is more dangerous than a uniform change throughout the country.

Certainly, the Mexican Committee for the Defense of Culture and Language, like similar French attempts to defend the French language against impurities, raises ludicrous images: pompous pedagogues railing against a lunch stand's menu listing "hot dogs" or "hamburgers," and attempting to invent equivalents for English technical terms. But, as the organization U.S. English has shown in its careful and judicious defense of the language, a native version of a committee to defend the English language need not be nativist.

Personally I am optimistic: I don't see Spanglish as

anything other than a way station on the road to the full use of English. It is not inevitable that areas of the United States will become permanently Spanish-speaking. But English will not automatically remain the dominant language of the United States in the face of continuing inaction and inattention. Preservation of English requires continuing effort and much work. If we believe the effort to preserve English as our national language is worthwhile, then we should not hesitate to undertake the work it will require.

Richard Rodriguez, in the powerful autobiography *Hunger of Memory*, understands and explains the dream of bilingualism and thus the power that it has held over so many who have supported it: bilingualists promise that "the barrio or ghetto child can retain his separateness even while being publicly educated" and that "there is no private cost to be paid for public success." It is the dream of immigration that there be no pain, no price paid by anyone, neither by the immigrant nor by the society, for the gains to be made. But Rodriguez found bilingualism to be a false dream: "Only when I was able to think of myself as an American, no longer an alien in gringo society, could I seek the rights and opportunities necessary for full public individuality."[17] The danger of surrendering to the dream of bilingual education and bilingual voting is that those who are trapped by it will remain apart, unassimilated into public life.

In America, language integration is an integral part of political integration, an integral part of our national cohesiveness. And it is notable that we as a country have been unsuccessful in integrating many Hispanic—particularly Mexican—immigrants into our political and cultural life.

We have always believed that immigrants who came to the United States were coming here for good, to become part of this country. Pat Burns of the Federation for American Immigration Reform (FAIR) has described it to me as the "deal" we have made. "We've accepted immigrants more easily and in greater numbers than any other country," he said, "and in return we've asked them only two things: to speak English and to become citizens. Citizenship is part of the deal." Unlike other immigrant-receiving countries, which severely restrict the ability of immigrants to become citizens, we have made the process easy and have encouraged immigrants to become American citizens. In fact, among most nationalities, only about one-third of permanent resident aliens became citizens on historical average—but we accepted that pattern as the normal one. But only about one-twentieth of permanent resident aliens from Mexico become citizens—a dramatically lower rate.

Do Mexican immigrants feel less attachment to the United States than do other immigrants? Do they feel that at some time, perhaps when they retire, they will return to Mexico? Or do they just not feel "American"? I have no answer to these questions; there is not enough information, there are not enough studies, to tell why Mexican migrants have such a low level of commitment to citizenship in this country.

But surely their children, who when born here are automatically citizens of this country, must feel an attachment? Again, I do not know. James Lamare, in a disturbing study of Mexican-American children in the schools in El Paso, Texas, in 1978, does little to reassure us. Lamare divided Mexican-American children into generations according to whether they themselves were immigrants or whether they were the first, second, or third generation of their family born in the United States. He found that "overall, Mexican American children, regardless of generation, show only limited commitment to the American political community. To be sure, each generation professes a preference for living in the United States, but only the mixed and second generation consider this to be the best country. None of the five cohorts prefers the label 'American' over identification tags more reflective of their national origin. Lastly, no generation exhibits a strong sense of trust in others."[18]

Certainly, it is tragic if any group of immigrants to the United States does not feel American even after three generations. But how should we react to such news? What should we do in response?

It should be obvious that the process of becoming American is not an empty one. The "salad" model of American society, in which distinct ethnic and racial groups are assumed to live side by side, unaffected and unchanged by each other, is simply nonsense. People who feel "American" share some commonalities. Certainly, there are people who live in America who do not share these commonalities—and they feel like outsiders. Increasingly, the political power of more than fifteen million Hispanics is being used not to support assimilation but to advance "ethnic pride" in belonging to a different culture. The multiplication of outsiders is not a model for a viable society, and we should discourage it.

Learning English to become a citizen is a perfectly reasonable requirement that benefits both our society and migrants themselves. It is no kindness to ourselves or to migrants to pretend that English is unnecessary in this country. It is no kindness to Hispanic immigrants to add to their present ability to listen to the radio, watch television, vote, or get educated in Spanish. Americanization is not an illiberal or a xenophobic process. Through Americanization we reach out to migrants and welcome them fully within our society, and migrants reach out to us and enter fully into our society. Indeed, it is the very essence of paternalism to claim that any group of nationality of migrants is unable to become American. We think that America is a great country with a rich culture—and migrants who come here, who choose this country, must think so too, or they would not have undertaken the difficult job of uprooting themselves from their homes and moving to a foreign land. If immigrants do not feel that they are fully a part of this society, as American as everyone else, then we are failing. We should reexamine the methods we use to integrate immigrants into our country and the goals of those methods. Languages are social cement. If bilingual-bicultural education encourages a feeling of separateness and difference among its students, it is simply inappropriate for this country.

And if Americanization is breaking down, we should examine the process of immigration itself. One very good reason that immigrant groups may not be accommodating themselves to this country may be that the pace of immigration into certain cities and states is too rapid, that the continuing immigration stream is preserving the separatism of migrant groups. Both acculturation and immigration, after all, are demographic processes. They can be measured by numbers. We ignore those numbers at our peril. We cannot willfully pretend that those numbers have no relevance to our country, that America is uniquely immune to profound demographic change.

6

Jobs, Immigrants, and Americans

The immigration issue is also an employment issue. Today's levels of immigration cause not only social problems but serious economic problems, too. Illegal immigrants are taking jobs that can and should be filled by Americans. And large numbers of legal immigrants only worsen America's inability to create enough jobs each year for our own citizens.

We must understand the harsh geopolitical realities of the world we live in. The twentieth century began with two billion people. It will end with over six billion people. It began with population growth that added thirteen million people a year; it will end with over ninety million more people each year. It began with a world full of unexplored places. It will end with human footprints on every corner of the globe and on the moon as well. It is reckless public policy to believe that the United States can solve not only its own unemployment problems but also the Third World's. We can't, no matter how well meaning we may be.

America's structural unemployment has been growing steadily over the past several decades. The following list shows dramatically the new job crunch that has come to America under the six presidents since World War II.

President	Rate of Unemployment (percent)
Truman (1946–52)	4.2
Eisenhower (1953–60)	4.9
Kennedy/Johnson (1961–68)	4.9
Nixon/Ford (1969–76)	5.8
Carter (1977–80)	6.5
Reagan (1981–83)	8.9

Clearly, America is having increasing difficulty providing full employment for its own citizens, let alone for a flood of immigrants.

There are many reasons why tens of millions of people throughout the world can't find productive employment. Some economies are badly managed by ideologues who cannot adapt their theories to reality. Some countries have neither the natural resources nor the human capital (in the form of an educated, skilled labor force) to develop. Some countries undergo disasters, either natural or man-made. But in almost every case massive unemployment and underdevelopment are due not to a resource or capital shortage but to what biologist Garrett Hardin has called a "people longage." India, Hardin points out, is an immensely rich nation, full of natural resources—for a population a third its size. Even Africa's Sahel could support some people at a high standard of living, but its cyclical droughts will continue to cause cyclical famines as long as the region is overpopulated to the extent that it is today.

126

How can enough jobs be provided to cope with the continuing, inevitable, and rapid growth of the work force? That is the major labor problem that will face the world over the next few decades. Demographer Robert Fox of the InterAmerican Development Bank points out that the work force of Latin America was 55 million in 1950 and 99 million in 1975, and that it will grow to 197 million by 2000 and 300 million by 2025. Any prediction of work force size is largely a matter of guesswork, of course, but these figures are rather conservative; they are based on the International Labour Organisation's projections of work force participation rates, and for the year 2000 they are based on actual counts of the people who have already been born, not on projections of birthrates.[1]

Let's consider only Mexico and Central America, which must produce 1.2 million new jobs each year to put their exploding populations to work. It is doubtful that they can come even close to that number. The United States, during the 1970s and early 1980s, created an average of only 2 million new jobs a year, and the U.S. economy was fifteen times larger than Central America's and Mexico's combined. It defies imagination to think that these countries, with their high population growth, low economic growth, vast discrepancies between rich and poor, and legacy of political instability, could successfully create this many jobs every year for at least the next forty years. Yet that is what would be necessary to keep employment from exploding beyond its present already unacceptably high rates. Without strong domestic immigration controls, the United States will be inundated by this region's poor, looking for jobs.

But worldwide job requirements are even more staggering. In 1980, the International Labour Organisation (ILO) projected that 600 to 700 million new jobs had to be created worldwide by the year 2000—not to improve employment figures, but just in order to keep the world employment rate at its current level. The United States' best year for new job creation was 1977, when approximately 3 million new jobs were created. Simply to stay even with population growth, Latin America will have to create at least 4 million new jobs a year with an economy about one-fifth the size of ours. In Mexico, there will soon be as many new entrants into the labor market every year as there are in the United States, and yet their gross domestic product is only 5 percent that of the United States. Obviously, unemployment in Latin America will increase. And the unrest based on economic disaster will increase and be directed against all kinds of political systems and governments, not just against right-wing or left-wing regimes, totalitarian or democratic governments. Only those countries that are able to cut their population growth rates drastically can look forward to a better future, and even those countries will pass through very difficult economic times, will be unable to expand their economies fast enough to provide employment for an exploding labor force. Continuously rising unemployment will create ever-increasing pressures to emigrate—*if* the United States does not close the loopholes in legal migration laws and enforce those laws more efficiently.

Unemployment and underemployment are what immigration specialists speak of as the *push factors,* the elements that cause potential migrants to want to move from their homes. But push factors alone are not enough to cause migration. There also have to be *pull factors,* the elements in the receiving country that attract migrants and make it possible for them actually to move. The employment pull factor in the United States is the relative ease with which a legal or an illegal immigrant can enter the United States and find a job that will pay more than he or she would have earned in the home country.

But what do we know about the impact of immigration on Americans, and what kind of evidence do we have about this impact? Unemployment in the United States in late 1984 was 7.3 percent. Almost 8½ million Americans were unemployed. (And this was just the official unemployment rate, which does not count those discouraged workers who have dropped out of the labor force and who are no longer actively searching for work, though they want it and would readily work were they to find a job.) In November 1982, unemployment had reached 10.7 percent, about 11.9 million people. Population growth and resource depletion are long-term problems, and they are remote from the day-to-day experiences of most Americans. But most of us are confronted every day with the necessity of earning a living, and competition in the work force is easily understood by all of us. The size of the American work force is not limitlessly elastic; its expansion has an impact on us all; and immigration has a direct impact on the expansion of the work force.

The United States cannot try to solve the world's unemployment problems by absorbing the world's unemployed. It would be disastrous even to try. As syndicated columnist William Raspberry wrote: "Illegal aliens may provide temporary relief for employers who have trouble filling their bottom of the barrel jobs, but in the long term they spell not relief but trouble."[2]

Our economy was vigorous and active during the late 1970s. Until growth was stalled by the recession of 1981 and 1982, we were creating jobs at a rate of over two million a year. But during that period legal and illegal immigration were well over a million a year. Not all immigrants worked, of course, but some labor economists believed that about one million new legal and illegal immigrants enter the work force each year.[3] That means that half of all new jobs were absorbed by new immigrants alone. And, simultaneously and relentlessly, U.S. unemployment moved up.

Vernon Briggs, professor of labor economics and human resource studies at Cornell University, is an expert on immigrants in the labor market. I have known and relied on his work for many years, and while I was writing this book he summarized many of his findings for me.[4]

When we discussed the impact of immigration on the labor market, Briggs distinguished between legal and illegal immigrants. In his opinion, the evidence on the labor market impact of immigration is very spotty even for the effect of legal immigrants.

> There is no time series on the economic behavior of immigrants when they enter the labor force; they are just grouped in normal market data. But some information which we have gathered from special studies of the work intentions of legal immigrants before they actually arrive indicates that the labor force participation rate of immigrants approximates that of native-born Americans. In fact, however, postarrival experiences have shown that the labor force participation rate of immigrants is higher than that of the population as a whole. What seems to happen is that the intentions they had when they entered the country are changed by their experiences here. When the family migrates here, fewer wives and young family members intend to enter the work force than actually do enter it after they have lived here for a few years. The same kind of labor market participation seems to be true of refugees as of other legal immigrants, although, again, the data are difficult to gather and interpret.

The United States—and this is especially startling to foreign observers of our immigration system—pays little attention to the labor market implications of selecting immigrants. We don't examine the skills we need in our labor pool and then choose people who have those skills to immigrate. We do almost the opposite. Family reunification has been the major, almost the sole, criterion for entry. We let into America not those whom we as a nation need, but those who simply want to come. There is little or no matching with the occupations and training that the United States needs and that are in short supply, there is no market direction, and there is little thought of how the immigrants will fit into our economy. Only 5 percent of all legal immigrants are screened by our labor department to find out their skills and where they might be productively employed.

But legal immigrants take jobs from Americans whether they are chosen for their skills or for their relatives. As Briggs points out:

> That there is no screening for labor market impact doesn't mean that there is no labor market impact. Legal immigrants do get jobs. In fact, to some extent they go disproportionately into the professional, managerial, and skilled occupations. Some people suggest this is because of the complexity of the legal immigration system. One has to be fairly well educated to figure out how to manipulate the system, and one has to have some income to hire a lawyer, among other things, to get through the system. This means that after a few years in this country legal immigrants have a good chance to equal or exceed the incomes of the general population, as studies by Barry Chiswick and others have shown. But there's a bias here that selects those who are better-off and better educated in their own societies. Legal immigrants are not randomly selected.

Of course, because of the difficulty of assimilating into a new society, because of language barriers, and because many professional degrees are not transferable between societies, many legal immigrants enter our labor force at a lower occupational level than they had in their own societies, even though their wages in the United States may be higher than what they were earning at home.

Legal immigrants are always thought of as hard workers, as ambitious, achieving people. That stereotype persists because many immigrants fit it. Not just the complexities of the American immigration system, but the difficulties of any migration tend to select those who are ambitious and who have energy and drive. That is why new immigrants are pictured as builders, as achievers, as contributors to America. Certainly no one begrudges them their ambition; no one claims that their hard work and dedication constitute unfair competition with American workers. But the question is not whether an individual migrant contributes to a workplace or to America. The question is the impact of massive flows of immigrants. The problem is not the impact of an individual who may be a desirable worker and eventually a desirable citizen, but the impact of hundreds of thousands of such workers every year.

About that problem, Briggs commented,

> When you count the numerically controlled visas, the nonquota relatives, and the refugees who are admitted legally each year, only about 5 percent of the people who are admitted come here because they have a skill in short supply in the United States or because they are exceptionally qualified to perform some work or because they are especially distinguished in their professions. That raises the question of displacement effects. That is, it's very hard to say that there aren't citizens who would work in the occupations legal immigrants choose. That isn't to say that there should be no legal immigration. The real question in my mind is whether one can defend the disproportionate emphasis on family reunification, with no labor force guidance, when there are such large labor force implications. I think that in any system other than immigration that would be indefensible; it would be called nepotism. But nepotism in immigration has been very pop-

ular politically, because we're admitting potential migrants who have relatives here who may already vote, instead of admitting migrants who have skills and can make a contribution to the economy but who have no relatives here.

Along with many other labor specialists, Vernon Briggs is convinced that the U.S. system of legal immigration should respond to America's labor needs—and to the *lack* of need for new workers that our current unemployment rate demonstrates.

I don't think it makes much sense to have the number of immigrants coming into the labor market be unaffected by the conditions of unemployment in the country. Annual immigration ceilings ought to be flexible administratively, not politically, not through the Congress. When unemployment goes up, immigration ought to go down—and it should be an automatic response determined by a bureaucratically administered formula, not by political pressures. There will be a bit of a lag, obviously. That is, if unemployment goes up this year, then the number of legal immigrants goes down next year; and vice versa. Conversely, when unemployment goes down, then legal immigration can go back up. This is what Canada has done, and it has worked well for them.

In Canada, in fact, one bureau manages both employment and immigration, and automatic adjustments of immigration levels are worked out by that bureau with little political pressure from their Parliament. "This reflects reality," Briggs said. "It simply doesn't make sense, when most immigrants are going to go to work, to allow a large number of legal immigrants to come in irrespective of what the economic environment is in a given year. It isn't fair to the immigrants, and it certainly isn't fair to the workers who are American citizens who have to bear the results of it."

When we examine the consequences of our immigration policies, we must look at all of them, including the consequences for other nations. When I stress that immigrants should be selected for what they can offer America, I don't want to overlook the international results of that. Many Third World countries have argued that they are already losing their more skilled, more ambitious, and more motivated workers through emigration. And, they say, they are losing the investment in human capital they have put into raising and educating these workers. Some of these countries have even demanded compensation from developed nations for the skilled emigrants they admit.

It is difficult to say how seriously some underdeveloped countries themselves take this argument. Few among them, after all, are attempting to regulate or limit emigration. But there is truth to the argument that a country such as the United States, with many skilled professionals, benefits unduly when it accepts the migration of engineers from India or doctors from Africa. Trained, educated, skilled workers are much more needed back home.

How much does the United States contribute to what is sometimes called the *brain drain* from the Third World? Are we, for example, admitting students from poorer countries and training them in subjects and professions that suit them for jobs only in a developed, technological society like ours? Yes, we are. In her study of foreign students in the United States during the 1980/81 school year, University of Maryland anthropologist Nancie L. Gonzalez found that 25.8 percent majored in engineering, 17.4 percent in business and management, and only 2.8 percent in agriculture, 3.6 percent in health-related fields, and 3.8 percent in education. "To the extent that these students expect to be employed in or on behalf of the U.S. companies, we might expect a concentration in these subjects,"

Gonzalez commented. "Employment opportunities in their own countries might be expected to exhibit a somewhat different educational demand profile."[5]

Skilled migrants themselves sometimes argue that they are trained in specialties that are of little use to their home societies; a specialized cardiac surgeon is certainly less useful to most African countries than a general practitioner would be, and it may be true that cardiac surgeons could not find jobs that would fully utilize their skills in hospitals in their home society. But that does not mean they would be of more benefit as cardiac surgeons in Dallas or Los Angeles than as general practitioners—or even nutritionists or nurse-midwives—in Lagos.

American colleges and universities have not faced up to this problem. Our universities and graduate schools must learn to perform a delicate balancing act between guiding foreign students into professions that would be useful to their home countries (at the risk of denying them entry into what may seem to them to be more glamorous and more advanced specialties) and allowing foreign students to explore the full range of knowledge available to Americans. We have to acknowledge that when we select immigrants to the United States for the benefits they will bring to this country we run the risk of consciously encouraging the brain drain from poorer countries, and we have to guard against it.

But what about the sheer numbers of immigrants? A few sociologists and economists argue that the United States will have a labor shortage in a generation, sometime after the turn of the century, because of our relatively low birthrate.[6] Because of this prospective shortage, they conclude that the ceiling on legal immigration should remain very high, or even be raised. "I would say, let's wait to do that until that shortage happens," Briggs responds. One reason for waiting is obvious: importing twenty- and thirty-year-old workers now won't help fill a shortage of younger workers in the year 2010—they won't be young workers then.

It does not make sense either to act now to solve a problem that may well never materialize. "There are all kinds of things that can happen," Briggs added, "both on the supply and the demand side. Maybe the labor force will contract, and maybe we shall need less labor in the future. We are now at a stage at which technological change in the marketplace is very rapid, and this change may significantly reduce the demand for labor, or shorten the workspan of workers. My view is that the system should be flexible, and that the best way to preserve flexibility is to make year-to-year changes in immigration levels, not to base immigration on predictions of our labor needs decades hence." For the past several decades, the American labor force has grown much faster than all the most reliable predictions forecasted.

Even if there should be a prospective labor shortage in our future, I don't think it would be a very serious problem that we should fear unduly. A labor shortage simply would mean that wages would rise, particularly for the young, unskilled workers who do manual labor—the very group that now has the highest rate of unemployment and the lowest rate of pay. That doesn't seem very bad to me, and I find it difficult to understand why anyone except their employers would want to forestall it by importing more workers.

In fact, however, some conservative economists argue that American wages are too high now, and that high immigration is good because it keeps wages lower. The economic law of supply and demand leads us to believe that the best way to lower the price of anything is to increase its supply, and increasing the number of workers in the labor force through large-scale immigration is attractive to some conservative economists.

If legal immigrants are not especially selected for their

skills, then adding them to the labor force simply expands the number of workers without improving its average quality. (On the other hand, if the immigration system were changed to favor legal immigrants with special skills and occupations for which there were shortages in America, then the first generation of immigrants would make a special contribution to the U.S. economy. Even if this happened, however, the second generation, the immigrants' children, would not make any special contribution; there is no reason to believe that children of immigrants would necessarily have different skills from their contemporaries or would choose occupations their contemporaries would shun.)

However, I think it's a pretty fair assumption that most Americans would rather not have their wages lowered. And it's in the best interests of the majority of Americans—most of whom live on wages rather than on income from investments or savings—to ensure that they don't get paid less for the work they do.

Some economists make a second argument, which has a superficial attraction, to defend high levels of legal immigration. They say that workers are productive; in effect, they make their own jobs. New workers are also consumers, after all; they add demand to the economy as well as adding their own labor. Therefore, increasing the number of workers in a country's economy should speed the development of that economy.

When you think about it, though, this is a specious argument. It leaves out something important. Simply adding more bodies to the work force doesn't increase the per capita wealth of the country unless a number of economic conditions are met. One is that the new workers have to be more productive, on average, than the older workers. If new workers are added at the bottom of the economic ladder, in occupations that are less skilled and less productive than the average job in the society, then their average productivity will be less than the society's average, even if the new workers are more productive than others doing the same jobs. Adding the new workers will bring down the per capita gross national product of the country.

A second economic condition to be met is that adequate capital be available to provide new jobs for the new workers. Energy and ambition alone do not create employment opportunities—if they did, millions of currently unemployed Americans would have been able to make jobs for themselves. It costs money to make a job. Creating a new job in a highly skilled, highly technical industry can cost hundreds of thousands of dollars, and the average job in America takes tens of thousands of dollars of capital to create. If the money isn't there to create new jobs, simply adding new workers won't increase the national productivity or the wealth of the country.

In the United States today, neither of these two conditions is being met. While legal immigrants may approximate the skill levels of Americans, and while they may demonstrate some special qualities of drive and ambition, their occupations are not matched to the skills needed in our economy; and illegal immigrants work primarily in the unskilled sectors of the economy, which are less productive. Our high level of unemployment is proof that the capital does not exist to create new jobs for all available workers.

At least four elements are necessary for an economy to grow: labor, energy, natural resources, and capital formation. The pace of economic growth is set by the element in lowest supply. If an economy has plentiful resources, energy, and capital, but has few workers, then increasing the number of laborers will make that economy grow. But in an economy like ours, which is limited by the energy, resources, and capital available to it, and in which workers are in oversupply and many are unemployed, adding workers will simply lengthen the lines of the unemployed. Lamm [12]

Most of what I've said about the impact of legal immigrants also applies to illegal immigrants. But there is another set of arguments over the impact of illegal immigrants. Economists Kyle Johnson and James Orr, in a paper for the U.S. Department of Labor, give a fair statement of how some economists present this argument: "the U.S. economy simply cannot make the adjustments that will be needed to fill some occupations. No matter what wage is offered (presumably within some 'reasonable' limits), some jobs are simply too demeaning, dirty, or of a 'dead end' nature to be filled by resident U.S. workers."[7] Economists who make this argument, say Johnson and Orr, also assume that these dirty jobs are essential to various industries in this country, and that industries have to fill these jobs in order to offer more important and productive jobs to American workers. Since the economists who believe this assume that Americans won't do these jobs but that the jobs must be filled, the solution is to have them filled by immigrants.

Why would immigrants do dirty jobs? Essentially, because they're immigrants: either they're too new to this country to know any better, or people from their countries have a traditional work ethic that Americans have lost, or they're so unskilled that nobody will offer them a better job. And if they're here illegally they can be forced to take dirty jobs, and they'll be unable to complain. Johnson and Orr associate these arguments with John Kenneth Galbraith's *Nature of Mass Poverty* and Michael Piore's *Birds of Passage*.

The biggest problem with this argument is that it's wrong. The history of the economic advancement of legal immigrants shows it hardly applies to them at all. And it's also inaccurate about the work behavior of illegal immigrants in the United States. Most urban illegals do not work at such low wages or in such undesirable jobs that Americans would not take them. In 1980, *The New York Times* reported that aliens seized in Chicago "in recent months were found to have average earnings of more than $9,000 a year while working for plastics and electronics companies, foundries, meat-packing plants, rubber products manufacturers, snack food and candy producers and the like."[8] Former senator Walter D. Huddleston (Democrat-Kentucky), a leader in bringing the problem of illegal immigration to the attention of Congress, noted in a speech on the floor of the Senate in 1981 that, according to INS statistics, "almost two thirds of the illegals who were employed were working at wages over $3.35 [the minimum wage], and many of these held jobs paying over $7.25 an hour."[9] And in Houston, a Rice University study surveyed the construction industry in 1981 and found that one-third of all workers in commercial construction were illegal immigrants, making wages of between $4.00 and $9.50 an hour.[10]

These figures tend to contradict our stereotype of illegal immigrants. Historically, they have worked as stoop laborers in the fields, and the few illegals who came to the cities worked as dishwashers or busboys. Because it was once true, we tend to believe that the majority of illegals still work in these kinds of occupations. In fact, INS apprehension statistics show that the majority of illegal immigrants work in cities, in heavy and light industry, construction, and the service sector. Less than one-half of apprehended illegals work in agriculture, and studies generally agree that less than one-quarter of unapprehended illegals actually do agricultural work. In fact, illegals tend to take better jobs than we think they do.

What about the "dirty" jobs that illegals do take, though? Would unskilled Americans take them, if illegals weren't available? Vernon Briggs noted that it has been alleged that they will not,

> but so far there is no empirical support for that position at all. There is nothing to support it. It's a very hard question for economists to handle. If there were

a shortage of workers to do these jobs, an economist would expect the wage rate to go up. If the wage rate went up, then he would expect more people to do that work. But what is being alleged by people who argue this position is that Americans won't do certain kinds of work no matter what the wage rates are. They won't collect garbage; they won't work in restaurants. The evidence just doesn't support that.

In San Francisco, whenever there are openings in the sanitation department, workers line up by the thousands to apply to collect garbage. There, the occupation is unionized; it's high paying and has good fringe benefits. The bottom line is not whether people are willing to collect garbage; it's whether we are willing to pay fair wages for useful work. Many low-wage workers in this country do very useful work, whether it be picking vegetables or picking up garbage. Their work is indispensable, and the tragedy is that they're paid so little. And the main reason they're paid so little is that there are so many workers available to do jobs in these low-wage labor markets. Their work is needed, and their jobs cannot be moved to other countries. We're going to have restaurants in the United States, and we're going to have hotels, and we're going to need farmworkers to grow and pick our food.

"In every occupation in the United States, a majority of the workers are U.S. citizens. You can't name a single occupation in which they aren't," Briggs pointed out from his study of U.S. Census Bureau data. "This includes farmworkers. In the South and East, for example, many of them are black, and you know that in most cases they're not illegal immigrants. Even in the Southwest most agricultural workers are citizens. This doesn't mean that illegal immigrants don't have a major impact on these occupations—but it does mean that millions of Americans are also doing this work."

Then why do many employers prefer to hire illegal immigrants? "Because they work scared," Briggs said. "They are fearful that they may be deported or that they may lose their jobs if they complain, cause difficulty, or if they unionize. Sometimes they perceive that they are going to be in the country only for a short period, so they don't see a need to unionize or to improve their jobs, but they tend to stay on or to come back to the country again."

Illegal immigrants have two primary effects on American workers: they can make them lose their jobs because an employer prefers illegal immigrant workers, and they can make their wages and working conditions go down because illegals will accept lower pay and worse working conditions. Direct displacement of American workers is hard to prove, and harder to set a number on. Vernon Briggs said, "Of course Americans workers are displaced by illegals. Nobody knows how much displacement there is, and displacement isn't one for one—one American doesn't lose a job for every illegal who gets a job—but displacement is substantial."

The evidence that illegals displace American workers is largely anecdotal. But the anecdotes are strong ones. In late 1982, Jack Sheinkman, the secretary-treasurer of the Amalgamated Clothing and Textile Workers Union, surveyed trade union leaders across the nation. He found that 72 percent of them said that illegal aliens were to their personal knowledge taking jobs away from American workers in their localities. The majority of volunteered reports of illegal aliens given to the Immigration and Naturalization Service come from Hispanic Americans, who are competing directly with illegal workers for low-wage and semi-skilled jobs.[11]

One example of what can happen when American workers see themselves being put out of work by illegal competition took place in California in late 1983. Striking agricultural union workers, both farmworkers and canning

industry workers, physically attacked their illegal alien re-
placements several times. Growers and canners had used
the opportunity of a tight job market for low-income workers in order to cut wages and to replace union workers.
Americans—white, black, and Asian—found themselves
competing with an unusually large influx of Mexican and
Central American illegal workers who came to the fields
because of the devaluation of the Mexican peso and economic difficulties in Central America. Southern Californian
growers responded to the labor surplus by cutting wages,
and some of the sharpest labor confrontations in years resulted.[12]

In August 1983 there was another important incident.
Lydia Jackson, a cleaning woman at National Airport in
Washington, D.C., lost her job. The janitorial company that
hired her was replaced by a company composed of non-
union Vietnamese and Cambodians. "Blacks are taking the
bad enough jobs as it is now, but now they cannot even
count on jobs in cleaning," she was quoted as saying. Pat
McDonough, of Local 82 of the Service Employees International Union, said, "It's a concrete situation where
American workers are being displaced. They [the employ-
ers] get a more docile work force and don't have to pay the
minimum wage."[13]

In Colorado, in July 1984, forty-three illegal aliens from
Mexico and El Salvador were apprehended as they worked
on a traveling roofing crew. They were based in Texas and
came to Colorado to do roofing work in the aftermath of
severe early summer hailstorms. They earned up to $100 a
day per person—even while, as of June 30, 438 Colorado
citizens were registered with the state employment service
as unemployed and seeking roofing jobs.[14]

But the garment industry provides the most extreme
example of how American workers are forced out of their
jobs by competition from illegal aliens. During the 1950s
and 1960s garment industry sweatshops had been almost

eliminated in the United States. Some brave union organizers and workers faced violence, racketeering, and even some murders to clean up the garment industry. But during the 1970s sweatshops made a big comeback. New York State's attorney general, Robert Abrams, has said that "the sweatshop is almost as big a problem as it was at the turn of the century." And the major cause of this change is the influx of illegal immigrants—willing and able workers who will endure sweatshop working conditions and wages—into the major centers of sewing and clothing manufacturing in the United States, New York City and California.

The worst part of this situation is that one of the brave unions that originally eliminated sweatshops, the International Ladies Garment Workers Union, has been a collaborator in their return. That union has decided to protect and encourage illegal aliens in the garment industry; instead of resisting the displacement of American workers, it has welcomed any illegals who will enroll in the union. But because many of its locals represent an illegal work force, the union cannot guarantee the wage stipulated in the union contract, or even the minimum wage, cannot supervise working conditions, and cannot cooperate with the government to enforce laws governing wages, hours, and working conditions. The union local, in effect, becomes a partner with the shop contractor or subcontractor in exploiting garment workers. A union that cooperates with the system of illegal immigration cannot represent American workers effectively; therefore American workers in the garment trade are displaced, illegals are hired in preference to Americans, and wages are lowered and working conditions worsened.[15]

We all pay when illegals take jobs from Americans, including for the high cost of the resulting unemployment. Let me make a very conservative estimate of the taxpayer cost of the unemployment caused by illegal immigration. Imagine there were only six million illegal aliens in this country, that only half of them worked, and that only half of those who worked were taking jobs that Americans would take. That still adds up to a million and a half jobs. In 1981, the Congressional Budget Office estimated that each unemployed person received about $7,000 per year in unemployment and welfare benefits. A million and a half unemployed people times $7,000 equals 10.5 *billion* dollars in taxpayer subsidies. And each estimate in this calculation is low, rather than high. There is no way to use reasonable assumptions about the effect of illegal immigrants on the work force and to arrive at a lower figure.

I'm impressed by the evidence that competition with illegal immigrants lowers the wages paid to American workers. If you compare two similar cities with different proportions of illegals, the difference is obvious. In the mid-1970s, economists Barton Smith and Robert Newman compared the hourly wages in Houston and Laredo. Both cities have significant illegal immigration (remember the Rice University finding that in 1981 a third of construction workers in Houston were illegal immigrants), but Laredo has an even higher percentage of illegals than Houston. Smith and Newman used Bureau of Labor Standards statistics to show that hourly wages for semiskilled labor in the two cities differed by over 60 percent, from $3.00 to $1.90. They were aware that factors other than illegal immigration could have caused this difference, and they held those factors constant. After accounting for occupation, education, race, sex, age, and other social and demographic characteristics, they found that workers in the border area earned approximately $1,679 less per year, on average. And for the semiskilled laborers they studied, this represented roughly a 20 percent annual wage difference.[16] Laredo laborers' income was cut by a fifth because of competition from illegals.

If you compare the same industry in similar cities, you'll find the same kind of loss. Around Los Angeles and in

Riverside and Orange counties in southern California, there are a dozen or so recreational vehicle plants making off-road vehicles and modified vans. Illegal aliens account for more than half of their assembly-line work forces. According to United Auto Workers (UAW) union officials, recreational vehicle plant employees in this region earn about two dollars an hour less than workers doing the same work in northern California, where there are fewer illegal immigrants.[17]

Some studies have tried to prove that illegal immigrants do not take American jobs or lower wages by comparing unemployment rates or wage rates in various cities. But I've concluded, after reading these studies and the comments of their critics, that all these attempts have made serious mistakes in both their assumptions and their methods. The most widely quoted of such studies makes a fatal mathematical mistake.[18] Others studies have compared vastly mismatched cities; they have, for example, chosen as low-immigration cities a group of older, industrial cities in the Northeast and as high-immigration cities a group of younger, high-tech Sunbelt cities.

In addition, a city or area with a high level of illegal immigration may have a relatively low unemployment rate—but that rate can conceal a high rate of unemployment for the workers who compete directly with illegal aliens for jobs. These groups—unskilled service workers or industrial workers, for example—may have a rate of employment that is two or three times higher than the total rate. Unemployment in southern California may be 5 percent, as compared with 9 percent in New York, but the unemployment rate of black or Hispanic workers in southern California will still be 12, 13, or 14 percent.

Not all of that differential in unemployment rates will be due to illegal aliens, of course. The important factor is the total size of the labor market—the number of workers relative to the number of jobs that are available to them.

More careful and more objective large-scale studies remain to be done; until they are done, all the most reliable evidence proves that illegal immigrants hurt American workers.

There is a tricky and clever restatement of the argument that Americans won't do dirty work and that illegal immigrants are needed to do it. This version of the argument doesn't say that Americans won't work hard or do dirty jobs at all; it says that they won't do them at wages low enough to meet foreign competition. Therefore, the argument runs, the industries in which these jobs are located would be lost to foreign nations unless illegal immigrants are allowed to come to the United States to do them.

I have three reactions to that argument. First, as I've said, most workers in every industry in the United States are citizens. Even in the garment trade, even among migrant agricultural workers, Americans are in the majority. Americans will do the jobs.

Second, some industries are going to leave the United States anyhow. It's inevitable. Working and wage conditions in other countries are so deplorable that it's impossible for us or for any country with occupational health, safety, and wage and hour laws to compete with them. And we shouldn't try to compete with them. Some companies are going to leave the United States to take advantage of deplorable working conditions. And our reaction should be to say "good riddance" to them. If a company says it can't pay a fair minimum wage, we shouldn't say, "All right, then pay less." We should let that company go out of business. The same is true of health and safety regulations. If a company can't afford to run a healthful and safe plant, we shouldn't allow them to run an unsafe one. We should let them close. We'll be better off without them.

Letting go of dying companies and industries may cause some economic dislocations in the short term. But in the long run it will contribute to the health of our economy. If we become dependent on illegal immigrants, on the other hand, if we can't operate our businesses with citizens, if many of our companies can't pay the minimum wage, then we shall have serious long-term problems in the United States.

And third, there are very few kinds of industries in this country that are really in danger of dying. Many industries in which illegal aliens are concentrated can't leave the United States. Farms, restaurants, and hotels must stay where they are. If they had to, even many marginal manufacturing industries would simply adjust to hiring Americans and paying fair wages. Most companies would try to avoid moving out of the country—it's as difficult and disruptive for a company to move as for an individual. Today they are simply taking advantage of the fact that illegal aliens are readily available in order to lower wages. In fact, the lower wages that can be paid to illegals do not seem to keep costs lower. There is no persuasive evidence that meals or hotel rooms cost less in New York or Los Angeles, where many illegals work, than in Indianapolis or Cincinnati. And there is no evidence that employers find it difficult to get enough workers to run restaurants or hotels in Toledo or Boise because there are no large numbers of illegals available there.

I don't see any evidence that there are many marginal industries in the United States being preserved through illegal immigration, and I don't think the few that may be saved through massive illegal immigration should be saved. The future of American industry shouldn't depend on our degrading the pay and conditions under which Americans labor. I have seen dozens of different plans to make America more productive, to increase the international competitiveness of American industries, to increase our foreign trade, and to improve our economic outlook. Each plan has its trade-offs, its disadvantages as well as its advantages. But one thing that none of these plans recommends is that the United States become a Third World nation of low-skilled labor and marginal manufacturing industries, a nation producing the raw materials for better educated and more skilled nations to refine. If, as most knowledgeable people believe, our economic future lies in highly technical fields, in information technologies, then we must educate America's own work force more widely, train and upgrade the skill levels of our own workers. We must not open our doors to more and more unskilled laborers to try to preserve marginal industries.

Because the fact may be that we face not a labor shortage but a glut of unskilled laborers. I sought out Gail Garfield Schwartz, a Washington economics consultant, after reading her book *The Work Revolution*[19] and asked her what the ramifications of technological change were for workers and for immigration. She told me that "in the future, the number of jobs which will be available and the compensation and on-the-job satisfaction that they will offer will change very radically. Technology will take away a great proportion of the relatively 'simple' jobs in manufacturing, office, and service work, in the way it has already changed warehousing. The actual, participating, active labor force will shrink. People won't be looking for jobs, since the job opportunities won't exist. On the other hand, the people will still exist; they will just be unemployed, and they will have all the disaffections that people who can't get satisfying job opportunities now have." The range of jobs changed by technology, she believes, will be broader than most planners now envision.

> When most people think of "unskilled" workers, they think of messengers or counter clerks at fast-food restaurants. To my mind, "unskilled" also means most people who work on, for example, automobile assembly lines; their tasks can be learned within a matter of weeks with no formal education or training and even without very much manual dexterity. A great many more jobs are unskilled than are formally classified as

unskilled, and there is no question that they will be destroyed by technology, that they will be done by robots and automated machinery. There is no point in hiring somebody at $20,000 or $25,000 a year plus fringe benefits to do a job that a robot will do for three shifts a day with no holidays, no sick days, and no coffee breaks. Of course, new businesses will be formed with new jobs, but relative to the amount of output, fewer workers will be needed. And people without skills will not gain entry into the "high-knowledge-content opportunities" that will be developed in science, technology, microbiology, agribiology, engineering, financial services, and so forth.

Dan Stein works for FAIR, the Federation for American Immigration Reform, which has often argued the economic case against massive illegal immigration. In a background paper for FAIR, Stein asks a series of questions about the possible effects of large-scale immigration on the future of our work force. He starts with this assumption: "A continued rapid entry of unskilled workers will increase the already high unskilled/skilled worker ratio. A glut will adversely affect the future shape of American industry—guiding it toward and sustaining labor intensive industries and technologies. Political pressure to keep a surplus of unskilled/semiskilled labor employed could slow down the pace of modernization." And he then proceeds to list the issues this assumption raises:

What is our future need for unskilled and semiskilled labor? What will happen to laid-off workers in the mature manufacturing sector? How many more will be displaced due to the introduction of robotics and other forms of automation? Will they lower their expectations to compete with illegal and recently arrived legal immigrants? Should we attempt to continue to compete with newly industrialized countries by importing large amounts of cheap labor to sustain marginal industries? If so, how will a glut of unskilled labor affect the nature and direction of our industrial growth? What will we do with this burgeoning excess of unskilled labor? Will there be political pressure to expand the availability of public works or other unskilled jobs? What are the advantages of a capital intensive economy and a stable work force? To what extent is a shortage of unskilled labor an "engine of ingenuity?"[20]

Let me get back to that question of "dirty work." Americans will do dirty work. Americans are good, enthusiastic, hard workers who will do low-paid, unskilled work if it is made available to them. Every empirical study that has been done proves it. In early 1980, Ohio University did a study for the Department of Labor on much-maligned young workers. It reported that a majority of young people and teenagers would be willing to take low-paying jobs in exactly the areas in which illegals are concentrated: fast-food restaurants, cleaning establishments, supermarkets, dishwashing. A substantial number of teenagers were willing to work below the minimum wage. The younger the worker, the lower the wage and level of job he or she would be willing to accept. And young workers who are members of minority groups would take lower level work than young white workers.[21]

In early 1981, *The Los Angeles Times* surveyed unemployed workers. It found that 75 percent were willing to apply for jobs paying between $3.35 an hour (the legal minimum) and $4.50 an hour. More than 48 percent would work in restaurants, and 40 percent would apply for garment industry jobs. But the general public, when surveyed by the newspaper, did not understand unemployed peoples' willingness, eagerness, to work. Nearly half, 48 percent, believed that illegal aliens took only jobs that Americans wouldn't accept.[22]

What is true is not that Americans won't work hard, that we won't do dirty work, that we won't take low-paying jobs, that we have become lazy and spoiled, but that many middle-class people have become estranged from the millions of Americans who now do exactly such work every day. As former undersecretary of labor Malcolm Lovell has pointed out, "In 1981, close to 30 percent of all workers employed in this country—some 29 million people—were holding down the kinds of low skilled industrial, service, and agricultural jobs in which illegal aliens typically find employment. In addition, it cannot be claimed that Americans will not take low-wage jobs. In 1981, an estimated 10.5 million workers were employed at or below the minimum wage ($3.35 an hour). An estimated 10 million more workers were employed in jobs earning within 30–40 cents per hour of the minimum wage."[23]

It's necessary to stress that Americans will do hard work in dirty jobs because the advocates of illegal immigrants have perversely tried to turn the natural urge of American workers to better themselves into a negative quality, an undesirable trait. Chicago columnist Mike Royko, on October 1, 1982, wrote about the plight of an American citizen who was laid off from his $5-an-hour job in order to make room for illegal aliens. Royko struck at the heart of the argument:

> In hard times like these—with hundreds of desperate job-seekers showing up whenever some factory advertises a few jobs in the paper—I don't think there are many paying chores that jobless people of this country will turn down. . . . Every time I've written about the illegal alien problem, and the impact it has on U.S. citizens like Charlie, I hear from people who tell me I have no compassion for the downtrodden. That's not

true. It's just that I have more compassion for a U.S. citizen who is currently downtrodden than for somebody downtrodden from another country who is in this country in violation of our laws. And one thing I've noticed about those do-gooders who argue that we should do almost nothing about stopping the flow of millions of illegal aliens. Unlike Charlie, the do-gooders have jobs.[24]

It is the near invisibility of lower-class American working people to the rest of American society that allows many of us to give our compassion more easily to illegal aliens than to the U.S. citizens whom they displace from the workplace. Even the U.S. Civil Rights Commission shared this blindness, and it did so even before President Reagan reorganized it to deflect its concern from the plight of minorities. In *The Tarnished Golden Door*, its report on immigration, the commission recommended against employer sanctions laws that would make it illegal for American employers to hire illegal aliens. In a stinging dissent from these recommendations, Commissioner Frankie Freeman wrote that they were "unfortunate in that they are fashioned on false premises and totally ignore certain fundamental facts." She continued:

> In following this approach the majority would ignore the fact that employers who knowingly hire undocumented aliens do so not out of compassion for the oppressed, but out of simple greed. The majority would ignore the fact that their exploitation is made possible because the fear of detection and deportation prohibits undocumented aliens from protesting unsafe working conditions or wages below the minimum required by Federal law. Perhaps the most distressing aspect of the majority's opinion is it ignores the reality that undocumented aliens tend to be concentrated in

the lowest paying jobs and displace American racial and ethnic minorities who traditionally have been employed in those fields, Hispanic and black Americans. . . . While the plight of the oppressed throughout the world is central to the principles of any supporter of civil and human rights, it does not follow at all that the plight of the poor and oppressed of our country should be ignored by the one agency that has traditionally championed their cause.[25]

Roger Conner is executive director of FAIR. He holds that there may perhaps be an even less attractive motive behind the negative view of American workers. In a conference at Howard University on immigration policies and black America, Conner argued that the unfavorable comparison of American low-wage workers to illegal immigrants is based on racial discrimination. Conner referred to a survey by the *Chicago Tribune* of employers who hired illegal immigrants: "They asked these people, are your people taking jobs Americans would take? Sixteen of the twenty-one personnel directors surveyed said 'no.' And when they asked why there were no Americans who could and would take those jobs, here's what they said: 'I don't think black people want to work in Chicago.' 'The blacks are the most unreliable help you can get, whereas the illegal immigrants are reliable.' 'The black people we've got here are uneducated and unskilled.' 'Black workers have high absenteeism and poor work habits.'" Conner commented: "Familiar stereotypes? You bet. They've always been there, and they've always been used by employers who did not want to hire black Americans. But now, you see, there's a new twist. They're saying that because we have these new illegal immigrants present here, who are willing to work at desperation wages under desperation working conditions, if Americans are not willing to work at the same desperation wages and under the same desperation working conditions, then Americans are lazy. It's a classic example of blaming the victim." And he observed that "illegal immigrants do not take jobs Americans won't fill; they *make* jobs Americans won't fill."[26]

There is an overwhelming logic to Conner's argument. Massive numbers of illegal aliens create a vicious labor market cycle. Large numbers of illegals depress wages and lower working conditions in numerous industries; at some point the wages and working conditions become so bad that American workers are unwilling to accept them. Then the "unavailability" of American workers is used as an excuse to justify even more illegal immigrants, who in turn drive wages and working conditions even lower, resulting in even fewer Americans willing to take those jobs.

I want to be sure that this is clear, and that what I am saying about the economic effects of immigration is not exaggerated. I do not believe that massive immigration is the only cause of unemployment or poverty, but I know it is a significant cause of them. I do not think we can cure the ills of unemployment by eliminating illegal immigration, but I know that allowing it to continue certainly makes unemployment worse. I do not think we can ensure better future living standards for Americans just by controlling illegal immigration, but it is certain that living standards will fall if we do not control it. Immigration control is not the single key to solving economic difficulties, but it is imperative that the immigration problem be solved as a step toward solving many social and economic difficulties.

It's the low-skilled, low-wage workers in the United States, who are already the worst off, who are made worse off by massive immigration. It seems as though there is a class bias behind our ambivalence toward immigration policy in the United States. If illegal immigrants were doctors and lawyers, professors and business executives, there would be no debate on this issue. Employer sanctions would be in place, the border would be controlled, and the money would be available to enforce our laws. We wouldn't tolerate this kind of invasion of white-collar and professional occupations. But because immigrants enter the blue-collar, service, low-skilled, and low-wage occupations, there is a tendency for the middle and upper classes to say that the illegals are just taking jobs that American workers won't take.

And low-wage workers themselves are often confused about what the problem is. They frequently can't figure out why their wages are so low—unless they're working side-by-side with illegals. They are not in a situation in which they can intellectually rationalize their positions, and many of them even blame themselves for their status without trying to question why it is so difficult for them to get or hold a job or to get out of the low-wage market.

Let me turn the argument around. If an influx of illegal professionals could lower the wages of the overpaid, of doctors and lawyers, rather than the wages of the poor, then there might be some economic benefit to their coming to this country. But doctors and lawyers would not allow that to happen. Instead, it is low-wage labor markets, the wages at the bottom, that are being depressed. Illegal immigration widens the differences between classes in the United States; it keeps down the price of hiring a maid or a gardener for the rich while it makes things worse for the poor. Instead of being a "free lunch" for our economy, illegal immigrants are becoming an indigestible and unassimilated lump in the body politic.

We can solve the problems caused by massive illegal immigration into the workplace by a simple change in the law that I've already mentioned, employer sanctions. When the last comprehensive revision of immigration law was passed by Congress in 1952, many acts of aiding and harboring illegal immigrants were made criminal, but not the act of hiring an illegal alien. This exemption, this omission of employment, has been called the "Texas Proviso" because its leading supporters were Texas ranchers and farmers who used illegal Mexican workers. It has continued to plague enforcement of our immigration laws ever since.

Most illegal immigrants come to the United States because they know they can get work here. Most employers of illegal immigrants hire them because it is not illegal for them to do so. The advantages they get from employing illegal immigrants—lower wages, less pressure to improve working conditions, and so forth—are secondary. The important thing is that they are not breaking any law. Americans are law-abiding people. Most of us pay taxes voluntarily, obey traffic laws and stop signs, and do not commit crimes. And almost all compliance with laws is voluntary. Only a small portion of tax returns are audited each year; only a small number of traffic intersections or stretches of highway are guarded by patrol officers. If it were made illegal for employers to hire illegal aliens, most employers who now hire them would stop doing so—immediately and without any pressure.

There would still be employers who would knowingly break the law, of course, and there would still be a problem locating and identifying illegal aliens who used forged or false or stolen identification to pass themselves off as citizens or legal resident aliens. But the enforcement problem would be much more manageable in comparison with the enforcement problem that exists today. In Chapter 8 I'll discuss the question of employer sanctions in more detail.

The work force problem caused by massive numbers of legal immigrants is just as important, but it will be quite a bit harder to solve. In the future, the United States Congress and the administration will have to take action on legal immigration, too. We take too little account of the effect on American workers of the yearly admission of hundreds of thousands of legal immigrant workers. I believe that the United States must adopt a point system for the admission of immigrants similar to the one used in Canada, and that the particular skills or services this country needs should be scored by a point system. The total number of legal admissions ought to be set by a formula that would follow closely the level of unemployment in this country.

These changes are coming. The American public, as the polls show, is increasingly concerned. Members of Congress and the Reagan administration are becoming aware that there is a direct connection between levels of immigration and the welfare of American workers. I'll discuss some additional possible solutions and how employer sanctions would work in Chapter 10.

7

Social Services, Aliens, and Americans

Immigrants—including many illegal aliens—are increasingly demanding social services, and, more and more often, they're getting them even when the law says they're not supposed to. It's hard to know how big the problem is, and people on both sides of the debate have made exaggerated claims. But it is clear to me that the United States, with a gigantic federal deficit and too many claims on existing social service and welfare programs, cannot ignore the growing burden caused by large numbers of immigrants, particularly illegal aliens. Illegal aliens are not the chief cause of the rise in welfare costs in America, but they do constitute a significant part of the cost of welfare in many areas and states. And the problem is growing yearly and adding to the total welfare burden on tax-paying Americans.

What do these costs add up to? Rice University economist Donald L. Huddle estimates that illegal immigration costs U.S. taxpayers $25 billion dollars a year. Huddle reaches that figure by adding the cost of unemployment benefits and social services paid to illegals to the cost of these benefits paid to the American workers displaced by illegal aliens, then adding the tax revenue lost from the underpayment of taxes by illegal aliens.

The social services and welfare burden of immigrants has grown because migration is a dynamic, ever-changing process. Many scholars of migration describe its stages in this way: first, single men arrive in a developed country to find work. These young men usually think their migration will be a temporary thing; many of them believe they will return to their home countries. But they develop ties to the new country, and they form new relationships with each other. The second stage of the process begins when these single men send for their families from their home countries to join them or when they marry locally and begin to have families in the new country. In the third stage the migrant community finally acknowledges that it is permanently settled in the new country. In the early years of a migrant stream, when most migrants are young, single, working men, migrants make few demands on the host country's social services. But the permanent migrant community of the later stages is far more expensive for the wider society.

Three distinct groups of immigrants make different kinds of demands on our social welfare programs: legal immigrants, refugees (who are also legal immigrants, but who are treated very differently), and illegal immigrants. Because each group has a different impact on welfare, each group has to be examined separately.

I'll start with legal immigrants. No one has done a comprehensive study of how many or what kinds of social services are used by legally admitted immigrants. It's a good assumption that a twenty-year-old native-born American and a twenty-year-old person who immigrates to the United States will use about the same kind and quantity of social benefits during the rest of their lives. The same is probably true of an infant born here and an infant immigrant. In other words, most social scientists would assume that legal immigrants would use social benefits in about the same way and in about the same proportion as their demographic peers among native-born Americans. It is true that legal immigrants have "sponsors" who have technically pledged their support for these immigrants during their first five years of residence in the United States, so the level of use of social services should be lower for five years, but this technical requirement is almost never enforced.

Most immigrants who are admitted as refugees will need a lot of welfare services; when the United States admits them, it is generally expected that they will be in desperate need or they wouldn't have qualified as refugees. Refugees require intensive education, medical care, and monetary support for the first several years that they are in this country. In recent years, legally admitted refugees have been supported by social services that cost, on average, well over twice the average annual income of Americans.

Through the 1950s, we admitted refugees to the United States without the promise of governmental aid. It was felt that the demands of humanitarianism were fully satisfied simply by allowing them admission. But we entered a new era when we admitted the Cuban refugees of the 1960s. Our consciences and the modern standards of American communities required then, and have required ever since, that the federal government provide a great deal of assistance to the refugees whom it selected and brought to the United States. The problems of refugees, the kinds of financial assistance they require in order to integrate fully into our society, are separate from the question of illegal aliens, but they are just as vital to the question of distribution of social benefits.

Dozens of refugees can be fed, housed, and supported in a camp in Somalia or in Pakistan for the cost of resettling one refugee in the United States. Resettling refugees in developed countries is a very poor solution to refugee problems because of its high cost and because of the political and personal difficulties involved in the movement of tens of thousands of people. Those whose first concern is for the welfare of the largest number of refugees, those actually involved in helping massive groups of refugees, know that most refugees must be repatriated to their home countries or resettled in neighboring developing countries—they try to keep resettlement in the developing countries to a minimum.

But the United States will always admit refugees, regardless of the cost, availability, or preferability of other kinds of assistance. Prior to 1980, the number of refugees was kept relatively manageable by the quota assigned to them under our immigration laws. In 1980, spurred by the crisis of Vietnamese "boat people," refugees from South Vietnam who were taking a dangerous route of escape to other Asian countries, Congress passed a new Refugee Act which both raised the quota to a "normal level" of 50,000 annually and established a procedure to sidestep that ceiling. In 1980, about 167,000 refugees were admitted to the Untied States, and the annual number of refugees has since dropped to only slightly under 100,000. The immediate impact on state and local welfare agencies was devastating.

In late 1981, the National Association of Counties reported on the first few months of large-scale refugee admission: "Beginning in mid-1979, when the Indochinese 'boat people' began to arrive in the U.S. at a rate of 14,000 per month, the welfare dependency rate of refugees increased dramatically. As of August 1979, this rate was 37 percent; by November 1980, it had increased to over 49 percent." In November 1980, 94.3 percent of all Indochinese refugees in Rhode Island were receiving cash assistance; the percentages were 87.2 in Minnesota and 72.8

in Oregon. In Orange County, California, 32.1 percent of all welfare cash assistance recipients were Indochinese refugees; in San Francisco, 20.9 percent. The National Association of Counties found that "41,188 Indochinese refugees were on cash assistance as of September 1, 1976. By November 1, 1980, the number of recipients had grown to 208,747, an increase of 167,559."[1]

In a second report in late 1981, the NACo concentrated on data from San Diego and San Francisco counties and found that "Indochinese refugees were applying for public assistance soon after their arrival in the United States. In both of these counties, the majority of refugees applying for public assistance have been in this country for thirty days or less. Indeed, 29 percent of refugees being added to the public assistance rolls in San Diego County applied for aid within ten days after their arrival in the U.S." The NACo reported that "more than ninety percent of refugees initially resettled into San Diego and San Francisco have been applying for public assistance within weeks after their arrival in the U.S. Such findings indicate that—at least in San Diego and San Francisco—refugee reception and placement grants, administered by voluntary resettlement agencies, are failing to keep refugees off welfare."[2]

Refugees created a social burden for local governments on the East Coast, too. On September 17, 1981, Barbara Glaser, the director of Social Services for Arlington County, Virginia, reported that between 30 and 50 percent of the refugees in her county were totally dependent on welfare, depending on the population figure used for refugees. And 39 percent of her agency's total expenditures were for refugees, though the refugees accounted for only 15 percent of its caseload. With the influx of refugees, the rate of tuberculosis in Arlington increased from an average of 5 percent per 100,000 before 1975 to 43 in 1980. Because of the high incidence of tuberculosis and other communicable diseases among the refugees, public-health services had to be redirected toward them, both for their own well-being and to contain the risk of infection to the native-born population. Therefore, services to nonrefugee Arlington citizens were reduced. And, Glaser reported, the school system had to expend far more than the normal outlay of means and personnel to meet the needs of the refugee children.[3]

Obviously, refugees compete with American citizens for the services they receive. This is true both for public services and, less visibly, for private charity. A church may have a choice between running a soup kitchen in the inner city or sponsoring refugee families, between donating clothes to poor citizens or funding English-language education programs for refugees. Such choices have to be made when refugee admissions into the United States are as high as they were in the early 1980s, when they are so high that neither public nor private charity can provide the intensive educational, housing, food, clothing, medical, and cash assistance that refugees require. If we don't want to skimp on services for the poor in this country, we have to make more realistic assessments of how many refugees can be aided this intensively, and then keep our admissions within these realistic levels. The refugee aid debacle of the early 1980s must not be repeated.

Illegal immigrants also use social services, and two major controversies have arisen over this issue. First, the claim has been made that illegal immigrants don't use any appreciable amount of social services in the United States. Advocates of that position sometimes claim that illegal immigrants pay more in taxes than they receive in benefits. I think that's a specious way of stating the issue, but it has to be answered. The second controversy is whether or not illegal immigrants are "entitled" to welfare benefits that are available to the people who live in the United States legally. This is both a legal question and a moral one, and its answer is both legally and morally complex.

Do illegal immigrants use a significant amount of social services? The stereotype is that they don't. The old and outdated, but still prevalent, image of illegals is that they are young men who come to the United States to work, not to get on welfare, and that they are afraid of coming to the attention of government agencies. It's true that it is difficult for healthy young men to claim many social services, and a population consisting predominantly of healthy young men would use very few services and receive very few benefits. It has been true in the past, and to some extent is still true, that illegals tend to shun doing anything—such as applying for benefits—that would call the attention of the authorities to them.

But the profile of illegal immigrants has been changing over the past two decades. As I said at the beginning of this chapter, migration is a process, and we're no longer in the first stage of that process. Illegals today are both men and women, both youths and the elderly, not just working-age men. There are many more families among illegals today than there were in the days when most illegals were stoop laborers. There are many more illegals in the cities than there are on farms. There are many more people, therefore, who need social services. And over the past two decades many more service organizations have arisen encouraging illegals to apply for social benefits, instructing them how to do so, bringing court suits applying for benefits and asserting illegals' rights to them, and publicizing among illegals the fact that most social organizations will not report them to the Immigration and Naturalization Service and are in fact forbidden by their own internal regulations from doing so. Recently, therefore, the picture has changed. Many more illegals receive social services and welfare benefits of various kinds than ever before.

Few studies have examined the groups that receive welfare benefits in order to determine how many illegals are among them. Most researchers in this field are advocates of immigrants' receiving these benefits, and the research they do is frequently skewed in favor of demonstrating little use, but great need, among illegals.

I found David North, of the New TransCentury Foundation in Washington, D.C., to be one of the few independent and reliable researchers in this field. North has written extensively on immigration and immigration policy for several government agencies, especially the Department of Labor, as well as for private organizations such as the Ford Foundation and the German Marshall Fund. In a conversation I had with him, North said that there are few good figures on illegals' use of social services because of "decentralization and inertia. Social services are generally delivered by state and local government or by school districts, so a whole muster of people at the state and local levels must cooperate. Secondly, the forms which could be used to identify illegal aliens are certainly hard to change, if not cast in concrete, and they generally were written before there was much interest in this question. Further, not an awful lot of executives in the social service business want to find out the extent to which their systems have failed in the past by letting in people who are ineligible for benefits.

"The laws themselves," North said, "are inconsistent, sometimes silent on this issue." He pointed out that the federally mandated, federally funded programs like Aid for Dependent Children and unemployment insurance made it illegal for illegal aliens to receive benefits. But, he said, a lot of state and local programs don't. "Several states continue to let illegal aliens use general assistance programs, which are the catch-all, state-funded welfare funds. We also find that illegal aliens are still eligible for the earned income tax credit, the 'negative income tax,' despite the efforts of former senator Walter D. Huddleston and a unanimous vote of the Senate.

"Generally, I would say, illegal aliens have shown more interest, more willingness to apply, less fear of the government than we all figured that they would just a few years ago." I asked North about the common argument that illegal aliens pay more in taxes than they receive in social benefits. "I unwittingly helped set that argument in motion several years ago," he said,

> when Marion Houstoun and I did a survey of illegal aliens for the U.S. Department of Labor. Our focus was the U.S. labor market, and we were essentially talking only to undocumented workers, as opposed to the whole illegal alien population. That study dealt mainly with the depressing effects of the illegals on the labor market. But in the course of it we asked illegals whether they had had income taxes withheld. About 72 percent said yes. And we asked whether they had had social security taxes withheld, and about 77 percent said yes. Then we asked them whether they'd used hospitals, schools, and income transfer programs. About 40 percent had been served in medical facilities, a much smaller percentage had children in U.S. schools, and a very tiny percent had used income transfer programs.
>
> Now, these findings have been widely misused. Marion Houstoun and I pointed out that this was exactly what you would expect to find in this population. They were over 90 percent male, largely between 18 and 35, most of them did not have a family with them, and they were by definition employed. That caveat of ours has been largely ignored.
>
> Other people have since spoken with the same kind of people and gotten the same kind of data. Surveys sponsored by the Mexican Government and the U.S. Civil Rights Commission have covered the same ground and gotten the same findings. The problem with all these surveys is that the kind of people they talk to predetermines the answers they'll get. What you

need to do is either look at the whole illegal alien population, including the unemployed, women, children, and so forth; or survey all the clients of the systems which pay these benefits and deliver these services, and find the illegals among them. This is the kind of survey which I have advocated.

Whenever somebody really looks, looks hard, at the people who use social services, he finds that a surprising number of illegal aliens use them. David Heer, for example, surveyed illegal aliens who gave birth in Los Angeles County Hospitals. This population is almost the exact opposite of the group in the North-Houstoun survey—a much more likely population to be drawing from income transfer programs—and, in fact, they were drawing on them substantially. Another study, done by Van Arsdol, of people seeking to legalize their status at a migrant service agency in Los Angeles, also showed substantial use of services. In these two instances, the Heer and Van Arsdol studies, we're dealing with a resident illegal alien population that is identified in some way other than by being picked up by the Immigration Service—which concentrates on picking up both men and workers. The INS doesn't raid hospitals; it raids fields and factories.

The best single summary of recent data on the use of social services by illegal immigrants is a short booklet by Roger Conner, the executive director of FAIR. Conner argues that "illegal immigrants, like all other immigrants, adapt to the societies in which they live. As illegal immigrants are increasingly institutionalized in the United States, as they are increasingly made to feel 'at home,' they behave more like the native population. They lose their fear of approaching the 'system,' of dealing with the government, and they lose whatever 'cultural reluctance' they may have had about accepting benefits to which they increasingly feel they are entitled."[4]

Conner cites several studies that show increasing use of welfare by illegals, some of which David North had mentioned to me. Here are three examples: Maurice D. Van Arsdol, Jr., and his associates studied illegal aliens in Los Angeles who came to a migrant service center called One-Stop Migration. In this sample, 8.9 percent of the males and 18.5 percent of the females were either current or former recipients of welfare. Charles Keely and his associates studied unapprehended illegal immigrants from the Dominican Republic and Haiti who were living in New York City in early 1977. Keely found that 29 percent of the Dominicans and 13 percent of the Haitians reported that they were current or former users of welfare. David Heer's study of illegal aliens who gave birth in Los Angeles County public hospitals found that 19 percent were current recipients of food stamps; 19.9 percent were enrolled in the Medi-Cal Program, California's version of Medicare; and 18.4 percent of those who were unmarried, who had U.S.-born children aged two or more, and who had been in the United States for over a year were receiving Aid for Dependent Children.

The lesson is simple. If you look at employed young men, whether they're illegal, legal, alien, or native, you'll find that they use very little welfare. But if you look at the whole population of illegal aliens in the United States, you'll find that a substantial number of them use one or a number of the social service programs that are intended for citizens. If you survey the people who use these social service programs in the cities and states with a substantial illegal population, you'll find a number of illegals among them. And if you look at illegals over the past couple of decades, you'll find that the number using welfare has kept growing.

Conner also notes some government agency studies that have discovered a large number of illegal aliens using social services. In the spring of 1982, the state of Illinois sampled the people who applied for unemployment insurance and who identified themselves as aliens. In the first week, the state tested one Chicago unemployment insurance office. Out of 198 people who identified themselves as aliens, 101—a little more than half—turned out to be using fraudulent "green cards," the identification cards issued to legal resident aliens. Next, the state surveyed all of its alien unemployment insurance applicants on April 1, 1982. Out of 257 alien applicants on that one day, 119 were using counterfeit green cards. Conner points out that, assuming this were an average day, over the course of a year about 29,988 illegal aliens would apply for unemployment insurance in Illinois.[5] The district office of the Immigration and Naturalization Service estimated that Illinois was paying about $66.2 million a year in unemployment insurance alone to illegal aliens.

David North conducted a study of unemployment insurance in California. He followed apprehended illegal aliens who reported having Social Security numbers. He found that 77 percent of them returned to California in the five years following their first apprehension. Forty-nine percent of them later filed for unemployment insurance, and 35 percent of them actually received benefits.[6] These findings should teach social service program administrators to use some caution to screen out illegal alien claimants. California unemployment insurance officials were either less concerned about illegal immigrants than California welfare officials—or less vigilant in guarding their programs against them—because there was no evidence in the unemployment insurance study that even one of the alien applicants was denied payments because of being an illegal. In late 1983, the district office of the Immigration and Naturalization Service finally announced that it intended to survey alien applicants for unemployment compensation in California.

North was able to get the Internal Revenue Service to cooperate in surveying how this group of apprehended illegal aliens behaved when it came to paying their taxes. He found that 69 percent of the sample study group of 517 aliens had had taxes withheld from their salaries at some time over a fourteen-year period. But it isn't enough just to find out how many paid some taxes. In 1979, for example, 226 illegals in the study group filed tax returns. Of these, 204 got tax refunds, and nearly a third of those who received refunds also received Earned Income Tax Credits, the program designed to distribute federal funds to the working poor. "The balance sheet that year showed that members of the study group had combined tax withholdings by IRS of $304,331, received $96,795 in refunds and another $19,637 in Earned Income Tax Cerdit payments, for a net payment of $187,889."[7]

North's unemployment insurance study and Conner's book both give brief descriptions of the Los Angeles County program that tries to identify illegal aliens who apply for government benefits. Los Angeles County undoubtedly has more than a million illegal alien residents, and its efforts to keep illegals off its welfare rolls are the most comprehensive in the nation. The county asks all benefit applicants to document their eligibility by showing either a birth certificate or naturalization papers if they are citizens, or a green card if they are legal aliens.

Here's how David North described what happened when Los Angeles began this requirement:

In the 12 months ending June 30, 1980, 19,088 applications for benefits were withdrawn by aliens in Los Angeles County after that request was made; presumably they were illegals. The number of aliens withdrawing claims in Los Angeles has risen in recent years, but the percentage of alien claims withdrawn has remained fairly steady at 17–18%.

After the self-identified illegals withdraw their claims, about 7,000 or so alien applications remain to be processed each month. Theoretically, each application could be sent to the local INS district office for verification, but that would be a sea of paper. What does happen is that county welfare workers sort out the more suspicious applications (filed, for example, by persons who say that they have lost their green card and cannot remember its number). Several hundred such forms are sent to INS each month for checking.

An INS clerk running a computer terminal sorts out the easiest cases—those known to the computer as being legal residents. The rest are invited to come to the INS office to prove their legal presence. If INS finds them illegal, or if they do not respond to the invitation, they are taken off the welfare rolls. In the year ending June 30, 1980, according to County records, 2,135 of the referred applicants proved their legal status to INS, while another 2,405 turned out to be illegals. The 2,405 welfare cases actually identified by INS were merely the tip of the iceberg; the bulk of those denied benefits, 19,088 of them, identified themselves as ineligible rather than face an examination by INS.

Each application denied or withdrawn saves the taxpayers $215.76 per month or $2,589.12 per year, the County estimates. If one multiplies $2,589.12 by 19,088 cases, the result is $49,421,123.55. That sum, in 1977, would have more than funded the entire, year-long AFDC programs in the states of Montana, Nevada, South Dakota, and Wyoming combined.

The $49,000,000 cost-saving estimate is a conservative one, for two reasons: first, it is the savings for denying 12 months of benefits. It has been estimated by other knowledgeable sources that a typical successful L.A. County welfare application triggers a 19-month period of benefits payments. If one were to factor in this element, the savings for a year's group of denials would be worth more than $75,000,000.

Secondly, the $49,000,000 in savings ignores the 2,405 illegal migrants who were determined to be illegal by INS. The overburdened INS office takes, on average, close to six months to handle these welfare referrals, and while that process continues, so do the welfare checks. But even if the savings for these 2,405 were calculated assuming only six months of benefits saved, that would be an additional $3,000,000 or so a year.[8]

By fiscal year 1983, California had started a statewide program based on the one in Los Angeles County. The state program referred 25,821 applications for welfare benefits to the Immigration and Naturalization Service. The INS found that 19,676 (76 percent) were ineligible. The INS and the California Health and Welfare Agency estimated that just these disqualifications—not including those applicants who withdrew their applications—saved $120.8 million in welfare benefits.

Obviously I'm particularly interested in social services in Colorado, and Colorado is an important example for other states because it isn't a "high-impact" state. It isn't Texas, or California, or Florida, or New York. What is true about illegal aliens and welfare in Colorado is likely to be true about most states. In Colorado, the food stamp program didn't ask people about the nation of their birth, much less about their immigration status. When a pilot program in 1983 required noncitizen applicants for food stamps to present their green cards, a number of illegal aliens dropped their claims, and an unknown additional number stayed away from the food stamp offices. Of those who did proceed with filing applications, 23 percent of the nonrefugee foreign-born applicants were ineligible on immigration grounds. Colorado has less than 1 percent of the nation's foreign born, but using the same simple methods in Colorado's AFDC program alone could save the state three quarters of a million dollars a year. Colorado does have an agreement with the Immigration and Naturalization Service to run continuing checks on unemployment insurance benefits, and that program helps to keep down claims by illegals. A recent study by the INS of 488 illegals in Colorado found that only 2.5 percent of them had actually drawn unemployment insurance.

There may be few systematic studies—I've cited most of them—but there are a lot of stories which convincingly indicate that illegal aliens are using a lot more social services than we used to think they did. Here are just five samples:

1. The Arizona Hospital Association surveyed five hospitals in the state, and found that these five hospitals alone had $4.4 million in unpaid hospital bills from illegal aliens in 1982, up from $1.2 million in 1975. Paying patients were charged an extra $10.10 per day of hospitalization to make up for the unpaid bills by aliens.[9]
2. In Washington, D.C., the number illegal Salvadoran children enrolled in public schools has grown to over 1,380, and superintendent of schools Floretta D. McKenzie has said that they are "putting a tremendous strain on our budget."[10]
3. Robert White, director of the Los Angeles County Department of Health and Human Services, estimates that the county paid $35 million in medical obstetrical costs alone for illegal aliens during fiscal year 1983, and that 67 percent of the babies born in county hospitals were to illegal alien mothers. Of the babies born at County-UCLA Medical Center in fiscal year 1983, 88 percent were to illegal alien mothers.[11]
4. In September 1982, the attorney general of Illinois, Ty Fahner, began indicting illegal aliens who, us-

ing fraudulent identification, had gotten hundreds of thousands of dollars in student grants by claiming U.S. citizenship or resident alien status. Fahner charged that abuse of student aid programs could easily run into millions of dollars nationwide.[12]

5. And in Denver, Colorado, our large public hospital, Denver General, admits an average of eleven illegal aliens a day. The taxpayers of Colorado paid an average of six hundred dollars for each admission.

When I asked David North whether illegal aliens pay more in taxes than they receive in transfer benefits, he replied cautiously.

There are enormous problems answering that question, but in a sense the answer doesn't really matter. First, if one works in a country, he assumes the obligation of paying taxes to it. Second, some kinds of services are provided to everybody whether they are here legally or not. This includes such things as the army, the navy, and the air force; the highways, bridges, and streets; the police department, fire department, and garbage pick-up. These are provided to everyone, and we all should be paying for them—the services provided by government are much broader than direct benefit programs or income transfer programs, and the comparison shouldn't be between taxes paid and direct income transfer programs alone.

Third, most taxes paid by illegals are paid to the federal government, and most of the direct benefits they receive are provided by state and local governments—there is a disproportionate distribution of taxes and benefits which works to the disadvantage of municipalities and states. Illegals are probably paying much more in taxes to the Social Security trust fund than they're getting back in benefits. But at the state and local levels there are very low contributions—some sales taxes and some property taxes on the dwellings which illegals rent, perhaps—and it's the local officials who have to pick up the police costs and the health costs and, if they're not careful, the income transfer costs.

But, fourth, how the balance comes out shouldn't be the deciding point. Because there should not be a drain on the social service system by individuals whom the society and government have decided are not eligible to participate in the social service system. How the balance comes out isn't relevant to that question.

And, North said, American society shouldn't be making a "tax profit" on illegals. "Even if illegals are helping underwrite a benefit program, that's inappropriate. Americans shouldn't subsidize our programs by relying on contributions paid by a group that's here illegally. We should be paying our own bills and not getting ourselves subsidized by what is essentially a disadvantaged illegal alien population."

The use of social services by illegal immigrants is usually against the law, as North pointed out. But illegality is not necessarily a deterrent for illegal immigrants. After all, they have already broken one very important law—that against their coming to the United States—and most of them have violated another law—that against their working here. The odds against their being apprehended are long, and if they are apprehended their punishment is likely to be light. Why shouldn't they conclude that the government of the United States is an easy mark? Why shouldn't they believe that they should get what they can? Certainly their past experience, and the accumulated experience of illegals over the past twenty years, has not taught them to be in awe of the legal system of the United States.

Groups like the Mexican-American Legal Defense and

Education Fund (MALDEF) and the League of United Latin American Citizens (LULAC) say that illegal immigrants are going to be part of our society in the future, that the American public does not have the will or the resources to deport illegals, and that denying social services to illegals now is both mean-spirited and harmful to our own society because it deprives people who are going to become part of this country. David North answers that

> the assumption behind that argument is that once un- documented people get far enough within our borders that the Border Patrol won't catch them, the game is over as far as society is concerned, and they are going to be here for the rest of their lives. That's not neces- sarily right. Factually, for one thing, there is a lot of temporary and seasonal migration ebbing and flowing across the border. Someone who is here legally and permanently has equities in our system, claims for support in times of trouble, that are much, much greater than the obligations we have to people who are here temporarily and illegally. We shouldn't lump to- gether everybody who happens to be in this country at any one time in terms of our obligations to them.
>
> Secondly, the argument makes an assumption which is contrary to fact: that we are not in the pro- cess of excluding from our society people who are here illegally. In fact, more than a million times a year we do apprehend illegal aliens and either deport them or allow them to depart voluntarily. And so it is falla- cious to base one's view of the rights of illegals in so- cial service programs on the position that no one will be expelled or that no one is leaving on his own.
>
> Clearly some kinds of services should be con- veyed to everyone whether the community has 2 per- cent illegals or 100 percent illegals. These are the in- frastructure of a community and the protective services

the community requires: roads, bridges, police, and firemen. But when you talk about social services, those which are provided to individuals or families rather than to the community as a whole, we have to distinguish between what should be offered to everybody and what shouldn't be. I think we have a humane obligation to provide emergency medical care to anybody who needs it, but this does not obligate us to provide elective medical services. The Supreme Court has decided that it is in the long-term best interests of our society to provide education to the minor children who are illegal aliens who have not been expelled. While I have questions about the long-term implications of that decision, I am impressed with the thought that it is better for the United States government to increase the enforcement of its immigration laws than to delegate that responsibility to thousands of boards of education around the country.

But, on the other end of the spectrum, if somebody is supported by our system through food stamps and housing assistance and cash assistance, as some people are who are here illegally, then that person is likely to stay. We are interrupting the cycle of natural emigration. People don't come here if they expect hard times. The United States had negative rates of immigration during the Great Depression of the 1930s; more people left this country than came here. People are less likely to come here if they perceive that they will have difficulty in supporting themselves, and we have no obligation to make it easy for illegal immigrants to come here. But we do just that if we provide cash and in-kind benefits that will cause people to stay who would otherwise go home because they couldn't make it in the United States. I see no problem with denying cash and food benefits to illegal immigrants, and I see a great potential problem in providing them.

Instead of a system by which we discourage people from staying in the United States, we have a lackluster, laissez-faire attitude of not being very stringent about providing these services and benefits. We may be encouraging illegal immigration because these benefits are available in some of the more casual states. It is very clear that we are holding on to people who are here illegally—which is certainly not our policy—by making it very easy for them to receive benefits. That anomaly can be cleared up simply by being a little more vigorous in our distribution of benefits.

What I'm advocating is not a bureaucratic nightmare. It's not all that difficult. Most people seeking benefits, including most aliens seeking benefits, have bona fide cases. But for a minority there are such questions, and these questions can be cleared up quite simply. What the state of Colorado is doing in the Aid for Dependent Children program is a good example. If an applicant says that she was born outside the U.S., she is then asked to fill out a paper on which she says when she came to this country and under what circumstances she got her legal status. And then she is asked to supply photostatic copies of the legal documents which support her claim. What happens is that about half of the illegals of whom that form is required drop their claims when they are told that their status will be checked against the computer in the Immigration Service. The other half of illegals are sorted out when the documentation that they present turns out to be fraudulent upon examination by an expert.

That's all you have to have people do in any social service system. Have the applicants fill out a piece of paper and photocopy supporting documents. That saves a lot of money. I think that every income transfer system which is available only to people who are here legally should use this kind of form. What Colorado and Los Angeles County are doing is simple, inexpensive, and cost-effective—and it does not encourage people to stay here when they are down on their luck.

Now, the federal government has not pressed this issue. Where it is pursued, it is because farsighted state and local governments have decided to do it. I would see nothing wrong with Texas doing it, and Arkansas not bothering, until and unless it is shown that that would cause illegals to flow into Arkansas in the same way that refugees have been shown to move because of greater social services available in some states. What's also important is that one more page in a form, or one more question for those who were born in the United States, doesn't discourage any eligible applicants for benefits, or disadvantage them any further.

The Supreme Court decided that illegal aliens were entitled to free public education on July 15, 1982, in the cases of *Plyler* v. *Doe* and *In Re Alien Children*. Those two cases had been brought by illegal aliens from whom the state of Texas had attempted to collect tuition for educating their children. Texas argued that illegal aliens, whose very presence in the United States was against the law, were not entitled to free public services; and that since the state did not have the power to expel illegals (only the federal government has the constitutional power to regulate immigration) and since the federal government did not intend to reimburse the state for the public services it provided to illegals, the state should be able to charge fees for the services it gave. After all, if parents whose legal residence was in Colorado sent their children to schools in Texas, they would have to pay tuition. Why shouldn't the same logic require that parents whose legal residence was in Mexico have to pay tuition for sending their children to schools in Texas?

Lawyers for the illegal aliens argued that denying free public services to illegal aliens was discrimination, a denial of the Equal Protection Clause of the Constitution. In a five to four decision of the nine justices, the Supreme Court held that illegal aliens were in fact covered by the Equal Protection Clause—at least in the case of education for minor children—and were entitled to free public education.

It's not really clear what additional rights under our Constitution this decision might give illegal aliens. There are several years of litigation ahead over various programs and benefits before all the implications of the decision will be finally revealed. Chief Justice Warren Burger, who was in the Court's minority, wrote that "the Court's opinion rests on such a unique confluence of theories and rationales that it will likely stand for little beyond the results in these particular cases."[13] On the other hand Justice Powell, in his decision concurring with the majority, opened the door to many future benefits. He wrote: "If the resident children of illegal aliens were denied welfare assistance, made available by government to all other children who qualify, this also—in my opinion—would be an impermissible penalizing of children because of their parents' status."[14]

In the first flush of victory after the Court's decision, lawyers for illegal aliens promised a rash of suits. John Huerta, an associate counsel with the Mexican-American Legal Defense and Education Fund in Los Angeles, said in one interview that "anything that's not based on a federal regulatory scheme is possibly subject to challenge," and in another interview called the suit only a "first step" toward obtaining public assistance for illegal aliens on the same basis as other residents. He particularly cited two cases that had already been filed by MALDEF, one seeking unemployment compensation for an illegal alien in Illinois and another attempting to force state junior colleges in California to stop charging higher tuition fees for undocumented aliens than for citizens of California.[15]

It will take years to determine the cost of providing free public education to illegal aliens and to decide who will pay those costs. Laws have been introduced in Congress to give federal reimbursement to states for the money they are now mandated to spend. Testifying on behalf of one law that would provide funding for educating illegals, Congressman Tim Wirth of Boulder, Colorado, said,

> Regardless of how one feels about this decision, there is no doubt that this left the state, the local school districts, and the local taxpayer with a heavy financial burden to bear. As a result of the recession and of limits on spending abilities, state and local governments are already scraping the bottom of the barrel without having the additional financial burdens of this decision placed solely on their shoulders. The cost of educating alien children is estimated at $2,500 per child. In my own state of Colorado, where it is estimated that roughly 5,000 alien children are attending public schools, this education is costing the state approximately $12 million.[16]

For states such as Texas, Florida, and California, of course, the costs are much higher. In 1980, Texas officials estimated it would cost $94 million a year to educate illegal alien children in that state, and Houston school officials testified that it would cost $21.8 million a year to educate the 14,000 illegals they estimated would be covered by the decision.

Federal funding eases the tax-collecting responsibility of states and local governments and places the funding responsibility on the federal government, which is also responsible for enforcing the laws against illegal immigration. But simply shifting the burden of tax collecting from state and local governments to the federal government will not lessen the actual cost of providing these services.

The real solution is to enforce the laws against illegal immigration and to cut the numbers of illegal aliens who demand social services. In the debate over the school funding law, Congressman Ron Mazzoli (Democrat-Kentucky), the House sponsor of the Immigration Reform and Control bill, said: "I do not suggest that the state of Texas and other states do not have specific problems, but they are dealt with, we think, very correctly and in a comprehensive fashion in the immigration reform bill; and to deny that immigration bill the opportunity to be heard and perhaps to solve these problems, at least to advance a comprehensive approach to these problems, is to simply put off until later what one of the other gentlemen has said is a ticking time bomb."[17]

Roger Conner of FAIR, in his booklet on how illegals are "breaking down the barriers" against their use of social services, places the importance of the welfare issue in perspective:

> There are several reasons to oppose illegal immigration: the impact of illegal immigration on the poor in America, its impact on our population growth and environment, its erosion of our national sovereignty, or the fact that it is a socially evil system which encourages exploitation.
>
> The mounting costs of social services should be added to these reasons. I am not suggesting that costs are the major reason to work against illegal immigration. I am saying something far less sweeping but, I believe, far more compelling: if illegal immigrants could be exploited to subsidize benefit programs, it would be unworthy of us to tolerate illegal immigration for these subsidies. But is is mistaken to believe that illegal immigrants are being efficiently and effectively exploited for the economic benefit of our government. Those who use that supposed benefit to apologize for the other

social ills of illegal immigration are simply misled. Illegal immigrants aren't a bargain.[18]

Finally, there is some evidence that illegal aliens and some groups of legal immigrants are significantly less productive and earn less money than other immigrants. Economist Barry Chiswick studied recently arrived refugees and legal Hispanic and Filipino migrants, and found that these three groups had been less successful economically than other immigrants.[19] Interestingly, these three groups represent a large percentage of the legal immigrants currently coming to the United States.

America assumes in its egalitarianism that all immigrants and refugees will go through a cycle of poverty, will work hard, and will end up as productive taxpayers. But that assumption ignores the fact that some groups in America demand more social services, commit more crimes, achieve less education, and, if Chiswick is correct, are less productive in the workplace. America has its own native "huddled masses" who have yet to find adequate employment. We should attempt to find productive jobs for our own unemployed and social service clients before our government willfully blinds itself to the fact that millions of uneducated and low-skilled illegal immigrants move across our border every year and that many will become welfare burdens in the future.

Illegal immigrants will always remember the conditions in the home countries that encouraged them to leave— but their children will not have those memories. They will demand their share of America's benefits. Roger Conner, reacting to the 1981 riots in Great Britain, observed: "The British riots have many causes, among them a high rate of unemployment and racial antagonism, but their root cause is massive immigration to England in the 1950's and 1960's. Because they were better off than they had been in their home countries, those early immigrants were able to endure their plight in the slums of English cities. But their children, the rioters of 1981, are not willing to endure the deprivations their parents did. They are not grateful to England because their parents were allowed to migrate there—with their job opportunities and horizons so limited, they cannot be expected to be grateful."[20]

We have been blinded to the problems ahead of us by the motto on the Statue of Liberty and by our own past success. But America of the 1980s is vastly different from America of the 1880s. Now we have social service and welfare programs that are easy to deceive and exploit. We have a cash-wage economy with high unemployment, vastly different from the empty frontier that greeted previous immigrants. And we have a new social phenomenon wherein all groups can "demand" almost instant entry into the American middle class, not as a result of hard work but as a matter of entitlement.

We are sowing dangerous seeds.

8

Rewriting the Law

A nation must have a border, just as a house must have walls and a door. The basic element of national sovereignty is the power to control admission into a country. All countries must set limits on who can and will enter and become citizens. The United States, by this definition, today just barely qualifies as a country. This chapter will explain what we have to do to reclaim our sovereignty, our control over our own borders—the laws we need to cut legal immigration and to control illegal immigration and the important evidence of public opinion polls, which shows that we Americans want these changes made.

I have so far argued that there are many sound reasons—demographic, environmental, resource, economic, and social—why we must limit immigration to the United States. And there are good historical reasons, as well: the United States has regulated immigration by qualitative laws ever since 1875, and we have had quantitative limits on immigration since the Quota Act of 1921. Today, nations universally limit immigration. A prerequisite for being a sovereign nation-state is having defensible borders and a definable group of citizens—in other words, a nation does not exist unless it has the power to say who belongs within it and who doesn't. The United States is the only democratic nation in the world that does not place a comprehensive limit on all categories of legal immigration.

Why has legal immigration to the United States grown so large? Is it possible for us to write good, fair laws to place reasonable limits on legal immigration? What must those laws include? Currently the laws of the United States limit immigration to 270,000 people within six categories, which are called *preferences*. Four of the preference categories are for relatives of U.S. citizens and of permanent resident aliens, and two categories are for workers with special skills that are believed to be needed in the United States. In theory, other applicants for immigration can be admitted if the quota of 270,000 immigrants a year is not filled by those who qualify for one of the preferences, but the quota is always filled by those with preferences.

Legal immigration to the United States is now always over at least 600,000 a year—more than 10,000 a week— and in 1980 it was over 800,000. That's a long distance from 270,000. For those not familiar with the loopholes in immigration law, it may seem puzzling how legal immigration can consistently grow to well over twice its legal limit. The answer to this puzzle is that two categories of legal immigrants are exempt from the preference categories and are not limited by the law: close relatives of U.S. citizens and refugees. And these two categories have ballooned far out of proportion to anyone's wildest expectations. Senator Edward Kennedy was the primary sponsor and the floor manager of the 1965 changes in the immigration laws, which established immigration categories in approximately their present-day form. He said then that he expected that immigration in the unlimited categories of relatives would never reach, and certainly never exceed, 100,000 a year. It has recently been double that figure. Senator Kennedy was also the primary sponsor of the 1980 amendments to the immigration laws, which removed the firm ceiling on refugee admissions from the 1965 law. In 1980 he said that the "normal flow" of refugees should be no more than 50,000 a year; since the new law was passed, the average flow has, again, been more than double that number.

Because these exceptions are the reason that legal immigration has grown out of control, the way to bring it back under control is to place a comprehensive ceiling over all categories of legal immigration, eliminating the unbounded exceptions. Former senator Walter D. Huddleston had proposed just such a comprehensive ceiling for many years, and a variant of his proposal was included in the Senate version of the Simpson-Mazzoli bill. If we had a comprehensive ceiling, this is likely to be how it would work: Congress would determine a single number as the maximum ceiling for immigrant entries into the United States during any year. Close relatives of U.S. citizens would then get first preference for immigration, instead of being outside the preference categories, as they are now. There would not be any limit on how many close relatives could come from any particular country or geographical area, and—except for the total number set by the comprehensive ceiling itself—there would not be any limit on how many immigration places could be given to these close relatives of U.S. citizens. Other categories of migrants—relatives of permanent resident aliens and needed workers— would be treated as they are at present.

One salutary side effect of putting close relatives under a comprehensive ceiling would be to help cut down on today's widespread marriage fraud. The category of close relatives of U.S. citizens includes the spouses, minor children, and parents of citizens. Marriage fraud for immigration has boomed because those who qualify for admission in this unlimited category do not need to wait for admission to the United States, and because those who apply to immigrate as spouses of citizens receive only a perfunctory investigation. This exception for spouses has made it tempting and profitable for aliens to bribe Americans to marry them or to pretend affection for Americans and defraud them into marriage, simply for the right to immigrate.

No one has a direct interest in enforcing the law against marriage fraud at present, because any number of spouses of U.S. citizens can be admitted without cutting down on other admissions. If all categories were under one ceiling, however, the number of those who could be admitted in other categories would be limited by how many close relatives were admitted. Then the permanent resident aliens who apply for the migration of their relatives and the employers who apply for potential employees would have an interest in seeing that there was much less marriage fraud than there is now, and the INS would receive the money and the mandate to investigate it.

Today refugees are the other unlimited immigration category. Under any proposed comprehensive ceiling, refugees would still be given preference; the question is whether to place them within the ceiling or to leave their admissions unlimited. Prior to 1980, the annual ceiling on refugees was 17,500. After the 1980 amendments, the "normal flow" of refugees was supposed to be 50,000 a year, but there were three different escape clauses, which ensured that refugee admissions would never really be limited by this annual ceiling.

Most of Congress is in favor of keeping refugees outside the ceiling, and there are reasons for wishing to do so. Some refugees are frequently in actual physical danger, and the emergencies that generate some refugees cannot be apportioned in neat yearly bundles by any law passed by the U.S. Congress. But every year there are millions of refugees who could legitimately be admitted to the United States, and our experience with refugee admissions has been that their number will continue to grow unless placed under a firm ceiling.

It is a fact, however, that only a small portion of refugees can be aided by migration to any country, including to the United States. The economy of the United States can't match the problem outside our borders. The number of refugees we admit to our country, therefore, will always be only a small fraction of those who would qualify for or benefit by admission. We have to recognize, therefore, that we cannot solve the world refugee problem, or any substantial part of it, through immigration to the United States, and that we may actually increase refugee flows if we try to do so. We have to be clear-eyed and realistic about this.

The problem of refugee flows requires a comprehensive solution, and that solution must include two primary elements: first, international pressure on countries that generate refugee flows, in order to discourage them from creating more refugees and to ensure that they will allow the peaceful and generous repatriation of their refugees; and second, aid to refugees who have already migrated to countries of first asylum. This means that in international organizations, such as the United Nations and the World Bank, and in bilateral contacts with countries that are expelling refugees, other nations have to link their political and economic relations to the treatment of refugees. It also means that developed nations have to give generous financial aid to Third World countries that resettle refugees from their neighboring countries.

As I said in the last chapter, voluntary repatriation—that is, allowing refugees to return to their homes—is the best solution for refugees themselves and for all nations, including countries of first asylum and eventual receiving nations. Obviously, refugees who are resettled in European countries or the United States will not return to their home countries in large numbers. That is just one more reason to prefer that they be supported in countries neighboring their home states. Voluntary repatriation is the most important element of a durable solution of refugee problems. To achieve large-scale repatriation of refugees, there must be effective international agreements, backed up by enforceable economic and diplomatic sanctions, against any nations that deliberately expel minorities or create refugees, or prevent their return. It would be a futile and ultimately useless exercise for the United States to promote international refugee resettlement programs if we did not simultaneously promote international efforts to increase repatriation.

The United States is by far the largest receiver of refugees as permanent immigrants; all other Western nations together accept fewer than half the refugees we alone take. Expatriation of refugees to the United States and to other Western countries is the most costly and the least efficient, and therefore the least desirable, element of a durable solution to refugees' problems. But the United States will continue to accept some fraction of the world's refugees as immigrants, selecting them by a political process. Some people might wish that there could be some "pure" selection system divorced from external influences. But there isn't. Others may claim that the Refugee Act commits the United States to accept all political refugees in the world. But it doesn't. We shall continue to give preference to those groups of refugees for whom the United States feels particularly responsible; those for whom we feel particularly close ties; those whose support of democracy results in their exile by our political enemies; and those for whom some group of Americans will act as advocates. And other refugees, who may have equally worthy and compelling claims of persecution, will continue to be denied admission.

The important thing is that the number of refugees

must be limited by law. If it is not, the political pressure will be for higher numbers, because there are millions of refugees in tragic circumstances who have articulate advocates in this country; and there will be no countervailing political reason to limit admissions.

The solution, therefore, is to limit admissions while providing for emergencies. Refugee admissions should be included under the single, stable, comprehensive ceiling on immigration, but the number should fluctuate with need rather than be limited to a set percentage of the ceiling. Flexibility for emergency situations can be provided if there is an immediate need for more admissions, but these additional admissions must be immediately subtracted from the other preference categories or the system will be continually abused.

If close relatives of U.S. citizens and refugees are brought under the comprehensive ceiling and made into the first and second preference categories, some of the preference categories that exist now should be modified or eliminated. Currently, there are more qualified applicants for migration places than we can accommodate, and the number of applicants keeps growing. Together with Senator Huddleston and many others who have studied the growth of legal immigration, I am convinced that we can cut that rapid rate of growth in immigrant applications if we can find a way to break the links of what is known as *chain migration*.

Chain migration works this way: a recent immigrant to the United States who has permanent resident alien status can apply for the immigration of his wife, his minor children, and his parents, and—this is the important fact for chain migration—if he has received citizenship he can also apply for the immigration of his adult brothers and sisters under the fifth preference category. His brothers and sisters can, in turn, apply for the migration of their spouses and minor children. When his wife arrived in the United

States and receives citizenship, she can apply for the migration of her parents and her brothers and sisters. Her brothers and sisters can then apply for the migration of their spouses and minor children. And so on and so on. The chain is unending.

We now give migration preference to close relatives of U.S. citizens and permanent resident aliens for humanitarian reasons. We do not believe that families should necessarily be divided by migration. But I think that the humanitarian desire to keep families together should apply only to immediate, nuclear families. There is no compelling reason to extend the chains and to give preference to adult brothers and sisters.

Advocates of the fifth preference argue that the nuclear family is a "culture-bound" definition of close family ties. They argue that in other cultures family ties are much closer, so a much wider family circle should be considered as the close family; therefore, when considering where family ties can be humanitarianly severed, we should adopt the much wider definition that the migrants themselves may have. In fact, many say, our family definition is even now much too restrictive. In many other cultures people whom we would consider distant cousins are thought of as close family members, and these cousins should probably also be given preference.

This is simply not a compelling argument, and it strains the bounds of generosity unnecessarily. While humanitarian motives may compel us to offer preference to a migrant's close family members, there is no humanitarian reason that someone who moves to this country to better himself should not have to make any sacrifices, or why a migrant should never have to live at some distance from any members of his extended family. The best way to cut long waiting lists within preference categories is to cut the long links of chain migration, and the best way to do that is to limit immigration preferences to the people who form the basic family unit *in America*. The fifth preference should be eliminated.

I've left the most important question about a comprehensive ceiling for last: What number should we choose as the ceiling, and how should we go about choosing it? No number is magic; no number is the "right" one; and there is not even one right method for choosing a number. But the aim of setting the ceiling is clear, and the goals that the ceiling should fulfill are inarguable. The ceiling should be set in the long-range interest of the nation as a whole, and the process by which the number is decided should consider the demographic, political, economic, and resource realities of this country.

If the United States had an overall national population policy, it would be easier to determine how to study and weigh all these factors and how to devise a rational process of setting an immigration ceiling. But this country does not have a population policy, and therefore we are unable to make sound, demographically based decisions on immigration levels. Zero Population Growth and many other population and environmental organizations have advocated what has been called a "global foresight" bill. This bill would enable the federal government to collect information about natural resources, the environment, and population in order to arrive at a reasonable national population policy. Interestingly, Arnold Torres, the executive director of the League of United Latin American Citizens, testified against the global foresight bill in July 1984. He objected to collecting information about the impact of increasing population upon the environment because it could be "used to further the purposes of Simpson-Mazzoli by using new immigrants as 'scapegoats' for scarcity in natural resources."[1]

There is no good reason for the United States to have a larger population than it does today; we would gain no benefit just from having more people live in this country.

Therefore, it might seem reasonable to set immigration at a level equal to emigration, as the organization Negative Population Growth recommends. There are two objections to this. First, unfortunately, there is no record of how many people emigrate from the United States each year. For many years, the Census Bureau estimated the number at 40,000 a year, and it now estimates that there are 100,000 a year. But no agency actually counts emigrants or collects any figures to substantiate these estimates, though, of course, we could determine the number of emigrants if we wanted to do so.

The second, more serious objection to setting immigration equal to emigration is that it would be politically impossible to get Congress to pass a ceiling as low as 100,000 or to get the president to sign it, even though the great majority of Americans might prefer the ceiling to be at that level. The congressional instinct for compromise is simply too strong, and the number of organizations and lobbyists advocating outlandishly high ceilings is too great. For example, Arnold Torres has said that any comprehensive ceiling lower than 1 million a year would be unacceptable to his organization.

The best way to set a ceiling number might be simply to put it at the historical average of immigration levels, at least until a comprehensive population policy could be agreed upon to determine demographically what the most beneficial level of immigration might be. I would advocate, therefore, that we limit immigration by setting the ceiling at a historical average. During the 1970s, legal immigration averaged nearly 450,000—449,331, to be exact. Over this century, between 1901 and 1980, legal immigration averaged a little under 400,000—394,154—a year.[2] Some number between 400,000 and 450,000, therefore, might be a politically acceptable ceiling on immigration. Some people would certainly object that this number was arbitrary. Of course it is; any number would be arbitrary. But until we have a global foresight policy which could establish some demographically valid criteria for setting a ceiling, choosing an arbitrary number is the best we can do.

Four hundred thousand legal immigrants annually is still a very large number—8,000 a week—and well over the number of permanent immigrants the rest of the nations of the world together accept. Four hundred thousand legal immigrants a year is also well above the level we should have for long-range population stability in this country. But if practical considerations make it necessary to set a ceiling at somewhere between the historical averages of 400,000 and 450,000 immigrants a year, then it is reasonable to accept that number in order to get the principle of a comprehensive ceiling into the law—and to forestall the certainty that immigration levels will continue to rise steadily and rapidly if we don't have any firm ceiling.

When we put a comprehensive ceiling in the law, as we must soon, we'll run the danger that opponents of immigration control will try to subvert it by amending it in the legislative process. For example, they will accept a ceiling of 400,000 or 450,000 and then propose amendments to the ceiling which will again place close relatives or refugees outside it. If that kind of ploy succeeds, then all we shall have accomplished will have been to raise the current ceiling on limited preference categories from 270,000 to the new ceiling level. That kind of maneuvering faces any legal reform; those of us who understand the need to bring legal immigration back under control will have to guard very carefully against it.

Advocates of higher immigration levels may also attempt to set the immigration ceiling as a percentage of our total population. If social assimilation of new immigrants were the only consideration, this could have a superficial appeal: If the country can easily absorb two or three new immigrants a year for every thousand people in our population, why not use that percentage as a ceiling? The answer, of course, is that social assimilation isn't the only consideration. Setting immigration as a percentage of our population would mean that immigration would grow larger and larger as our population grew, when for environmental and resource reasons it should become smaller.

We can bring legal immigration back under reasonable limits with only two relatively modest changes. First, we should establish a comprehensive ceiling on all categories of legal immigration, with no exceptions for *any* group, including refugees and relatives, and we should eliminate the preference category for all adult brothers and sisters of American citizens. That ceiling should probably be set initially somewhere between 400,000 and 450,000 immigrants a year. Second, in the long run we should establish sound demographic, economic, and social criteria by which a mandated agency free of political pressure can continually adjust the level of immigration to balance unemployment and environmental concerns, to ensure that it continues to benefit the people of this country.

We can take similarly reasonable and simple steps to improve the laws on illegal immigration. In the past the federal government has attempted to control illegal immigration in the most humane and least intrusive manner. It has concentrated its enforcement—what enforcement there is—at the borders of the United States; it has preferred to prevent illegal immigrants from entering the country rather than to apprehend and deport them after they have arrived here and disappeared. While the Border Patrol is terribly understaffed and underfinanced, the internal investigation unit of the Immigration and Naturalization Service is in even worse straits. Until an experimental increase of a couple of hundred investigators authorized by Congress in 1984 takes effect, there will continue to be fewer INS investigators for the whole country than there are special police patrolling the few acres of Capitol Hill in Washington, D.C.

The effect of this neglect is that, once illegal immigrants have made it across the border without being detected, they are virtually assured of never being apprehended. We have tried to enforce immigration laws as if we were playing a game of tag, with the entire country as a safe home base. When illegal immigration is low and under control, it is possible to concentrate almost all our resources on the border. But when illegal immigration is massive, we must apprehend illegals within the country. Deliberately neglecting to do so sends potential illegals the message that illegal immigration is easy—and that we have no serious intention of enforcing our laws.

There's a possible problem with enforcing immigration laws in the interior of the country. Identifying illegals without discriminating against citizens is hard. How will the INS investigators know which individuals to apprehend? In practice, the INS has hobbled itself to a great extent in order to avoid any hint of intrusiveness or of interference with American citizens or permanent resident aliens. The proof that these restraints work is that, out of the more than a million apprehensions made by the INS every year, mistaken apprehensions of Americans or permanent resident aliens have never been a serious concern. The law allows the INS to pick up individual illegal aliens on the streets or in their homes and to conduct street sweeps or neighborhood sweeps where illegal aliens are known to congregate or live, but the INS does not use these methods even though they would be effective. Within the United States, it apprehends illegal aliens almost solely at their workplaces. And the INS receives so much information, so many tips, that it is unable even to investigate employers unless it knows that they employ large numbers of illegal aliens.

The INS concentrates on workplaces because it is less likely to impinge on American citizens there, because it is the least intrusive method of operating—and also because jobs are the primary magnet that attracts illegals to this country. As I said in Chapter 6, employers hire illegal aliens because they can pay them lower wages and place them in worse working conditions than American workers would accept. And employers hire illegals because they are unfairly exempted from the law that forbids American citizens to aid illegal immigrants in breaking the law; that is, it is not illegal to hire them. If this exemption were simply ended, if employers were required to obey the law along with the rest of us and were forbidden to employ illegal aliens in preference to American citizens, most of them would do so. As I have argued earlier, most Americans are law-abiding, and most employers would obey an employer sanctions law. The INS could then concentrate on the small percentage of employers who would continue to flout the law, and its ability to target the employers would make internal enforcement many times more effective than it is now.

It has been objected that many European countries have employer sanctions laws that have been laxly enforced and therefore have been relatively ineffective. This is not a serious objection against employer sanctions laws; all laws require some enforcement in order to be effective. It should not be a surprise that poorly enforced laws are relatively ineffective. Obviously the United States would have to devote some work to making an employer sanctions law work.

Associations of employers and some lawmakers have raised another objection to an employer sanctions law, which seems to me to be transparently false but has been given much currency. The objection is that the employer sanctions law turns employers into agents of the INS, and that they shouldn't be put into that position. The Immigration and Naturalization Service, so this argument goes, has the responsibility for enforcing laws against illegal immigration, and requiring employers to cooperate in this endeavor forces them to be policemen.

In fact, employer sanctions laws do not require employers to enforce the law. They require employers to obey the law, and the distinction is an important one. People who argue that employers shouldn't have to obey an employer sanctions law are not usually radical libertarians who would object to employers' collecting withholding taxes or obeying child labor laws or obeying OSHA regulations. At bottom, what most of them are really saying is that illegal immigration is not a serious enough problem to justify making employers go to the bother of obeying a rather simple law or of giving up their illegal alien employees.

In summary, an employer sanctions law closes the most important loophole in the laws against illegal immigration. It is the most important single tool that the INS can be given to become more effective. It is very likely that the combination of voluntary observance of the law by American employers and the improvement in the efficiency of the enforcement efforts of the INS would drastically cut the incentive for potential illegal immigrants to attempt to come to the United States and would allow us to bring illegal immigration back under control.

Will the American public support making these changes in the law? Will we support putting teeth in the limits on legal immigration and support strong laws against illegal immigration? Do we have the national will to enforce these laws? Any effort to amend the laws or to give additional resources to the Immigration and Naturalization Service would be futile if the American people did not really want to enforce the laws. Prohibition stands as the preeminent example of a law that led to disaster because the people of the United States did not want it. Any law that attempts to prohibit something that most people really want will have similarly disastrous consequences. If the American people really didn't mind illegal immigration, or if we were uncertain about whether or not it were a serious crime with serious consequences, then passing new laws would only compound the hypocrisy that already existed.

Some serious scholars of immigration, for example Edwin Harwood of the Hoover Institution, believe that public ambivalence toward illegal aliens will prevent any effective enforcement of immigration laws.[3] And advocates of illegal immigration have seized on public sympathy for individual illegal aliens to argue that the American people really do want illegal immigration. They also argue that Americans wink at illegal immigration because they believe it lowers the wages of busboys and so makes fancy restaurant meals cheaper, or because they think designer-label jeans that sell for sixty dollars would cost even more if the subcontracting garment shops couldn't get illegal aliens to make them for three dollars apiece. In fact, while there is public sympathy for individual illegals, the American people are not naïve enough to believe that the savings obtained from exploiting illegal workers are passed on to them, or that the hotel rooms they rent or the salads they eat are substantially cheaper because low wages prevented Americans from working as hotel maids or lettuce pickers.

I am convinced that the American people do want illegal immigration brought under control. Public opinion polls provide the best evidence of this. Numerous polls over the past several years have had consistent findings. Ever since legal immigration began to grow so quickly and illegal immigration began to be obviously out of control these polls have uniformly shown that the American public wants strong measures taken to reform our immigration laws and policies.

Do Americans want illegal immigration controlled? Yes. Do they want legal immigration quotas reduced? Also, yes. The Roper Polls of June 1977 and June 1980 asked respondents whether they agreed with various measures to control population growth. Among those measures were two that dealt with immigration. When asked whether they agreed the United States should "make an all-out effort to stop the illegal entry into the U.S. of one and one-half million foreigners who don't have entry visas," 91 percent said yes in both 1977 and 1980. When asked whether we should "reduce the quotas of the number of legal immigrants who can enter the U.S. each year," 75 percent agreed in 1977; 80 percent agreed in 1980.

Do Americans want employer sanctions? Yes. The Gallup Poll asked its respondents about illegal immigration in a series of three polls in October 1977, November 1980, and October 1983. When people were asked whether it should "be against the law to employ a person who has come into the United States without proper papers," 72 percent said yes in 1977, 76 percent said yes in 1980, and 79 percent said yes in 1983. When people were asked whether all citizens and permanent resident aliens should have an identification card like a Social Security card to make it possible for employers to tell who is an illegal immigrant and who is not, 63 percent said yes in 1977, 62 percent said yes in 1980, and 66 percent said yes in 1983.[4]

Do Americans care about immigration? In October 1980, the Roper Poll asked people what topics they would like to see debated in the upcoming presidential debates between President Carter and his challenger, Ronald Reagan. Among a list of eighteen topics, immigration placed sixth in interest, above cutting income taxes, above foreign policy, and above the then-recent Russian invasion of Afghanistan. (And it should be noted that most of the topics that rated above immigration then would not be considered more important now. They were: how to deal with inflation, what to do about the U.S. hostages in Iran, how to deal with recession, how to solve energy problems, and what to do with regard to the military and defense.)

A 1982 Field Poll of Californians found that 62 percent believed "the number of immigrants now permitted to enter this country should be decreased." Seventy-six percent agreed that "severe penalties should be imposed on employers who hire illegal or undocumented immigrants." In an NBC/Associated Press Poll in August 1981, 65 percent of respondents thought "the U.S. should allow less immigration to this country." A *Washington Post*/ABC News Poll in March 1981 found that 59 percent of respondents agreed that "immigrants are taking jobs that could go to Americans."

One of the most important findings of the polls is how strongly Hispanic Americans support immigration reform, in sharp contradiction to the rhetoric of those Hispanic politicians who claim to speak for them. In the Gallup Poll of October 1983, 75 percent of the Hispanic respondents favored a law making it "against the law to employ a person who has come into the United States without proper papers." Seventy-five percent also thought "everyone in the United States should be required to carry an identification card such as a Social Security card."[5]

A poll in June and July 1983, which was commissioned by the Federation for American Immigration Reform (FAIR) and conducted cooperatively by Democratic pollster Peter D. Hart and Republican pollster V. Lance Tarrance, found that 66 percent of Hispanic citizens thought "illegal aliens hurt the job situation for American workers by taking jobs Americans might take," and 54 percent thought that "illegal aliens cause U.S. wages to be lower than they would be otherwise." In addition, 66 percent of Hispanic citizens favored penalties and fines for employers who hired illegal aliens, 55 percent thought immigration laws should be tougher, and 63 percent favored "major increases in spending to enable the Border Patrol to stop illegal aliens from entering the U.S." Fifty-one percent of Hispanic citizens thought the United States should allow fewer legal immigrants each year, and only 12 percent thought we should allow more. Forty percent thought the United States should allow fewer legal immigrants from Mexico, and again only 12 percent thought we should allow more.[6]

These findings agree with a survey taken of Hispanics in Texas in the summer of 1978 for the Immigration and Naturalization Service. Over 69 percent of Hispanics in the border counties of Texas favored an employer sanctions law; fewer than 11 percent felt the number of visas for people coming from Mexico should be increased; and more than 53 percent felt we should spend more money for enforcement at the border. Television's Spanish International Network, SIN, had roughly the same results in their May 1984 poll of Hispanic Democrats: 60 percent favored fines for employers who knowingly hired illegal aliens, and 41 percent favored a "national i.d. system." The Hispanic Opinion and Preference Research, Inc., poll taken in April 1981 found that 70 percent of Hispanics did not want Latin Americans to be given preferential treatment in immigration.[7]

So many numbers tend to blur into one another after a while, but they all point to a single conclusion: both Hispanic Americans and the American people as a whole clearly want both illegal and legal immigration controlled.

The evidence proves that the American public will strongly support the few basic reforms in immigration laws that I am proposing—and that we'll support enforcing these laws. Certainly we'll continue to feel ambivalence when confronted with a sympathetic, attractive, hard-working family of illegal aliens with close ties to an American community, whose only crime was to cross the border without proper documents. And we shall undoubtedly find ways to show mercy toward them and to temper the enforcement of the law. But the sympathy expressed and the mercy extended should never be mistaken for a spineless lack of will, for a tolerance of lawlessness, or for an apathy toward criminality.

9

Enforcing the Law

We can improve the enforcement of our immigration laws just by improving the management, resources, and policies of the Immigration and Naturalization Service and the Border Patrol—without adding new laws and without creating new bureaucracies. To explain how we can do that, I'm going to rely heavily upon two very well informed people, the commissioner of the Immigration and Naturalization Service and the president of the Border Patrol Council, the union of Border Patrol officers. I'm also going to discuss how the increased enforcement of U.S. immigration laws would affect our relationship with Mexico.

The job of the Immigration and Naturalization Service and the Border Patrol is to enforce the immigration laws of the United States, to be a police force that guards the borders and the interior of the United States. While the INS is to some extent a service agency—it processes applications for immigration and for the naturalization into citizenship of permanent resident aliens—90 percent of its resources and personnel must go into its more important tasks, policing the borders and the interior.

Alan C. Nelson was appointed commissioner of the Immigration and Naturalization Service by the Reagan administration. He has attempted to improve the management of what, for a very long time under both Republican and Democratic administrations, has been a lackadaisically and rather haphazardly run division of the Justice Department. The INS had been something of a stepchild of Justice—the INS got the hearthchild's leftovers after all the more glamorous, more politically popular law-enforcement priorities had received their funding and attention. The INS had earned a reputation as one of the worst-run agencies in the federal government because of this official neglect and also because of public inattention to immigration law enforcement. Ironically, this inattention may have been the fault of the INS's own earlier success. The enormously successful law-enforcement drive spearheaded by the Border Patrol in the early 1950s kept illegal immigration from becoming a serious problem for almost fifteen years, until the middle of the 1960s.

But as a result of that lack of attention, even as illegal immigration soared between the 1960s and the 1980s, the number of INS internal investigators actually dropped. By the early 1980s, the number of Border Patrol officers, who had to patrol both the Mexican and Canadian borders, was smaller than the number of *transit* police on New York City's buses and subways. For the entire 2,000 miles of the southern U.S. border, only about 350 Border Patrol officers could be mustered during any shift. But the recent combination of the rapid growth of illegal immigration and public demands for enforcement of the laws led to a slight upgrading of the Service's importance within the Justice Department, an upgrading that Commissioner Nelson was able to utilize to increase funding for and staffing of the

INS and to promote the modernization of its methods and facilities.

Alan Nelson argues convincingly that there have been improvements in the Service over the past few years, and that the improvements will continue. "We are getting additional resources, and attention, and trust from the Congress," he told me.

> I think there's good bipartisan support for general increases in funding and manpower.
>
> We're moving to use new technology to enforce the law—not just computerization in the offices, but also additional light aircraft and helicopters for patrolling the border. We're installing better, more effective infrared sensors that will detect border crossers; and in a few places we're adding low-light television cameras that will enable central patrol stations to see exactly what's going on when a sensor is tripped, even in pitch darkness. And, in contrast, we're starting to use horses again in the border areas where horses are more effective than all-terrain vehicles.
>
> And we're acknowledging that we have to increase the manpower. Equipment isn't going to do the job if there aren't enough officers. We do need additional manpower in conjunction with this more advanced—and less advanced—technology and tools.
>
> Tied in with that, one of the things I feel best about is that we're reinforcing the enforcement posture in terms of prosecution. We are raising the level of interest among U.S. Attorneys for the prosecution of immigration law violations, especially smuggling of aliens. That helps. If people know that we take smuggling seriously and prosecute it as a very serious crime, that the law is strongly enforced and there are some heavy sentences pending, all our other efforts are going to be much more effective.

Nelson believes it will take time for the INS to rebuild a reputation for efficiency and good management. "It takes a long time for a reputation to change. The INS has been viewed in a certain way for a number of years, and it will take some time for the reputation to catch up with the improvements we're making. In addition, immigration is a problem, a complicated problem with no nice, easy solutions. That's not the fault of the INS. Massive illegal immigration didn't happen because the INS was badly run, but it's almost inescapable that it would be blamed."

While Nelson acknowledges that there was a good basis for the INS's reputation for bad management, he believes that charges of systematic corruption and brutality within the INS were always untrue.

> Look at the record with regard to incidents of brutality, for example. It's in the interests of some people to exaggerate charges of brutality or mistreatment leveled against the Border Patrol. But even so the number of incidents, compared with the number of border patrolmen and the number of aliens who are apprehended, is minimal. And the charges which have any substantiation are almost nonexistent. For every charge of brutality there are ten examples of officers going beyond their duty to save people from drowning, from burning cars, from the desert, from smugglers who have abandoned them in sealed vans.

> I've been on the border a number of times. And when you think about it, the human relationship between the Border Patrol and illegal aliens is an amazing one. It's really very friendly. The number of incidents of violence or antagonism is very small. They're trying to get in, almost uniformly, to get jobs. We're doing our job, and doing it professionally, and they know it and accept it. In most cases, they give us their cooperation.

Obviously, I'm biased, but I do think we've done a tremendous amount to turn around what had been organizational problems. We're making good progress. We have a long way to go, but we are instituting data processing, cutting down caseload backlogs, improving morale within the service, improving our legal structure, instituting better budget planning, and generally tightening up.

Most knowledgeable observers would agree with Nelson that things are getting better. There are still many problems, however, and there is disagreement in Washington over how fast the INS is improving. The service handles millions of files through old-fashioned, paper-shuffling methods, and it is years behind the rest of the federal government in the computerization and automation that would enable it to handle the geometric growth in its work load. Its pay levels are still much too low—for example, in California a new Border Patrol officer supporting a family of four would qualify for food stamps. And its public relations efforts don't adequately tell its story, considering the criticism that enemies of immigration laws continually direct at it.

Dick Bevans is a border patrolman and the president of the Border Patrol Council, the union that represents members of the Border Patrol. He told me that he agrees that additional technology and manpower will help.

The enhancement program that was passed by both houses of Congress in August 1984 is a good starting point. We got 900 additional people and additional resources to deal with the situation. For the next couple years, the new people are just going to be coming on board, so it'll be fiscal 1987 before we are going to be able to see the effects of the enhancement package.

That will give us a good yardstick to see what we're

able to do with more people and increased funding. But even the people and the funding aren't enough. We need some other basic changes.

We need a change in enforcement policies. Current law is adequate to deal with the situation. The problem is not bad laws, it's the policies that have arisen in interpreting the laws. The basic law would allow for effective enforcement. It's policies that have been adopted over a long period of time, over thirty years, that have crippled the law. And most of those policies aren't the result of adverse court decisions; they're internal policies of the Justice Department and of INS. They always take the line of least resistance. I've said for years that we do a disservice to the guys going through the Academy by teaching them the law. The law has nothing to do with it; administrative policy is our guide. The law would let us do things that just aren't done, that haven't been done for years.

The policies I'm talking about are those which decide who will or will not be prosecuted for repeated illegal reentries, or who will or will not be prosecuted for smuggling. Today, if the alien has any relative who's an American or a permanent resident alien, that lets him off. No, it's gone beyond that, because of the volume of illegal immigration. If there's not a large group of illegals involved, that lets them off. Whether there's an American immediate relative or not, whether there's monetary gain or not, no longer has anything to do with it. If there aren't big numbers involved, at least in the Southwest, the case isn't attractive to the prosecutors. We have Assistant U.S. Attorneys who are saying, "Hey, we've got smugglers who are bringing in loads of a hundred. What are you doing coming to me with a case involving just two people?"

The message that gets to the Border Patrol is, "Never mind quality; we want quantity. We want numbers. If you go delving into these little cases and work up complicated cases, you're just making a lot of clutter and a lot of fuss and a lot of bother." In some ways, of course, as the system is now that's realistic, because very likely nothing is going to be done about a complicated case that involves only a few people. If it goes to court, the U.S. Attorney is not going to be interested. If you send it up to the District INS Office, the adjudicators are going to say they don't have the time to investigate it. So you may as well take a simple case, with bigger numbers.

Or take the investigation of I-130 petitions, which are the petitions filed by U.S. citizens for their alien spouses. The marriage fraud rate has gotten to be ridiculous, and meanwhile examiners are put under very stringent time constraints limiting how long they can talk to these petitioners. The examiners' performance ratings are based on how many cases they can adjudicate in a set amount of time. Never mind quality; never mind any kind of in-depth questioning. The message to the individual investigator is that it will only cause a problem if he denies a petition, because denying a petition takes more time. The message is to rubber-stamp the petition and to move it along.

The whole system is geared to winking at the law, and that's the message that is being conveyed to INS employees by the people who make the policy: "Well, this is the law; however, this is our policy. Well, of course you are supposed to talk to these people who file petitions for a spouse; however, if you don't turn them out at five-minute intervals your performance rating will suffer, and you might not get your next in-grade raise."

Then there are policies about who will be formally detained, incarcerated, until they depart. Whenever the Service is short of funds for detaining illegals until we can formally transport them out of the country—and the Service is chronically short of funds—it turns them loose. It turns them loose with a letter saying, "You are ordered to depart the United States by such-and-such a date." Now, they came here illegally in the first place. How much attention do you think they are going to pay to that letter? It's a joke, and everybody knows it's a joke, and everybody knows that if we took immigration laws seriously we wouldn't turn them loose.

I remember a few years ago in the Eastern region we ran short of money. We were turning loose people who had very serious cases, people whom we wouldn't just give voluntary departure, people who would normally be locked up and held for formal deportation hearings. We were turning them loose with these letters. And about three or four months later the investigators in Buffalo, New York, were getting all of these kickback cases they were supposed to follow up on, cases of people who were supposed to show up at deportation hearings with their letters, people who had disappeared. Stacks of cases.

This thing about giving them a piece of paper is a joke. It's the INS version of creating a record, taking a number. That's all it is. It doesn't do anything effective to stop or to contain the situation. It just gives you credit for locating one, locating an alien. And then, once he's located, you say, "Tag, caught you," and turn him loose.

The law has teeth in it, but the teeth have been pulled by the Service and by the Justice Department. And the aliens are well aware of that. They tend to laugh at the whole thing. I understand the economics of it. It's difficult, after you've finally asked for more money for equipment and more money for people, to go back and ask for more money to keep the aliens in custody. But until you can actually ensure that at least the illegals you are able to catch have to leave the country, you haven't done anything.

Dick Bevans speaks as a representative of the officers on the line; he is free to criticize the policies dictated by politics and to analyze why they are adopted. "It seems apparent to me," he said,

that the current [Reagan] administration—this doesn't exclude previous administrations, but especially the current administration—has the attitude that what's good for some kinds of business is good for America. A portion of their constituency, the people who contribute to their campaigns and so on, has come to depend on illegals for their work force. They've come to feel that it's their God-given birthright to have a bunch of people who'll work for substandard wages under substandard conditions. And the administration doesn't want to antagonize them. It's one of those situations in which we'll make a token effort. We'll show the flag. But when it comes down to some meaningful enforcement, we'll start to get wishy-washy.

There are employers who work this thing like a revolving door. When I was on detail out in California a few years ago, there was a guy in Los Angeles who dealt in wrought-iron furniture and railings. The smugglers usually roll on Sunday nights, because we close down the border checkpoint at San Clemente on Sunday nights because of traffic. That's right, when the traffic gets too heavy, when all the visitors drive back to the U.S. at the end of the weekend, we just shut down and stop checking everybody, and do only spot checks. And, of course, all the smugglers know it. The standard procedure is that they bring the aliens in during the week to drop houses just south of the border, and then on Sunday night they roll them north to L.A.

So this guy who dealt in wrought iron would get a new crew in every Sunday night or Monday morning. And every Friday afternoon he would call Immigration to do a raid, thereby ducking a large part of his obligation in salary and so on, and so on. Nobody is around during the weekend, and then he's got a whole new crew come Sunday night or Monday morning. That's the way the guy operates. That example may be extreme, but there are a whole lot of them who operate the same way.

I knew a fruit grower in northern New York, where I'm based now. He's dead now, but I don't feel particularly guilty speaking ill of the dead, because I called him a son of a bitch when he was alive. He dragged Jamaicans in there to harvest. Up there they pay pickers by the tote box on the apples they pick. The pickers keep pretty close track of how much they pick. And a picker would go up to this grower and say, "Well, boss, you owe me for eleven boxes." And the grower would say, "The foreman says I only owe you for seven." "Well, no, boss," the picker would say, "I picked eleven." "Well, no, the foreman says. . . ." And he knew they were honest; and he knew they were going back to Jamaica. He knew they weren't going to get a lawyer to collect for the rest. We're talking fifty, sixty bucks for a tote box. The chiseling bastard would cheat a guy out of a hundred, couple hundred dollars for the summer, because he knew the guy had to take what he offered.

Like the wrought-iron guy, like the fruit grower, it's become a way of life for a lot of people, and those are the very people who make large contributions to keep the present administration in power. What the administration is doing, even with the enhancement package, with the additional funding and bodies for the INS, is making a flashy symbolic gesture. It's not the whole answer, and everybody knows it. Instead of losing two or three illegal entrants for every one we catch on the border, maybe we'll get it down to one for one, but the bosses are still going to have all the labor they want. The Border Patrol alone caught over a million last year. Even if we get the ratio down to one for one, that illegal labor force is still going to be there unless we have employer sanctions and some serious policy changes.

Bevans believes that his recommendations for enforcement would discourage not only the illegal aliens who were apprehended but also those who were considering coming here illegally.

We're sending mixed signals right now. We're not sending a clear, sharp deterrent signal. While we're increasing the force on the border, we're still going along with the policy of releasing people who should be detained with the letter I talked about. We're not saying to illegals that, "Hey, if you're caught we're going to take it seriously. We're not just going to give you a short bus ride to Tijuana." That clear signal is not there, and I think that's intentional. We're playing a game for the American public, throwing more money at the problem and pretending to solve it; but meanwhile, the other, attendant things that would solidify everything and send a clear signal are purposely not done.

Bevans told me that potential illegals are well informed about American policy, and that even small changes in policy affect the flow of aliens.

Even the smallest thing. Do you remember when the Carter administration ran up a trial balloon on amnesty in 1977? We had an influx that you wouldn't believe. They were trooping in ten-deep. And they weren't bashful about saying, when we interviewed them, "We came for the *amnestia.*" And what caused it was just the fact that Mexican radio stations had picked up the fact that there was some talk in Washington about an amnesty for illegal aliens. I'm sure that current plans for amnesty are increasing the flow. How serious our government appears to be about this whole thing has a lot to do with how many people come. If they believe that they're going to stand a good chance of getting caught, that we're going to take it seriously and impose some kind of punishment on them, it's going to slow them down.

Potential migrants' options are affected not just by our laws, but even by small points of administrative policy, according to Bevans and to the officers on the line. Some students of Mexican society believe that illegal immigration has become an ingrained sociological pattern of behavior over generations, and that changes in U.S. laws would have little effect on that behavior. That ignores, of course, the fact that the very purpose of passing laws is to change patterns of behavior. In the 1950s, southern segregationists argued that laws could not change the patterns of discrimination; but, of course, they did. Compared with achieving desegregation, it would be relatively easy to break habits of migration from Oaxaca, Mexico, to San Diego, California—if the laws forbidding it were seriously enforced.

To break the patterns of illegal immigration from Mexico, the United States should reinstitute a policy of "interior repatriation." When the INS apprehends someone who has come to the United States illegally from Sweden or India, that person has to return, either voluntarily or through deportation. The distance and expense of traveling from those countries tends to discourage repeated attempts at illegal entry. But a Mexican illegal alien who is apprehended in the United States is returned just across the border. "We're talking about the classic definition of a syndrome," Dick Bevans says, "if we're just shoving an illegal across the border. If you figure we're losing two or three for every one we catch, what are his odds if he comes back tomorrow night? If he misses tomorrow night, very likely the next night he's going to get through."

But most Mexican illegal immigrants are not from cities or towns just across the border from the United States. The northern states of Mexico are relatively sparsely settled. Most Mexican illegal aliens come from the central or southern states of Mexico, and they may travel thousands of miles to get to the border. If they were returned to their homes or to Mexico City, instead of to the closest point just across the American border, they too, like the Swede or the Indian, would be discouraged from making repeated attempts at illegal entry.

"The farther you can send them back into the interior of Mexico," Dick Bevans told me, "the closer they are sent back to their homes, the better. That's not saying they're not going to come back. But they're not going to come back anywhere near as soon, and they're going to need resources to get here again and again from their homes. It would go a long, long way towards slowing the traffic down."

Bevans brings up a good point. One of the major difficulties of enforcing our immigration laws is that we share a 2,000-mile border with a large, impoverished nation with an exploding birthrate. Would Mexico cooperate with the United States if we announced a policy of interior repatriation? Of course it would, if we insisted—but only under firm, consistent, and tactful pressure. It has cooperated in the past and it would cooperate again, if the United States really wanted it to. Mexico and the United States have a very sensitive relationship; we are divided by our very closeness. But our relationship with Mexico is vitally important to the future of our control over illegal immigration, so we must consider how the measures we take to enforce our immigration laws will affect our bilateral relations with that country.

In the first quarter of 1985, the United States and Mexico were involved in delicate maneuverings over the killing of an American Drug Enforcement Agency officer in Mexico City and over threats against other DEA and Border Patrol officers. The misunderstandings and difficulties involved when the United States enforced stricter searches on border crossers illustrate well the problems our two countries have with each other. On the one hand, it is in the interest of any American president to demonstrate a good relationship with Mexico; not only is there a large voting block of Mexican Americans who feel sentimental ties to the country, but also most Americans believe that we should have a friendly and close relationship with our closest southern neighbor. On the other hand, it is in the interest of any Mexican president to demonstrate independence and some amount of distance from the United States; not only is there a history of resentment toward the United States for the Mexican-American War and other past interventions in the government of Mexico, but also there is jealousy of the prosperous Colossus of the North. U.S. diplomatic rhetoric toward Mexico, therefore, is normally conciliatory, while Mexico frequently takes any opportunity to berate and scold the United States.

One outrageous example of such rhetoric was a resolution passed by the Mexican Senate on December 8, 1983, while the American Congress was considering the Simpson-Mazzoli bill (discussed in Chapter 8). It was addressed to Thomas O'Neill, the Speaker of the House, and it read in part:

1. That the Chamber expresses as a resolution our alarm and concern for the repercussions which will impact both countries if the Simpson-Mazzoli legislation is passed, since this transcendent matter should not be considered from a unilateral perspective, but rather should be treated from a bilateral and even multilateral perspective, taking into account the far-reaching migratory phenomenon of undocumented persons between our two countries.

2. That the recommendation of the Parliamentarians of the Western Hemisphere Conference on Population and Development held in Brazil November 5, 1982, be implemented. Those recommendations were approved by several U.S. Senators, and designed to discourage laws such as this [Simpson-Mazzoli], which directly and openly threaten the labor and human rights of migrant workers in the United States, and which create a repressive precedent of global repercussions.

3. That this matter be turned over to the Foreign Relations Committee of the [Mexican] Senate for detailed analysis, and that it be included as part of the memos to be treated at the next reunion of the Mexico/U.S. inter-parliamentarian conference.

4. That the Latin American Congress, the World Congress, and the Group of Parliamentarians for a New World Order be notified so that they may direct their concerns to the U.S. Congress and include the matter in their work agendas.

5. That the proper Mexican authorities be notified of this proposition so that the necessary mechanisms be implemented in order to inform the nation, the

U.S. Senators and Representatives, and, if possible, the American public of the concerns, intent, and actions of the [Mexican] Senate in regard to this grave matter that negatively affects our good neighbor relations.[1]

This kind of presumption and insult, however, is not typical of how the government of Mexico normally handles the problem of illegal immigration. When I visited with Manuel Garcia y Griego of the faculty of Mexico City's prestigious Colegio de Mexico, he insisted that, putting rhetoric aside, it is actually much more important to the government of Mexico than to that of the United States to demonstrate a satisfactory working relationship. "It's like Trudeau's metaphor," he said, "of sleeping with an elephant. For both Mexico and Canada, the United States is the elephant with which we sleep. The elephant may be very well intentioned, but you must always be alert to make sure that it doesn't roll over while it dreams."

Garcia contends that although the Mexican government cannot be perceived by its people as being too eager to please the United States, too responsive or sensitive to our needs, the government understands very well that it is against its own interests to antagonize the United States too much. And in fact the resolution passed by the Mexican Senate is something of an aberration in the way the Mexican government usually treats immigration matters.

The public posture of the Mexican government is consistent with the policy it articulates in private meetings with U.S. officials and representatives: immigration policy is *not* a matter for bilateral negotiation between countries. Any country's immigration policy is its own internal decision, and the principle of nonintervention in a country's internal matters prevents Mexico from consulting with or commenting on the United States' immigration laws or its enforcement of them. Only if the civil rights of a Mexican citizen are abridged by the actions of the U.S. government or by a U.S. employer should the Mexican government concern itself with American immigration policy.

It is in Mexico's own self-interest to take this position: Mexico certainly doesn't want its immigration policies to be subject either to international comments or to bilateral negotiations with its southern neighbors. Mexico itself, after all, is the rich Colossus of the North to the Central American countries of Honduras, Guatemala, El Salvador, and Nicaragua. And over the past few years the influx of tens of thousands of economic and political refugees from these countries has created enormous problems for southern Mexico.

In 1983 the Mexican government announced strict new rules for issuing visas, instituted close monitoring of refugee activities, and increased patrols along its southern border with Guatemala. On February 28, 1983, Minister of the Interior Manuel Bartlett Diaz described the impact of Central American refugees on Mexico in remarkably familiar terms; he said they had "taken jobs from Mexicans" and caused "social pressures because of all the excess of demand in all services."[2] And by the middle of 1984, Mexico was embroiled in a tense dispute with the Catholic Church over the government's efforts to move more than 46,000 interned Guatemalan refugees into camps farther away from the Guatemalan border.[3]

Either increased efficiency in the United States' enforcement of its immigration laws or the passage of an employer sanctions law might create temporary disruptions in Mexico, and we should certainly expect that there will be official and unofficial protests and some rather sharp words. But the possibility of sharp words should not be too frightening, especially when the Mexican government is constrained by its own awkward position, by its recognition of the internal nature of immigration laws, and by its desire to preserve good relations with the government of the

United States. The internal enforcement of American immigration laws does not depend on the approval of or the acquiescence of the government of Mexico, and a spate of unfriendly rhetoric will not disrupt working relations between our two countries.

Manuel Garcia y Griego told me that while a sharp and decisive change in American immigration policy would affect it adversely, Mexico would be able to adapt. And, he said, the most important element in the bilateral relations of the two countries is consistency. If increased enforcement were applied in temporary, inconsistent spasms, the economic and social effects on Mexico could be devastating. But if a policy of increased enforcement were announced and applied consistently, the people and the government of Mexico would adapt.

Consistency is a difficult thing for the government of the United States to achieve. Our government is not designed for consistency or efficiency. Instead, it has built into it a series of checks and balances among its branches and forces that seem intended, at times, to make consistency impossible—when they don't frustrate action altogether. But the enforcement of immigration laws requires that we practice consistency and firmness to achieve our aims.

Before the United States can enforce immigration laws effectively, before we can attain that necessary consistency, we have to demonstrate our national consensus on enforcing them. We have to demonstrate that we have the national will to support the Border Patrol and the Immigration and Naturalization Service even when they catch in their nets those sympathetic, friendly, ambitious, hardworking families who make such good photo opportunities for the local television news crews.

And, with good administration, adequate funding and personnel, a firm will, and a decent consideration for the dignity of both natives and aliens, the Border Patrol and the INS can do their jobs. We can improve the enforcement of immigration laws—even before passing a Simpson-Mazzoli bill or making other changes in immigration law. To summarize the recommendations from throughout this chapter, we would need to do the following:

1. Computerize the Immigration and Naturalization Service to enable it to get its paperwork done.
2. Ensure that all apprehended illegal aliens are held in custody until they are required to depart from the United States.
3. Increase the number of INS interior investigators so that they are able to devote adequate time to individual cases.
4. Ensure that all smugglers and habitual illegal border crossers are criminally prosecuted, and that U.S. Attorneys seek appropriate sentencing.
5. Reinstitute a policy of interior repatriation for Mexican illegal aliens.
6. Provide enough funding so that the Border Patrol can adequately patrol the southern and northern borders of the United States.

We can be optimistic. One danger of emphasizing the difficulties facing us is that the task ahead may seem impossible. But it is certainly possible to achieve a high level of enforcement. The borders of the United States *can* be adequately patrolled. Most of the southern border of the United States is guarded by a huge, hostile desert that discourages nearly all illegal immigrants. That is why 63 percent of all apprehensions along the southern border are made in a few locations that total just sixty miles in length. That funneling of illegals by natural barriers explains how Border Patrol officers can be so effective, how an individual officer can be responsible for so many apprehensions every year.

And it explains how a modest increase in funding and

manpower for the Border Patrol—accompanied by adequate support from the Washington bureaucracy, the courts, and the American people—will enable it to achieve control over illegal entries.

10

The Need
for Change

Writer John McPhee has compressed the four billion years of geologic time into the metaphorical six days of Genesis. Life wouldn't begin on earth, he notes, on Monday, the first day. It wouldn't appear until noon on Tuesday. Over the next four days, various life forms would develop. The dinosaurs wouldn't appear until Saturday at 4:00 P.M. and would be extinct by 9:00 P.M. Human beings would appear at three minutes before midnight on Saturday; the Industrial Revolution at a fortieth of a second before midnight. And, McPhee notes, we are surrounded by people who believe that the explosion in population and the consumption of resources that have taken place in that fortieth of a second are normal and can continue indefinitely.

These people are mad. All modern-day curves in population and resource consumption lead to disaster. The United States can ignore this and join the march to disaster, or it can attempt to save itself and as many others as will join us. It is my sad and reluctant conclusion that the economy within the United States cannot solve all the problems outside the United States, and that it would be foolish for us to try.

We call the poorest countries of the world "developing countries," as though the use of a progressive adjective could make a country progressive. But the overwhelming evidence is that most of these countries are not "developing" countries but "never-to-be-developed" countries. Most of the world's poor will stay poor for our lifetimes and for several generations to come, and there is nothing the developed nations can do to alter this fact. Our maximum generosity cannot make a dent in their poverty.

Some of these countries can and will help themselves. There will be success stories—South Korea, Singapore, Hong Kong. But most countries will not have the capital, the political culture, the government, or the knowledge to become developed countries. They will sink into squalor, poverty, disease, and death.

To help them, the United States and other developed countries must confront not only the problem of supply but also the problem of demand. If we try to supply only the food and capital these countries require, we shall invariably fail to help them, and we shall have engaged only in self-defeating generosity. We must never give food without family planning. That's throwing gasoline on the fire. That's feeding a cancer, for mankind has become a cancer on the earth.

It is not enough that we "mean well." We must also "do good." It is not enough to keep starving people marginally alive so that they procreate but never establish their self-sufficiency. That is the sin of softheartedness—it is counterproductive generosity that merely expands the number who will eventually die off.

Even if these countries had the capital, knowledge, and skills to become developed countries, the world does not have the resources to give everyone a "developed country" standard of living. Doing so would put an unbearable drain on the world's finite resources. To raise per capita energy consumption to the U.S. level, the world would need to burn 300 percent more coal, 500 percent more petroleum, and 1100 percent more natural gas. To believe that this could happen is more than wishful thinking; it is willful blindness.

In the last fortieth of a second of these first six days of creation, our civilization has been running a marathon as though it were a hundred-yard dash. We have treated the earth as though it were limitless. Even after satellite photos showed us the world as a finite sphere in the vast blackness of space, we continued to act as though we could endlessly abuse it. Each year our population grows; the deserts advance; the pollution seeps through the soil; the forests shrink; topsoil erodes; habitats degrade. Each decade a million species of living things become extinct forever.

We in the United States are unable to alleviate the suffering and starvation of the earth. But we have a humanitarian responsibility to use both our hearts and our heads to maximize the good we can do. In order to maximize that good, we need a heavy dose of reality. We need to understand the magnitude of the world's problems and the limits of our ability. Today we are just beginning to understand both of these concepts and to develop the moral codes, philosophical tenets, and political language to equip ourselves for the tough choices that face us.

The problem of immigration to the United States is only one of the areas in which we must make these tough choices. It is perhaps the first time we have had to confront the need to limit our impulsive generosity in order to preserve ourselves. That is why it has proved to be so difficult. It is also why the issues it poses must be faced squarely and honestly.

The inefficiency and cumbersomeness of the federal government frustrate me as I attempt to move Congress and the administration to deal with the immigration problem. The size of the problem has been growing for two decades, and the legislative and executive branches of the federal government have not yet been able to face it squarely and start to solve it. Individual members of Congress, strategically placed in positions of power in the Judiciary Committees, the Immigration Subcommittees, the Rules Committee, or the party structure have been able to delay and misdirect legislation. And the repeatedly expressed desire of the great majority of the American people for immigration reform has not been able to move those few individuals.

But sometimes, in the middle of any hard work, we have to take the longer view. The American political system is designed to frustrate fast action, not to encourage it. That is what the checks and balances among the branches of government are supposed to accomplish. That is why the Senate allows filibusters and why the chairs of House Committees and Subcommittees have broad power to block legislation that is proposed under their jurisdictions.

We talk about do-nothing Congresses and unresponsive federal bureaucracies, but in fact that is exactly the kind of slow-moving, considered government we want. The very glacial movement of the process is a guarantee that only the most necessary and the best legislation will be passed and will be funded. When we first hear the commonplace complaint that a session of Congress has passed well under 10 percent of the bills that were introduced during it, our first reaction may be "how terrible," but our second reaction is probably "thank goodness." We may, without too much irony, think of the huge and unwieldy mass of federal laws as being about the minimum we need to govern our large and pluralist population.

In this longer view, the hard work necessary to solve

a problem is justified, even though it can be frustrating. A problem develops through four stages before this lumbering dinosaur of a government can address it: first, the problem has to be presented and perceived clearly; second, it has to be demonstrated that there is a solution to the problem; third, it has to be shown that the solution to the problem doesn't create new difficulties that are worse than the problem itself; and fourth, the constituency supporting the solution has to convince the divergent groups in this society that have competing interests in the problem to accept the solution.

The first stage of the immigration problem developed slowly. In the early 1960s, there simply was no large-scale immigration problem in the United States. Legal immigration was barely over 200,000 people a year, and apprehensions of illegal immigrants were under 100,000 a year. Immigration, legal and illegal, was essentially under control. The immigration problem grew slowly over the past two decades. Until the Mariel boatlift (see Chapter 3) there was no single precipitating crisis that alerted and energized the public.

The second stage also developed slowly. After immigration was recognized as a problem, it took time to fashion a satisfactory solution. It isn't easy to locate and deport illegal aliens in an open and free society or to settle upon the least intrusive method of doing so. Forbidding employers to hire illegal aliens and penalizing those that do—the method agreed upon by both the Select Commission on Immigration and by the legislators who devised the Simpson-Mazzoli bill—promises to be the best method.

The third stage of this process has occupied Congress for the last three or four years. Members of Congress had to consider the ramifications of employer sanctions and determine how they would affect American citizens in general, employers as a special class, permanent resident aliens, and illegals themselves. The Senate and the House of Representatives devoted many hearings, many hours of debate, and thousands of hours of staff time to careful consideration of how employer sanctions could be implemented while protecting the rights of all of these groups. And it has reached good answers that satisfy most reasonable people.

But the fourth stage of this process, getting interest groups to accept the solution arrived at by the majority, has not progressed at all. In particular, Hispanic leaders have remained obdurate, have refused to accept any solution to the problems of massive illegal and legal immigration, and have even refused to admit that massive illegal and legal immigration are a problem.

Both the 97th and 98th Congresses, from 1981 through 1984, considered the Simpson-Mazzoli bill. In the 97th Congress, in 1982, the Senate passed it by a vote of 80 to 19. But the leaders of the House of Representatives did not move the bill to the floor until the last days of the session, and the Hispanic Caucus then deluged it with hundreds of minor, repetitive, and irrelevant amendments. The House dropped the bill after a few days of debate without ever voting on it.

In the 98th Congress, in 1984, the Senate passed the bill by a vote of 76 to 18. Late in its session, the House of Representatives also passed the bill, but in a version that differed slightly from the Senate's. Unless the Senate and the House pass exactly the same bill, the differing versions of the bill are referred to a conference committee that has members from both houses of Congress. This committee reconciles the differences between the two versions and refers the reconciled bill back to both houses, which must then pass the new reconciled bill. In 1984, the House members of the conference committee on the Simpson-Mazzoli bill raised small problem after small problem and were obstinately slow to compromise on very minor sticking points, so that when the Congress adjourned the bill died in the conference committee.

But it would be a mistake for someone interested in immigration reform to concentrate on the parliamentary maneuvering that took place in the last days of the 97th and 98th Congresses and to assume that it was the reason the United States has not had its immigration laws reformed. The real reason that the Simpson-Mazzoli bill did not pass in either session of Congress is that the leaders of the House of Representatives stalled it both times. They made the clock run out; they deliberately let it wait until the last few weeks of each session, when there would not be enough time for the bill's supporters to counter the delaying tactics of its opponents.

The blame for the lack of improvement in the border security of the United States and in the enforcement of the laws against the rampant rise of illegal immigration lies primarily with the Democratic Party and its leaders. I'm proud of the Democratic Party and so find this embarrassing to say, but the truth has to be faced. The Simpson-Mazzoli bill died in 1984 because Democrats caved in to pressure from a few Hispanic "spokesmen" who, as I've shown, don't speak for the Hispanic people of the United States.

In both the 97th and 98th Congresses, the Simpson-Mazzoli bill sailed through the Senate. Almost all Senate Republicans and a large majority of Senate Democrats voted for it; only a few members on the far right and the far left voted against it. Both times, the postponements in the House of Representatives were engineered by the Democratic leadership. The bill got no help and a good deal of hindrance from the Democratic power structure, and Democratic leaders such as Thomas P. "Tip" O'Neill, Speaker of the House; Peter Rodino, Chairman of the Judiciary Committee; and Claude Pepper, Chairman of the Rules

Committee, didn't lift a finger to expedite the bill. Outside the House, leaders of the party such as Ted Kennedy, Walter Mondale, Jesse Jackson, and Gary Hart worked to dismantle the law-enforcement portions of the bill or, failing that, to defeat it.

There is blame enough to go around. President Reagan never made immigration reform a priority of his administration, as Attorney General William French Smith urged him to. Reagan and his aides often hinted at possible vetoes of the Simpson-Mazzoli bill because of the cost of amnesty or some other reason, leaving its fate uncertain until the very end. Vice-President Bush campaigned before a Hispanic organization claiming that the administration would veto any immigration bill that discriminated against Hispanics—deliberately leaving the false impression that the administration thought the Simpson-Mazzoli bill did discriminate. But the administration would have signed a compromise bill if it had been presented with one. On this issue, at least, the hands of the Republicans are, if not clean, only smudged; and the fingerprints at the scene of the crime were all left by members of my own party.

Prior to the final consideration of Simpson-Mazzoli, both parties acknowledged the need to reform our immigration laws in order to preserve the American tradition of immigration. It was neither a Democratic nor a Republican issue, nor was it part of a conservative or liberal debate; it was not subject to partisan party politics. Throughout the Ford and Carter administrations, as study commissions set up both within the executive branch and independently with executive, congressional, and public members took the preliminary steps necessary to reform our immigration laws, both Democrats and Republicans, liberals and conservatives, cooperated with each other. So the opposition of the Democratic Party leaders is a terrible disappointment to those of us who are trying to keep the American tradition of responsible immigration free from partisanship. The pressure brought on Democratic leaders by a few activists within Hispanic interest groups has endangered that nonpartisan cooperation and brought the Democratic Party perilously close to dropping out of the national coalition for immigration reform and to defying the national consensus on the need for that reform.

The Simpson-Mazzoli Immigration Reform bill was a start toward getting control over illegal immigration, and the Senate version also included a ceiling on legal immigration that could help this country begin to regain control over our growing legal immigration. Everyone admitted that Simpson-Mazzoli was an imperfect compromise; no one liked everything it contained. Liberals were concerned about an increase in the foreign temporary worker program in the House version of the bill; conservatives were disturbed because the House bill gave amnesty to illegal aliens who entered the United States before January 1982—a relatively short time before the date at which the bill could have been passed. But the reason that Simpson-Mazzoli was killed was not that the members of Congress are unable to compromise on a bill that isn't perfect. It was killed because a few spokesmen for unrepresentative Hispanic pressure groups and a few members of the Congressional Hispanic Caucus do not want illegal immigration to be controlled. They, regrettably, do not want the borders of the United States to be guarded against illegal immigrants from Latin American countries (though a jaundiced observer could cynically suggest that they would willingly allow the illegal immigration of others to be controlled if they could ensure that Mexican and Central American illegals would be unaffected), and they will use any means within their power to attempt to defeat all efforts to control that illegal immigration.

In fact, as columnist Carl Rowan wrote, the opposition to the Simpson-Mazzoli bill was characterized by "a barrage of demagoguery and some shamefully misleading

statements," by "distortions and blatant misrepresenta-
tions."[1] Those are strong charges that require some sub-
stantiation. Here are some examples of the kind of rhetoric
and tactics that were used. The leader of the opposition to
the bill in the House of Representatives was Representative Edward Roybal of California. He said the bill "would
be the start of a police state in the United States of America."[2] That police state, he claimed, would be complete with
"dog tags or national identification cards."[3] He said it
"would definitely enslave the Hispanic in this nation."[4]
Representative Robert Garcia of New York also used strong
and completely false and misleading language to characterize the bill. He said the "legislation represents a giant
step backward for American immigration policy,"[5] and that
"for the first time since Jim Crow laws, we are setting apart
a group of people—twenty million U.S. citizens—for separate and unequal treatment."[6]

The language on the House floor was no more re-
strained and no more accurate during debate over the bill.
Congressman Henry B. Gonzalez of Texas claimed that
"Simpson-Mazzoli is, sadly, the latest in a long history of
immigration law that springs from the heart of the Know-
Nothings, those who feared and loathed all foreigners,
though they themselves were only recent arrivals. The spirit
and driving force of the Know-Nothings is present, alive,
and embodied in the Simpson-Mazzoli bill, an unworkable, unworthy addition to a body of law that has never been
distinguished by much, if any pretense toward justice, de-
cency, or workability."[7] And Congressman Roybal said of
the bill's system for aiding employers to determine whether
applicants for work were illegal immigrants, "It will be extended and extended and pretty soon we may face the
danger of ending up like Nazi Germany. History tells us
that Hitler recommended and put in place a system where
everyone had to carry a card. And that it did not work well.
You see the motion pictures of Hitler wearing a dog tag

over his neck because he wanted to show the German people that there was nothing wrong with everyone having to identify themselves."[8]

We should not be deceived; the opponents of Simpson-Mazzoli don't oppose just employer sanctions. They oppose any enforcement measures. They will also work just as hard to defeat realistic efforts to increase border guarding or to increase apprehensions of illegals within this country. The suggestions, the hints, that they might support increased border guarding or interior enforcement will evaporate into the ether when such proposals near reality. And their unfounded and unfair attempts to smear the bill's sponsors as somehow being racist were desperation measures that they undertook because they had no facts, no arguments, no statistics, and no reasoned response on their side—and because they had no alternative to offer to bring immigration back under control.

Representative Kiki de la Garza of Texas made that clear when he said in the course of the debate over Simpson-Mazzoli, "We are working at it and putting the dam where the water is hitting the ocean, and that is too late. It has gained too much momentum, and it is going to knock that dam down and it is going to go right into the ocean. You cannot stop it where it has all its momentum. It has all of the force that it gathered for thousands of miles. That is the flow of the undocumented. You cannot stop it on the border. You are not going to stop it there. You can put every employer in jail, you can penalize them, and that is not going to stop him. You have to find him a job where he came from. That has not been done."[9] In other words, Representative de la Garza and the others who opposed Simpson-Mazzoli offered in return neither additional border guarding nor additional internal enforcement. They offered only the prospect of tolerating illegal immigration for decades while American foreign aid programs tried to improve working conditions and living standards in the countries from which the illegals emigrate. They offered only a counsel of despair, only the advice to learn to live with illegal immigration because we could do nothing to control it.

The political mistake made by the sponsors of the Simpson-Mazzoli bill was that they never accepted the fact that they could not compromise with the bill's opponents. They filled the bill with laudable safeguards for Americans' essential liberties and with assurances that nothing in it could be used to discriminate against Hispanics. They offered solely those enforcement methods that would fall equally on all Americans. And they larded the bill with outright concessions to its Hispanic opponents, including an amnesty for illegal aliens that was broader by far than most Americans wanted. After all of these concessions, the bill's sponsors thought that its opponents would have to accept the best political deal they could possibly get. But none of these concessions could entice the bill's opponents into supporting it—because the bill still contained measures that would help to guard our borders. The "strong control measures," which the Hispanic Caucus had promised would be part of its long-advertised "Hispanic alternative" to Simpson-Mazzoli, turned out, when the bill finally materialized, to be merely very modest increases in the budget of the Border Patrol—increases that were earmarked for Spanish-language and cultural-sensitivity training for Patrol officers.

The sponsors of the Simpson-Mazzoli bill made one politically fatal concession to the Hispanic opponents of immigration reform—they coupled employer sanctions and measures to control illegal immigration with a massive amnesty for illegal aliens who already resided in the United States. Amnesty for the illegals who now live here was the highest political priority for the opponents of immigration reform, since they see themselves as advocates of the illegals as much as they are advocates of American Hispanics.

But it turned out that the overly broad and generous amnesty provision—and its tremendous costs—created so
much public and congressional opposition to amnesty that
the bill lost many supporters and gained practically none.
Scores of members of the House of Representatives voted
against the bill because of the amnesty, and few or none
of those who opposed immigration control changed their
positions and voted for it because amnesty was included.

This political miscalculation could have been avoided.
The fact is that a massive amnesty for most of the illegal
aliens in this country presents horrendous problems. The
amnesty could extend to uncounted millions of illegals,
ranging from those with long ties and histories of many
contributions to the United States to those who have only
the scantiest or most recent connection to it. The social
welfare costs of amnesty would be high and could be only
roughly estimated. The Immigration and Naturalization
Service does not have the manpower or the funds to ad-
minister the amnesty adequately. The voluntary agencies
that would "pre-interview" illegal aliens would pass only
their completed paperwork on to the INS, and these voluntary agencies—primarily Hispanic social advocacy organizations and the churches to which the aliens belonged—
could not be expected to review their cases with as much
skepticism and investigative care as the INS. Because of that,
amnesty would be an open invitation to widespread fraud
and abuse by ineligible aliens. It would be an insult to the
millions of aliens who had patiently waited their turn to
come to the United States under the law and to those who
were still waiting. It would be a reward for scoffing at and
breaking the law. And, most important, the amnesty would
be an open invitation for millions of others to come to the
United States illegally in hopes of another future amnesty.

The bill's sponsors acknowledged that a massive amnesty presented all these problems. But they were ready to
pay that price if they could ensure that the bill would pass

by including amnesty as one of its provisions. The bill, they reasoned, would enable the country to begin taking strong measures to bring immigration back under control, even with amnesty included. But instead of ensuring that the bill would pass, the amnesty ensured that it would fail.

The next time an employer sanctions bill or increased funding for the Immigration and Naturalization Service is proposed in Congress, it must not be coupled with a politically deadly massive amnesty for illegal aliens. Immigration control measures will have to be proposed separately, to stand or fall on their own merits, and so will amnesty for illegal aliens. If that means that amnesty cannot be passed, if millions of illegals in the United States are left in limbo because their cause will not generate enough support in Congress, that will have to be the result—and the blame for that should fall on the opponents of immigration reform who would not accept amnesty as their part of a political compromise, as their price for accepting better control over illegal immigration.

The next time an employer sanctions bill is proposed in Congress, the Democratic leadership of the House of Representatives must allow it to proceed to floor passage. It must break the stranglehold over the leadership of the Democratic Party that has been gained by the few activist Hispanics who oppose any control over legal or illegal immigration. These few activists have veto power in the party with regard to "Hispanic" issues, and they have succeeded in convincing the party that immigration is a Hispanic issue rather than an American one.

The extent of the problem this situation causes can be shown by one fact: in the Democratic primary campaign of 1984, all three major candidates, Walter Mondale, Gary Hart, and Jesse Jackson, opposed the Simpson-Mazzoli bill.

Jesse Jackson's opposition was in keeping with his basic ideology and general world view, and should not be surprising. As part of his primary campaign, Jackson even traveled to Mexico to denounce the Simpson-Mazzoli bill. There he displayed how poorly he understood the immigration issue and how out of touch he was with his black constituents' position on it by announcing that illegal workers "are not hurting our economy—they're a cheap labor base strengthening our economy."[10] He completely misrepresented the bill by claiming that it would require Americans to carry identification passbooks like those in South Africa.[11] And throughout his campaign he conducted a scare tactic against the bill, saying that if it passed "no Latino will ever be able to go to work or take a walk without the threat of harassment, arrest, or even deportation."[12]

Gary Hart is generally a supporter of the environmental movement and of its concerns for pending resource problems. But he did not appreciate population's contribution to these problems and refused to accept the connection between immigration and the increasing population of the United States. He was an active opponent of the bill in the Senate and argued that making it illegal for employers to hire people who were in the United States illegally was a threat to the civil liberties of Americans. And he argued before Mexican-American rallies that "The real solution for the immigration problem will not occur until the Mexican economy turns back up. If we want to solve immigration problems across the southern border, we ought to have a much more creative bilateral economic policy for development of the Mexican economy." Hart argued that until living standards are equalized between Mexico and the United States (and, presumably, between the United States and the rest of the underdeveloped world, though he has never made that inescapable conclusion explicit), "We're going to have this enormous immigration problem, and no legislation is going to solve that."[13] This economic equalization must mean that living conditions in the United States will fall to meet those of the undeveloped countries, because Gary Hart is certainly not so unrealistic as to believe that standards of living in the Third World will approach those of the United States within the foreseeable future. Hart has never admitted that this country experiences any serious economic or social problem as a result of tolerating massive illegal and legal immigration.

The third candidate for the nomination, Walter Mondale, is a practical politician who does understand the population problem and immigration's contribution to it. He is also very experienced at reading bills, so it can only be assumed that he understood that it contained nothing limiting the civil liberties of Hispanics or other Americans in any way. But in the Grapevine, Texas, primary debate on May 3, 1984, against Hart and Jackson, he claimed that the Simpson-Mazzoli bill would require Americans to carry an identification card, that it would "guarantee that employers will be very, very reluctant ever to hire an Hispanic or anyone else who doesn't look like he's an American, whatever that means," and that it somehow called for a "big roundup" of illegal aliens.[14]

Why would Walter Mondale distort and misrepresent the bill, and why would he oppose it actively? As he admitted in his second debate with President Reagan, his opposition to immigration reform was politically costly. It hurt him with both the general public and Hispanic voters.

But in the primaries, when he was seeking the endorsements of groups and organizations, the political benefit of Vice-President Mondale's opposing immigration reform was obvious. Though Hispanic-Americans are predominantly Democratic, Hispanic organizations were unreliable and unstable allies of the Democratic Party; the leaders of these organizations made their support for Democratic candidates contingent upon the candidates' pledges not to do anything to impede illegal immigration. Throughout the campaign and at the convention itself Hispanic organizations issued continual threats to withdraw support from the party if it did not abandon bipartisan support for immigration law enforcement. There was even a partially successful movement led by Mario Obledo of the League of United Latin American Citizens (LULAC) to organize a Hispanic boycott of the convention's presidential ballot because Mondale, though he opposed Simpson-Mazzoli, hadn't opposed it strongly enough.

As syndicated columnist Georgie Anne Geyer wrote, in a shrewd insight into the operation of Hispanic organizations:

> When you look at the Hispanic groups claiming they represent American Hispanics—groups such as the Mexican American Legal Defense and Education Fund, the League of United Latin American Citizens, and the National Council for La Raza—one finds that most were created artificially from the top down, rather than from the bottom up. Most started with grants from the Rockefeller and Ford Foundations and other American corporations.
>
> Their leadership is—and represents—a generation of young, upwardly mobile Hispanic American lawyers and professionals whom one might call "yuphies," or young urban professional Hispanics. They are using immigration to show their macho and their clout.
>
> Their campaign is utterly without grass roots input, and these groups have probably never been able to deliver the vote for anyone; yet, they were able to force Walter Mondale to his knees in California with threats of the Hispanic vote, and they were able to force Jesse Jackson to go against his own black constituency, who suffer tremendously from illegal immigration. This could not have occurred, of course, if any of the Democratic candidates had stood on principle and simply called the gigantic bluff.[15]

Hispanic organizations have an advantage in the Democratic Party, of course, because the Democratic Party has traditionally been the party of immigrants to the United States. When new immigrant groups came here and needed representation, when they needed political power, when they needed to find a way into the political system, it was the Democratic Party that was open to them, accepted them, and went out of its way to invite them to participate, to join, to wield their newly gained rights of citizenship.

No Democrat wants to end that tradition of acceptance and openness to new immigrant groups. But because of that tradition some Hispanic leaders were able to play very skillfully on the "Democratic dream," just as they play on the "American dream," to delay effective steps to control legal and illegal immigration. If the generosity of the Democratic Party has been its openness, the genius of the party has been in the balancing, the honest brokering it has done among the interests of its various constituencies. The party has advanced not by tilting to one interest or another, not by becoming captive to one single constituency, but by being able to balance interests and to represent all constituencies.

There is no conflict among the interests of working people, middle-class people, blacks, and Hispanic Americans on the immigration issue—all of these groups feel that immigration must be controlled. The Democratic Party must operate, as it has in the past, in the true interests of the people. It wouldn't be representing the interests of the working man and woman if it just took orders from organized labor unions. It wouldn't represent women if it just followed the official line of any single women's organization. And it wouldn't represent the interests of minorities if it blindly obeyed the commands of a few self-appointed spokesmen for those minorities who deliberately ignore the interests of the members of their own groups. It is incumbent upon the Democratic Party, it is its duty as the party of immigrants and of minorities and of working people, to represent the true interests of those immigrants and minorities and working people.

How can this political muscle be countered? Not by arguments, not by facts, and not by statistics. Those were all used in the debate over the Simpson-Mazzoli bill. The supporters of the bill had the best of the arguments. The supporters had all the facts and all the statistics on their side. But they lost because sheer political muscle was used against them and because they weren't able to mobilize the active, vocal support of the American people to counterbalance that muscle.

The past few years of immigration reform efforts teach one lesson for the future: when a good bill to control immigration is again proposed in Congress—and it will be proposed again because it is necessary for every sovereign nation to protect its borders—the political muscle of its opponents must be matched by the political muscle of its supporters. That is what we must have in the future. The arguments, the facts, and the statistics are not enough. We must also have the political passion. Opponents of immigration control won simply because they cared more strongly than supporters of it. In a direct democracy, the issue would be settled by a simple vote, the majority would rule, and our borders would be adequately guarded. But we live in a representative republic, not a direct democracy. Our feelings on issues have weight not just according to how many others share them, but also according to how strongly, how passionately, we all share them.

The people of the United States will be able to oppose the obstructionist tactics of Hispanic pressure groups on the leadership of the Democratic Party only when we speak out clearly and loudly on the immigration issue. At the 1984 Democratic Convention the entire nation could see exactly what kinds of tactics those groups would use and how far they would go. Hispanic groups were willing to embarrass

243

and oppose Walter Mondale, their friend and supporter, and to help Ronald Reagan, who opposed them on innumerable issues aside from the Simpson-Mazzoli bill, because they detected inadequate fervor, incomplete acquiescence to their demands, on Mr. Mondale's part. How can the general public counter such extreme tactics on the part of an organized special interest group?

In our political system, when arguments, facts, and statistics have proved inadequate, only votes can move politicians. We have to let members of Congress know that we are following their actions on immigration reform, and that they are going to be held accountable for how they vote—held accountable not just by a few Hispanic extremists but also by the majority of the American people, who want immigration reform. This means that we have to use all available means of getting to our representatives. And we have to work not just with Democratic members of Congress, who may be subject to countervailing pressures from interest group activists; we also have to continue to work with Republican members to ensure that they stay committed to immigration reform and continue to work for it. A representative can devote personal attention to any of hundreds of worthy issues, of which immigration is only one. Even stalwart supporters of immigration reform need to be reinforced, need to know that immigration is an important issue to their constituents.

We cannot ignore the issue any longer. Legal and illegal immigration are out of control. And study after study show that the people who are hurt most by uncontrolled immigration are those who need protection most: our poor, our minorities, working women, and teenagers looking for jobs. Unless we take positive steps to bring immigration under control, the situation will get much worse.

American society has often advanced through the raising of uncomfortable, even heretical issues—civil rights, consumerism, and conservation among them. As Abraham Lincoln said, "As our case is new so must we think and act anew—we must disenthrall ourselves." We must disenthrall ourselves now from the dream of unlimited immigration, a dream that will turn into a nightmare if we do not waken ourselves from it.

The effects of our lack of control over immigration penetrate every layer of our society; and we must face that problem now or miss our chance to fashion a compassionate and dispassionate solution to the problem. This country is now the largest recipient of immigrants in the world. We take more than the rest of the world combined. Yet most of the decisions that brought immigrants to the United States were not made here; they were made in Hanoi, Havana, Tehran, and a thousand other foreign cities—because we, the strongest nation in the world, have acted as though we had no right to protect our borders.

The American frontier is gone, replaced by an America of limits. Yet in the past decade more people came to the United States, legally and illegally, than during any other decade in our history. We have an unknown number of illegal immigrants living in the United States. Hundreds of thousands of people fly into the United States every year and don't leave. Immigration inspectors at airports and ports of entry catch almost a million people trying to enter the country illegally each year, and the Border Patrol now makes more than a million apprehensions a year.

What is the effect of bringing hundreds of thousands of new workers into the United States each year, with an unemployment rate that refuses to fall back even to 7 percent? How many of our unemployed would take jobs that are now taken by illegal immigrants? Each percentage point of unemployment costs the country twenty-five billion dollars in lost taxes and governmental benefits. How many billions of dollars and, more to the point, how many millions of American workers are we misallocating each year because of uncontrolled immigration?

And we have seen an equally dramatic increase in costs for social services for both legal and illegal immigrants. That has changed in the last few years. It may once have been true that illegal immigrants would not take benefits from the government. But studies that claim that illegal immigrants pay more taxes than they receive in social services are outdated; they are no longer valid. Los Angeles County saves $40 million a year just by denying benefits to the illegal aliens it is able to identify who do apply for benefits. The General Accounting Office estimates that as many as one-third of public housing tenants in some areas are illegal immigrants.

Pressures to immigrate to the United States have to be stopped domestically by American laws and American enforcement of those laws, because in the countries of the developing world the pressure to emigrate will continue to grow as their population explodes. Without action on our part, that pressure may prove to be irresistible.

Mexico, the country most often mentioned in connection with immigration to the United States, is a good case in point. The population of Mexico has tripled since 1945 and will double in the next twenty years. No reasonable amount of immigration to the United States could relieve that pressure. And that's the point: our immigration system today, as out of control as it is, does not serve the interests of the world's poor. Only a few fortunate souls are able to migrate here; hundreds of millions less well off will never have the chance to. Certainly the source countries for immigrants are not helped by our immigration laws; they lose their most productive and skilled workers, the people they need to develop their own economies. Certainly the American people are not helped by uncontrolled immigration. More people coming here means more population growth, more population pressure on our own resources, more energy and water use, more traffic, more fertile farmland used for housing, more unemployment.

Facing the reality of a harsh and overpopulated world is not easy. The ethics and politics of such a world are still being created. But to "do good," not just "mean well," we have to accept the responsibility of making tough choices, of limiting, and of acknowledging the overwhelming pressures of human population on earth.

Because of these pressures, because of that reality, we have to control and limit immigration. It is in our own interests, in the interests of our nation and our citizens, and it is in the ultimate interest of our world. Immigration reform is not the death of the American dream, either for Americans or for the potential immigrants who are prospective new Americans. It is the necessary precondition for the preservation of the dream.

Notes

1: How Many Can America Absorb?

1. Langston Hughes, "Harlem," *The Panther and the Lash* (New York: Alfred A. Knopf, 1967).
2. Daniel R. Vining, Jr., "Net Migration by Commercial Air: A Lower Bound on Total Net Migration to the United States," *Research in Population Economics* 4 (1982): 333–50.
3. William French Smith, "Remarks of the Honorable William French Smith, Attorney General of the United States, to the Joint Breakfast Meeting of the San Antonio Bar Association and the Greater San Antonio Chamber of Commerce," U.S. Department of Justice, 19 April 1982.

2: The Dispossessed

1. "Four to Be Tried in Sale of Mexican-Born Babies," *The New York Times,* 23 May 1984, A-16; "Witnesses Say Babies Were Sold," *Dallas Times Herald,* 13 June 1984, B-3.
2. Joseph Wambaugh, *Lines and Shadows* (New York: William Morrow & Co., 1984), pp. 20–22.
3. "Four Die When Train Traps Illegal Aliens on Trestle," *The New York Times,* 30 April 1984, A-11; "Alien Deaths Followed Long March in Texas," *The New York Times,* 2 May 1984, A-16.
4. John Kendall, "Youths Tell of Privations as Pickers," *Los Angeles Times,* 10 April 1979, I-3, 29.
5. Leslie Maitland Werner, "Justice Dept. Considers Possible Appeal of Sentences in Texas Slave Case," *The New York Times,* 11 February 1984, 13.
6. Judith Cummings, "Lawyer Defends Employers in Indonesian 'Slavery' Case," *The New York Times,* 1 February 1982, A-13.
7. Sasha G. Lewis, *Slave Trade Today: American Exploitation of Illegal Aliens* (Boston: Beacon Press, 1979).
8. Ray Gibson, "Deadly Factory a 'Huge Gas Chamber' for Illegal Alien Workers," *Chicago Tribune,* 23 October 1983, 4–9.
9. Bill Richards, "Governors' Decisions in Extradition Cases Vary All Over the Map," *The Wall Street Journal,* 25 May 1984, 1, 11.
10. Rinker Buck, "The New Sweatshops: A Penny for Your Collar," *New York,* 29 January 1979, 43.
11. "Garment Industry: If the Coat Fits—," *Los Angeles Times,* 9 September 1979, V-4.
12. Buck, "The New Sweatshops," p. 43.
13. Quoted in Lewis, *Slave Trade Today,* pp. 122–23.
14. Harry Bernstein, "Illegal Aliens Cost U.S. Jobs—Mar-

shall," an interview with Secretary of Labor Ray Marshall, *Los Angeles Times*, 2 December 1979, 1–26.
15. "Woman Gets Probation in Baby Smuggling Case," *The New York Times*, 25 August 1984, 5.

3: Lawlessness

1. Quoted in Michael Daly, "Los Bandidos Take the Town," *New York*, 26 October 1984, 67.

4: The Splintered Society

1. Michael S. Teitelbaum, "Right Versus Right: Immigration and Refugee Policy in the United States," *Foreign Affairs* 59, no. 1 (fall 1980): 26–27.
2. Leon F. Bouvier, "Human Waves," *Natural History* (August 1983): 12.
3. "Pro and Con: Teach Immigrants in Their Own Language?" *U.S. News and World Report*, 3 October 1984, 52.
4. Nathan Glazer and Daniel P. Moynihan, *Beyond the Melting Pot: The Negroes, Puerto Ricans, Jews, Italians, and Irish of New York City*, 2d ed. (Cambridge, Mass.: The M.I.T. Press, 1970), p. xcvii.
5. Michael Hirsley, "Hispanics Overwhelm Blacks in Miami Jobs Fight," *Chicago Tribune*, 18 January 1983, 4.
6. Bruce Porter and Marvin Dunn, *The Miami Riot of 1980* (Boston: Lexington Books, 1984), p. 195.
7. Ibid., p. 196.
8. T. Willard Fair, "Blacks Must Help Themselves," *The Miami Herald*, 14 February 1982, E-1.
9. Phillip Moffitt, "America, Where Are You Going?" *Esquire* (May 1983), 7.
10. Thomas B. Morgan, "The Latinization of America," *Esquire* (May 1983), 55.

11. Ibid.
12. "The Cubans: A People Changed," special section, *The Miami Herald*, 18 December 1983, 8-M.
13. Milton M. Gordon, "Models of Pluralism: The New American Dilemma," *The Annals of the American Academy of Political and Social Science 454* (March 1981): 178–88.
14. "Documents of the Chicano Struggle," *International Socialist Review* (June 1970): 30–33, 44.
15. Nina Glick Schiller, "Ethnic Groups Are Made, Not Born: The Haitian Immigrant and American Politics," in *Ethnic Encounters: Identities and Contexts*, ed. George L. Hicks and Philip E. Leis (North Scituate, Mass.: Duxbury Press, 1977), pp. 23–35.
16. Bouvier, "Human Waves," p. 12.

5: Language: The Tie That Binds

1. Thomas Muller, *The Fourth Wave: California's Newest Immigrants: A Summary* (Washington, D.C.: Urban Institute Press, 1984), p. 11.
2. Colin Greer, *The Great School Legend* (New York: Basic Books, 1972).
3. *Lau v. Nichols*, 414 U.S. 563 (1974).
4. Iris Rotberg, "Some Legal and Research Considerations in Establishing Federal Policy in Bilingual Education," *Harvard Educational Review* 52, no. 2 (May 1982): 157.
5. Keith A. Baker and Adriana A. de Kanter, "Effectiveness of Bilingual Education: A Review of the Literature" (U.S. Department of Education, Office of Planning, Budget, and Evaluation, Washington, D.C., 25 September 1981, Mimeographed), 1.
6. Mario Obledo, " 'We Will Change the Political Face' of the U.S.," *U.S. News and World Report*, 22 August 1983, 49.

7. "Pro and Con: Teach Immigrants in Their Own Language?" *U.S. News and World Report*, 3 October 1983, 51–52.

8. Burt Schorr, "Grade-School Project Helps Hispanic Pupils Learn English Quickly," *The Wall Street Journal*, 30 November 1983, 1.

9. Ibid.

10. The Twentieth Century Fund, Task Force on Federal Elementary and Secondary Education Policy, *Making the Grade* (New York: The Twentieth Century Fund, 1983), pp. 11–12.

11. "English Spoken Here, Please," *Newsweek*, 9 January 1984, 24.

12. Suzanne Daley, "Elizabeth Mayor Orders City Hall Employees to Speak English," *The New York Times*, 18 July, 1984, B-1; "English Only," *The New York Times*, 19 February 1984, 53.

13. Letter from Guillermo Lopez, Chief, Office of Bilingual Education, California State Department of Education, 7 November 1983.

14. Mario Obledo, "An Open Border Between the U.S. and Mexico," *Congress Report* (June–July 1980): 4.

15. Eugene J. McCarthy, "Is America the World's Colony?" *Policy Review* (Summer 1981): 123–24.

16. "New Tongue Heard on Mexico Border," *The New York Times*, 14 October 1983, A-12; Wayne King, "It's English and It's Spanish, and It's Officially a Problem," *The New York Times*, 2 August 1983, A-1, 10.

17. Richard Rodriguez, *Hunger of Memory: The Education of Richard Rodriguez* (Boston: Godine, 1981), pp. 27, 34–35.

18. James W. Lamare, "The Political Integration of Mexican American Children: A Generational Analysis," *International Migration Review* 16, no. 1 (Spring 1982): 174.

6: Jobs, Immigrants, and Americans

1. Robert Fox, "The Challenge of Numbers," *IDB News* (Washington, D.C.: InterAmerican Development Bank, December 1983), p. 7.
2. William Raspberry, "Should It Be Legal to Hire Illegals?" *Washington Post*, 8 August 1980, A-13.
3. Edwin Reubens, testimony before the Select Commission on Immigration and Refugee Policy, 29 October 1979.
4. Two of Vernon Briggs's books on immigration and economics are *Chicanos and Rural Poverty* (Baltimore: Johns Hopkins University Press, 1973) and *Immigration Policy and the American Labor Force* (Baltimore: Johns Hopkins University Press, 1985).
5. Professor Gonzalez's study was presented to the International Development Conference, 17–19 May 1983, in Washington, D.C., and reported in the *Conservation Foundation Letter* (June 1983): 6.
6. A more careful statement of this argument would be to say not that there would be a labor shortage, but that there will be an older work force as the large baby-boom generation grows older and is followed by smaller age cohorts.
7. Kyle Johnson and James Orr, "The Economic Implications of Immigration" (U.S. Department of Labor, Bureau of International Labor Affairs, Office of Foreign Economic Research, Washington, D.C., 15 July 1980, Mimeographed), 8–9.
8. John Crewdson, "Illegal Aliens Are Bypassing Farms for Higher Pay of Jobs in the Cities," *The New York Times*, 10 November 1980, A-1, D-9.
9. *Congressional Record*, 9 July 1981, S-7357–7358.
10. Unpublished study, Professor Donald Huddle (Department of Economics, Rice University, 1981).
11. Reported in FAIR *Immigration Report* (December 1982), p. 3.

12. Robert Lindsey, "Job Unrest Grows on Coast's Farms," *The New York Times*, 19 August 1983, A-1, 8.
13. Caryle Murphy, "Market Tightens as Immigrants Fill Local Jobs," *Washington Post*, 7 August 1983, A-1, 11.
14. Bill Walker, "Roofer, 42 Workers Held as Illegal Aliens," *Denver Post*, 24 July 1984, A-1, 19.
15. William Serrin, "After Years of Decline, Sweatshops Are Back," *The New York Times*, 12 October 1983, A-1, B-4; Serrin, "Combating Garment Sweatshops Is an Almost Futile Task," *The New York Times*, 13 October 1983, B-1, 4.
16. Barton Smith and Robert Newman, "Depressed Wages Along the U.S.-Mexican Border: An Empirical Analysis," *Economic Inquiry* 15 (January 1977): 51–66.
17. Robert Lindsey, "Strike at Southern Calif. Plant Puts Focus on Illegal Aliens' Plight," *The New York Times*, 4 May 1980, 22.
18. The mathematical mistake was the averaging of averages: the researcher added the percentage of unemployment in cities of vastly different sizes and divided by the number of cities, rather than weighting the percentages by the sizes of the cities. This procedure vastly understated the total unemployment in high-immigration cities.
19. Gail Garfield Schwartz and William Newkirk, *The Work Revolution* (New York: Rawson Associates, 1983).
20. Dan Stein, "Thoughts on the Labor Market Impact of Illegal and Inordinately High Legal Immigration," 28 April 1983, photocopy, 2.
21. Reported by Philip Shabecoff, "Count of Jobless Among Youths Called Very Low," *The New York Times*, 29 February 1980, A-1, 14.
22. Harry Bernstein, "75% of Jobless Would Accept Menial Work," *The Los Angeles Times*, 7 April 1981, 1, 10.
23. Malcolm Lovell, Jr., "Statement of Malcolm Lovell, Jr., Undersecretary, U.S. Department of Labor, before the Subcommittee on Immigration, Refugees and Interna-

tional Law, Committee of the Judiciary, United States House of Representatives, and the Subcommittee on Immigration and Refugee Policy, Committee of the Judiciary, United States Senate," 20 April 1982, photocopy, 3–4.

24. Mike Royko, "He Was Jobbed," *Chicago Sun-Times*, 1 October 1982, 2.

25. *The Tarnished Golden Door* (Washington, D.C.: U.S. Commission on Civil Rights, 1980), p. 147.

26. *Immigration Policies and Black America: Causes and Consequences*, Proceedings before the seminar co-sponsored by the Department of Human Development, School of Human Ecology, Howard University, and the Federation for American Immigration Reform (FAIR), 3 November 1983, p. 21.

7: Social Services, Aliens, and Americans

1. National Association of Counties Research, Inc., "The Impacts of the 36-Month Limitation on Full Federal Refugee Funding on State and Local Welfare Costs" (Washington, D.C.: NACo, August 1981, Mimeographed), 4.

2. National Association of Counties Research, Inc., "Analysis of San Diego and San Francisco County Data on the Length of Time Indochinese Refugees Have been in the U.S. Prior to Application for Public Assistance" (Washington, D.C.: NACo, September 1981, Mimeographed), 1.

3. Barbara Glaser, Director of Social Services, Department of Human Resources, Arlington, Virginia, "Statement for the Public Meeting on Refugee Admissions, Georgetown University Center for Immigration Policy and Refugee Assistance," 17 September 1981.

4. Roger Conner, *Breaking Down the Barriers: The Changing Relationship Between Illegal Immigration and Welfare*

(Washington, D.C.: Federation for American Immigration Reform [FAIR], September 1982), pp. 20–21.

5. Ibid., p. 19.
6. Ibid.
7. Ibid., p. 25.
8. David S. North, *Government Records: What They Tell Us About the Role of Illegal Immigrants in the Labor Market and in Income Transfer Programs* (Washington, D.C.: New TransCentury Foundation, April 1981), pp. 67–68.
9. "Your Taxes Pay Health Bills for Illegal Aliens," *The Arizona Republic*, 18 May 1983, A-14, 15.
10. Alma Guillermoprieto, "Salvadoran Refugees Straining D.C. Public Schools," *Washington Post*, 2 October 1983, A-19.
11. "Illegal Alien Delivery Care Documented," *Los Angeles Herald Examiner*, 5 March 1984, A-12.
12. Ty Fahner, Attorney General, State of Illinois, Public Information Releases, 30 September 1982 and 29 October 1982.
13. *Plyler, Superintendent, Tyler Independent School District, et al.,* v. *Doe, Guardian,* et al., Nos. 80-1538 and 80-1934, 15 June 1982, dissenting opinion of Chief Justice Burger, p. 3.
14. Ibid., concurring decision of Justice Powell, pp. 3–4, n. 3.
15. "Texas Isn't Shocked by Schooling Order for Aliens' Children," *The Wall Street Journal*, 16 June 1982, 24; "Ruling Likely to Affect Welfare," *Dallas Morning News*, 16 June 1982, A-1, 6.
16. *Congressional Record*, 13 September 1983, H-6773.
17. Ibid., H-6779.
18. Conner, *Breaking Down the Barriers*, p. 38.
19. Barry Chiswick, ed., *The Gateway: U.S. Immigration Issues and Policies* (Washington, D.C.: American Enterprise Institute for Public Policy Research, 1982).
20. *FAIR Immigration Report* (July 1981).

8: Rewriting the Law

1. U.S. House of Representatives, Committee on Post Office and Civil Service, Subcommittee on Census and Population, *Global Resolutions, Environment, and Population Act of 1983*, Serial No. 98-49 (Washington, D.C.: U.S. Government Printing Office, 1984), pp. 57–62.
2. Immigration and Naturalization Service, *1980 Statistical Yearbook of the Immigration and Naturalization Service* (Washington, D.C.: U.S. Department of Justice, Immigration and Naturalization Service, n.d.), table I, p. 1.
3. Edwin Harwood, "Can Immigration Laws Be Enforced?" *The Public Interest*, no. 72 (Summer 1983): 107–23.
4. "Stronger Policies on Aliens Favored," *The New York Times*, 15 November 1983, A-17.
5. George Gallup, "Gallup Poll: Americans Want U.S. to Get Tough on Illegal Aliens," *New Orleans Times-Picayune*, 13 November 1983, I-33.
6. FAIR, "Public Opinion on Immigration" (Washington, D.C.: Federation for American Immigration Reform, 1984).
7. Hispanic Opinion and Preference Research, Inc., "A Study of Hispanic Opinions and Preferences: A Preliminary Report," April 1981, photocopy, pp. 19–22.

9: Enforcing the Law

1. *Congressional Record*, 17 December 1982, H-10256.
2. Marlise Simons, "Mexico Moves to Stem Refugee Flows," *The New York Times*, 22 June 1983, A-3.
3. William A. Orme, Jr., "Rumors, Conflicts Complicate Mexico's Relocation of Refugees," *Washington Post*, 15 July 1984, A-21, 24.

10: The Need for Change

1. Carl Rowan, "Immigration Demagoguery," *The Dallas Morning News*, 15 June 1984, A-19.
2. "Hispanic Reps. Fight Immigration Bill," *Sacramento Daily Recorder*, 12 June 1984, 16.
3. "L.A.'s Roybal Targets Bill on Immigration," *San Francisco Examiner*, 4 June 1984, A-8.
4. *Los Angeles Times*, 23 July 1984, I-2.
5. "Hispanic Groups Charge Racism, Demand Immigration Bill Be Killed," *Sacramento Bee*, 8 June 1984, A-16.
6. "Fight Looms on Immigration Bill," *Washington [D.C.] Times*, 8 June 1984, 3-A.
7. *Congressional Record*, 11 June 1984, H-5560.
8. *Congressional Record*, 12 June 1984, H-5660.
9. *Congressional Record*, 11 June 1984, H-5573.
10. Fay S. Joyce, "Jesse Jackson Crosses into Mexico to Denounce an Immigration Bill," *The New York Times*, 15 May 1984, A-24.
11. Juan Williams, "Jackson Is Seeking Emergency Meeting on Immigration Bill," *Washington Post*, 17 June 1984, A-14.
12. Katharine Macdonald, "Jackson Says a Floorfight Might Be Waged over Rules," *Washington Post*, 20 May 1984, A-4.
13. Dan Balz, "Hart Espouses Aid for Mexico in Bid for Hispanic Votes," *Washington Post*, 30 April 1984, A-3.
14. "Excerpts from the Democratic Candidates' Debate in Texas," *The New York Times*, 4 May 1984, A-18.
15. Georgie Anne Geyer, "Control the Borders," *The Phoenix Gazette*, 19 June 1984, A-13.

Acknowledgments

We gratefully acknowledge the assistance of all those whose generous help made writing this book a pleasure—among them, especially, those from whom we quote so extensively: Richard Alvarez, Dick Bevans, Gerda Bikales, Vernon Briggs, Manuel Garcia y Griego, Alan Nelson, David North, and Gail Garfield Schwartz. Pat Burns and Dan Stein were particularly helpful in calling our attention to and finding long-lost sources; Nancy White in trying to keep our economics accurate; Linda Kovan in typing and library research; and Truman "Mac" Talley, our editor and publisher, in recognizing the importance of the subject. We thank Carrying Capacity, the population-environmental organization of which Gary Imhoff was executive director while we were writing this book, for understanding the relationship between massive immigration and the American environment and for allowing him to spend time on the book. And each of us thanks a Dorothy.

Index

Abrams, Robert, 144
affirmative action, 94
Afghans, in Pakistan, 16
Africa, population of, *xii*, 126
agriculture, 9–10, 147, 152
　blacks employed in, 141
　Green Revolution in, 6, 10
　illegal immigrants employed in, 18,
　　33–34, 44–45, 140–43, 214
　stoop labor in, 44, 140
Aid for Dependent Children (AFDC),
　166, 169, 172, 173, 179
Aiken, George, 32
Alexandria, Va., immigrants in, 101
Alvarez, Richard, 57–74
American Horse, Ben, 26
"Anglos," 100
Arizona Hospital Association, 174
Arlington County, Va., refugees in,
　163–64
Asians:
　discriminations against, 50
　illegal activities of, 51
　legal immigration of, 20
　violence against, 11

Assam, India, Bengali immigrants in,
　10, 95
assimilation, 3, 10, 77, 78–80, 82,
　196–97
　acculturation vs., 80
　defined, 93
　language problems and, 99, 100–
　　101, 104, 109, 111, 116, 123
　pluralism vs., 93–94
Atlanta, Ga., police seminar in, 51
Atlanta federal penitentiary, 65, 67
Atotonilco, Mexico, 34

Bailyn, Bernard, 104
Bangladesh, immigrants from, 95
Barbados, immigrants in, 81, 97
Barkley, Alben, 26
Batista y Zaldívar, Fulgencio, 70
Belgium, separatism in, 95, 99
Belize, immigrants in, 81, 97
Bengalis, in Assam, India, 10
Bevans, Dick, 209–17
Beverly Hills, Calif., Indonesians in,
　36

263

INDEX

Mexicans:
  in California, 101–102, 143
  smugglers and, 27–28, 32
  Spanglish spoken by, 119–20
  in Texas, 157
  in U.S., 15, 121–22
Mexico:
  American culture in, 84
  babies smuggled to U.S. from, 27–28, 48
  birthrate of, 7–8
  economy of, 23, 128, 221, 239
  illegal immigrants from, 15, 27–36, 38, 143, 157, 216–18
  immigrants from, 15, 27–36, 38, 106, 111, 121–22, 143, 157, 203–204, 216–18, 246
  population growth in, 7–8, 128, 246
  refugees in, 221
  resolution of Senate in, 218–20
  tax survey in, 167
  U.S. relations with, 218–22
  see also Border Patrol
Miami, Fla.:
  bilingual education in, 104
  blacks in, 85, 87–89, 91
  crime in, 4, 70
  Cubans in, 11, 56, 70, 85–93, 100
  employment patterns in, 87–89
  as foreign city, 85–93
  Haitians in, 87, 89–90
  Hispanics in, 11, 87–93, 100
  immigrants in, 4, 56, 70, 77, 85–93, 100
  language problems in, 89, 91–92, 100
  mayoral race in (1983), 11, 91
  Spanglish in, 119
Miami Herald, 88, 92–93
Miami Riot of 1980, The (Porter and Dunn), 88
Michaelson, Alvin, 36
Minnesota, refugees in, 162
Moffitt, Phillip, 90–91
Mondale, Walter, 232, 238, 240–41, 244
mordida, 30
Morgan, Thomas B., 91–92
Moynihan, Daniel Patrick, 20, 82–83
"mules," 55
Murphy, Mary G., 118

National Association of Counties, 162–63

National Council of La Raza, 94, 111, 241
National Institute of Education, 108
Nature of Mass Poverty, The (Galbraith), 139
NBC/Associated Press Poll, 203
Negative Population Growth, 195
Nelson, Alan C., 206–209
Newark, N.J., Mariel Cubans in, 50–60
New Bedford, Mass., rape case in, 52
"New Colossus, The" (Lazarus), 4
New Jersey:
  illegal immigrants in, 39
  Mariel Cubans in, 59–60
  Spanglish in, 119
Newman, Robert, 145
New Orleans, La., Italian immigrants in, 80
New York, N.Y.:
  bilingual education in, 106
  crime in, 59–60
  Dominicans in, 106, 169
  as foreign city, 85, 91, 93
  illegal immigrants in, 15, 41, 144, 148, 169
  Mariel Cubans in, 59–60, 65
  sweatshops in, 39, 144
New York magazine, 39
New York State:
  immigrants in, 50, 146, 214
  Spanglish in, 119
New York State Select Committee on Crime, 69
New York Times, The, 51, 139
Nicaragua, refugees from, 81, 221
Nigerians, illegal activities of, 51
North, David, 166–73, 175–80

Oaxaca, Mexico, immigrants from, 216
Obledo, Mario, 110, 118, 241
Occupational Safety and Health Administration (OSHA), 38, 42
Ohio University 151
oil, as fuel, 8–9, 227
O'Neill, Thomas P., "Tip," 21, 219, 231
Orange County, Calif., immigrants in, 146, 163
Oregon, refugees in, 162–63
Orr, James, 139

Pakistan:
  refugees in, 16, 162
  separatism in, 95

INDEX

State Department, U.S., 86
Steger, William M., 35
Stein, Dan, 150
stoop labor, 44, 140
Suarez, Xavier, 91
Supreme Court, U.S., 106–107, 178,
  180–81
sweatshops, 39–40, 143–44
Switzerland, multilingualism in, 99

Tarnished Golden Door, The, 153
Tarrance, Lance, 18, 203
Tarranova, Peter, 117
Teitelbaum, Michael, 78
television, Spanish, 92, 204
Texas:
  bilingual education in, 106
  education in, 106, 180, 182
  illegal immigrants in, 15, 18, 26,
    32, 143, 145, 157, 180, 182
  Mexicans in, 157
  Spanglish in, 120
  survey of Hispanics in, 204
  Vietnamese in, 11, 79
"Texas Proviso," 156–57
Texas State Department of Forestry,
  illegal immigrants enslaved by
  contractors for, 35
Tijuana, Mexico, California border
  of, 30–32
Torres, Arnold, 194, 195
Toynbee, Arnold, *ix*
Trudeau, Pierre, 220
tuberculosis, 163
Turks, in West Germany, 11–12
Twentieth Century Fund, 111
Tyler, Tex., slavery case in, 35

unemployment, *xii,* 11, 17, 133, 136,
  166, 169–70, 174, 181
  1946–1983, 126
  1982, 129
  1984, 128–29
  of blacks, *x,* 146, 154
  cost of, 144–46, 160, 170, 245
  in England, 184
  of Hispanics, *x,* 146, 154
  as push factor, 128
  technology and, 149–50
  of teenagers, *x,* 151
unions, 141, 142, 143, 146
  illegal immigrants in, 12, 41, 144
United Auto Workers (UAW), 146
United Kingdom, immigrants in, 95,
  184–85

United States:
  American culture in, 82, 84–85,
    97–98
  birthrate in, 16
  Canada's relations wth, 220
  citizenship requirements of, 115–
    16, 122
  emigration from, 195
  foreign students in, 134–35
  Hispanics in, 15, 78, 123, 184, 203–
    204
  labor shortage predicted in, 135–36
  Mexicans in, 15, 121–22
  Mexico's relations with, 218–22
  minimum wage in, 140, 151, 152
  new job creation in, 127–28
  polls in, 17–18, 201–204
  population of, 3, 5, 8
  pull factor in, 128
  separatism in, 95
  "Untouchables, The," 53, 70
  Urban Institute, 101
  U.S. English, 79–80

Vajda, Richard, 58
Valdivia, Guillermo, 34
Van Arsdol, Maurice D., Jr., 168, 169
Venezuela, immigrants from, 106
Vietnamese, 143
  "boat people," 162
  violence against, 11, 51, 79
Vining, Daniel, 14
Virginia, Vietnamese in, 51
visa abusers, 14

Waggnor, Randall Craig, 35
Wall Street Journal, 110
Wambaugh, Joseph, 30, 32
Washington, D.C., immigrants in,
  11, 77, 85, 93, 143, 174
Washington Post, 51
Washington Post/ABC News Poll, 203
welfare, 145, 159, 160, 161, 162–66,
  169, 171–173
West Germany:
  guestworkers in, 95
  Turks in, 11–12
White, Robert, 174
Whitman, Walt, 85
Wirth, Tim, 182
Wood, Robert, 112
Work Revolution, The (Schwartz), 149

Zangwill, Israel, 83
Zero Population Growth, 194